T0358291

———————————THE———————————

INTEGRATED
LEADER

A Foundation for Lifelong Management Learning

THE

INTEGRATED LEADER

A Foundation for Lifelong Management Learning

CHRIS DALTON, PhD

Henley Business School, UK

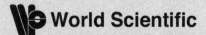
World Scientific

NEW JERSEY · LONDON · SINGAPORE · BEIJING · SHANGHAI · HONG KONG · TAIPEI · CHENNAI · TOKYO

Published by

World Scientific Publishing Co. Pte. Ltd.
5 Toh Tuck Link, Singapore 596224
USA office: 27 Warren Street, Suite 401-402, Hackensack, NJ 07601
UK office: 57 Shelton Street, Covent Garden, London WC2H 9HE

Library of Congress Cataloging-in-Publication Data
Names: Dalton, Chris, author.
Title: The integrated leader : a foundation for lifelong management learning /
    Chris Dalton, PhD.
Description: New Jersey : World Scientific, [2021] | Includes bibliographical references.
Identifiers: LCCN 2021013465 | ISBN 9789811229213 (hardcover) |
    ISBN 9789811229220 (ebook) | ISBN 9789811229237 (ebook other)
Subjects: LCSH: Leadership--Study and teaching. | Management--Study and teaching. |
    Executives--Training of. | Diversity in the workplace.
Classification: LCC HD57.7 .D3445 2021 | DDC 658.4/092--dc23
LC record available at https://lccn.loc.gov/2021013465

British Library Cataloguing-in-Publication Data
A catalogue record for this book is available from the British Library.

For any available supplementary material, please visit
https://www.worldscientific.com/worldscibooks/10.1142/12070#t=suppl

Desk Editor: Lai Ann

Typeset by Stallion Press
Email: enquiries@stallionpress.com

Printed in Singapore

Although at many times in recent human history societies have faced huge hurdles and felt they are unique in doing so, there are questionably few instances that compare with the challenges faced by leaders today. The present health crisis notwithstanding, the all-encompassing climate and natural world crises are monumental in scale as are many societal, belief system and political ones. *The Integrated Leader*, with immaculate timing and even better articulation, puts forward an argument for the only type of leadership that will now make a difference. It calls upon polymath leaders who simply put can and do 'connect the dots' for positive outcomes, and do so at a time when the dots are big, complex, overlapping, and impacting billions of fellow humans and the vast communities of countless other species. Put aside your other reading and embrace the challenge of becoming an Integrated Leader. We need you.

Ian Dunn
Chief Executive Officer
Plantlife (UK)

Clever and thought-provoking, this book and its approach is something I would draw on in my support of others as well as my own development. *The Integrated Leader* is a fresh and challenging manifesto for leadership that stimulates new thinking about people, personal development, systems, change, and much more. A stimulating blend of theory, examples, exploration, and provocation that invites the reader to think deeply about their leadership style and learning, it is a pertinent and relevant read — vital in understanding leadership more fully and critically in our hyper-integrated world.

The book poses powerful questions for leaders at any stage of their development and career stage.

Helen Gordon
Chief Executive Officer
Science Council

In a dynamic, increasingly complex world, leaders continue to search for ways to make a difference and have lasting impact. *The Integrated Leader* offers a compelling look into the importance of conscious awareness of both ourselves and the environments and systems in which we exist. This book is an important read for anyone curious about how they can become a more complete, more fulfilled leader and human being.

Geoff Brockway
Head of Learning & Development — Global Finance and GBS
AstraZeneca

Chris invites us in for something that feels like a tasting menu of eleven servings in three sittings. Emerging from a lifetime of insights on management theories, and acutely relevant and susceptible to the state of the planet today, he presents no definitive answers but challenges us to slow down and consider how we think about ourselves, our identity as leaders and our relationship with the ecosystem we are impacting. It takes courage to dine with Chris, but I highly recommend you invest the time to savor his reflections and allow them to challenge (and evolve) the self-awareness and interconnectivity of you and your organization.

Xenia Duffy
CEO and Chief Zebra
zeal, Denmark

All that matters is that
you have a good heart

(this motto found me in 1996
and has stayed ever since)

Contents

Acknowledgements   xi

Foreword   xiii

Preface   xv

Introduction   1

Chapter 0   The Integrated Leader's Manifesto   11

Part 1   Getting in Your Own Way   **17**

Chapter 1   The Beginner's Mind   19

Chapter 2   Punctuation   33

Chapter 3   Difference   59

Part 2   Getting Out of Your Own Way   **81**

Chapter 4   The Leader Complex   83

Chapter 5   Today is Not a Stepping Stone to Tomorrow   105

Chapter 6   Outside-In and Inside-Out   127

Chapter 7   The Familiar Self   153

Chapter 8   Universal Mental Health and Well-Being   175

Part 3 Don't Forget You're Change   **201**

Chapter 9   Let's Meet at Infinity   203
Chapter 10   Everything and Everyone Needs to Change   221
Chapter 11   The Principle Uncertainty   245
Appendix 1   A List of Human Universals   263
Appendix 2   A Learning Journal Extract   265

Glossary   267
Index   275

Acknowledgements

This book reflects my 25+ years of experience as a facilitator in post-experience management education. Many voices have influenced me over the years, and some deserve direct mention here.

For the main title, I am indebted to **John Whittington**, coach and author of *Systemic Coaching & Constellations*.[1] I had been struggling to express what was at the core of the personal development idea at Henley, aside from awareness. Awareness, yes, but of what? The key was the idea of integration. John and I had been developing a joint workshop for alumni of the Executive MBA at Henley, and on his suggestion the Integrated Leader concept fitted perfectly.

The manifesto for business leaders in Chapter Zero came from **Diana Naya**, an inspirational educator and yoga and mindfulness teacher from Spain.[2] Diana had already developed a manifesto for teachers and educators in her field, and it struck me how much of that would work well in management. She has been generous and gracious in reworking this wisdom to fit the concept and intention of the book.

I am grateful to **Tracey Mills**, who took time to offer feedback on the draft for this book, and to **Dr Tai Wei Lim** for encouragement and for connecting me with World Scientific as publisher.

---

[1] Whittington, J. (2020). *Systemic Coaching and Constellations* (3rd edition). London, United Kingdom: Kogan Page.

[2] Diana's web page is at: www.samyamayogaibiza.com.

Foreword

Personal development is often treated as a 'nice to have' in leadership. In fact, it's central and essential to any development that endures and is the difference that makes the difference. This simple truth is central to Chris's teaching and writing and runs through this insightful book.

Chris invites you to unpack one of the most loaded words in the English language — leadership — and find yourself within. He opens the door wide and then lets you find your own way around. There are timeless truths on every page and yet he manages to convey them as if we are hearing them for the first time, so they resonate deeply. This book offers an invitation to stop and think about how you think and connect to your emerging sense of authentic self.

If you want to know about being an authentic leader, it must include an investigation of how everything is connected, an openness to what is and what might be; in you, in others, and then in the wider systems we live and work within. Awareness of this is one of the foundation stones of Chris's fresh thinking and writing. As he guides you to enjoy the process of leading while staying open to the ever-changing systems that you inhabit, he offers support that will resource a journey of lifelong learning.

'Integrated' is not a destination, outcome, or goal. Neither is it an invention, but the discovery of something essential and true about the self and about the world. This is the great gift of this book and why there are more questions than answers. I encourage you to ask yourself each of them and, as you do, feel your inner integration process begin.

John Whittington

Preface

This is a contemporary search for the questions to which 'leader' or 'leadership' is the answer. It represents a shift in gears in personal leadership thinking and is written for anyone who wants to ask better questions of themselves. Most notably, it is written with these people in mind:

- Experienced and senior managers interested in making the most of their career in business and management, and who are already in leadership roles.
- Mid-career managers who are about to lead others and suspect that they first need to know how to lead themselves.
- Master of Business Administration (MBA) and Executive MBA students and alumni.
- Aspiring/new managers who want to build their personal development on a strong foundation of fundamentals.
- Educators, coaches, trainers, and policy-makers who want to know more about these ideas in personal development, management education, and management training.

Three Ways to get More Out of This Book

1. Allow everything to take the time it needs.

Insights can and often do come in a flash, but be wary of microwave personal development (PD) or pop-up leadership solutions.

Instant answers are like fast food — occasionally an option but rarely nourishing for long. Insights generally follow a lot of preparation and reflection on experience, and there is no formula for when a penny will drop. Nor is there one for how; PD is not a one-size-fits-all recipe.

Many organisations rush headlong from their point As to their point Bs and are moving so fast that they do not fundamentally learn, or grow anything more than the bottom line along the way. Every new business starts from the seed of an idea, which means it first emerges in harmony with an ecosystem. Many will fail to get going, while others will always fail to sustain growth beyond what their habitat or niche will allow. Those that thrive beyond the first four or five years will face new questions of purpose, direction, and growth, and this is where they may gradually start to feel the conflict with the world around them, with their competitors, with time, with resources, and sometimes sadly also with their most important asset, their employees. Even in larger, well-established businesses, epidemics of short-term thinking and quick fixes follow as they struggle and fail to keep up with a rapidly changing world. It is really no different for individuals. Many managers and leaders have a dread fear that they are missing out, that they are being judged as inadequate, and that if they do not learn the rules of the game, they will be rejected. Learn from this and allow personal development to flow through you. Take time to tune in to the world around you. Notice how when you slow down, personal development arises by itself quite naturally. People and the organisations they work for can find their own ways to develop if given enough time and the right support. To speed things up, slow things down.

2.   Write things down.

In leadership, as with other areas of life, new ideas flow when given space, permission, and stimulation. Inspiration can come from many unexpected places and directions. Thoughts come and go, and if triggers for certain thoughts feel significant, writing them down translates the data of fleeting impressions into information. Not everything can or needs to be logged, and the content of a reflective journal probably will not change your life, but the act of writing *will* improve your thinking. Whenever we write something down, we are processing our thoughts. Writing is a communication skill that an Integrated Leader can use to great effect. This is even more impactful when you take time to revisit your writing at a later time and review it.

3. Be present. Be curious.

No generation in human history ever had the technology and wealth that we possess. We are surviving longer into old age, but often we are failing to discover life before death. With so many distractions and calls on our attention, our minds are full but our days are poorer for it. For example, in modern life, we have reduced the idea of the present to a razor-thin fraction of a fraction of a second, hardly visible. Instead, our attention is consumed replaying the past or preoccupied with anticipation of the future in our search for control. Put that on hold, at least for now, and suspend any need to have the answers. Always look for the better question.

As a manager or leader, you probably already have a lot of effective strategies (and opinions) for fast sense-making, quick meaning-making, and confident explanation. These have been your route to functioning well in the world, and you are probably not too aware of many of them. You may feel that you do not need to, or cannot, change these too much, and yet you are likely to be an advocate of lifelong learning and growth. There is a conflict already.

I hope you enjoy reading this. It will not offer a programme to follow or a formula to apply. You must develop your own thinking. If some sections appear dry or abstract, feel free to return to these at a later point. Do not be bound by the convention of reading a book once, from start to finish, and then referring to it no more.

Chris Dalton

Introduction

I honestly believe it is better to know nothing than to know what ain't so.

Attributed to Josh Billings (1874)

This book presents a new perspective on being a leader and understanding leadership, personal development, and lifelong learning. People have a common sense understanding of what the words *leader* and *leadership* mean, and in most normal situations this is enough. However, the global challenges of technology, society, economics, and the environment mean we face ever bigger and trickier questions. We are now presented with two paths in how we apply leadership for the future.

Along one path, the realm of the leader looks quite fragmented. Their attention is therefore drawn to dealing sequentially with a system only as parts, a logic that follows the belief that organisations consist of separable bits and pieces. This is often efficient in the short term, and for problems where all the variables and boundaries are known. It leads to cultures where good leadership is good problem solving, and a good leader is the person who knows the algorithms. How effective is this in the long-term? Are organisations just complicated bits and pieces? Along the other path, the realm of the leader looks quite different. Here is a world where everything is integrated. Their attention is drawn to an understanding of the whole system, which may have many aspects, but is not just a collection of parts.

1

This book follows the second path. Because leadership matters, we must be precise in our understanding of what a leader is. While being systemic and integrated are not new to management thinking, something big and important is happening in the world, right here and right now, which makes what path we follow a very important question. It will be the leadership shown by *this* generation that will have repercussions for nurturing and sustaining the next. Before I define what I mean by the Integrated Leader, let me highlight some background of the current context that help set the scene:

1. *Our economic and social success is putting our natural environment in jeopardy.*

The Earth's resources were once thought of as limitless, and our ingenuity in finding ever more sophisticated ways and means of extracting, converting, and trading them has been inexhaustible. Achievement has come at a cost. We are meeting many unintended consequences, such as the rapid rise in global temperatures and the loss of sustainable habitats and stable environments that support life. There is even evidence that we are at the cusp of a new geological era called the Anthropocene epoch, in which human activity is visible in geological strata. Two hundred years of growth and technological progress have bequeathed a material standard of living, one of richness and convenience our ancient ancestors could not have envisaged. In the relatively recent switch from an agrarian and handmade economy in the 18th century to one thriving on machine-driven trade and industry in the 19th, certain core beliefs took root. Collectively we are now on the verge of radical change, to which we must adapt. Our unspoken assumptions that people will, and that individuals should, work for their own benefit, and that free trade and open competition will always result in 'better'. We have attained much in the way of prosperity and beauty, but also in violence and social division. Change is around us, and some of it is now irreversible. We are coming to realise that if nature is not healthy, then neither are we. As soon as we consider this, our lack of agency to redress this global imbalance is acute.

2. Work-related stress is on the rise. People frequently have no idea why they are working and get little joy from their jobs.

We have an epidemic of unhealthy physical and emotional states among many employees in the modern workplace, which of course also includes managers and leaders. Faced with what appears to be a relentless stream of complex events in the world, the individual human feels separate from it and almost powerless to intervene. One of the most pervasive myths of leadership is that the good leader must overcome their feelings, suppress or at least put aside their emotions, and confront the world head on to shape it to their will. As a result, many people are, at best, sleepwalking through careers and, by extension, through their lives. At worst, they feel that they are drowning. Our lack of agency to redress our imbalance is chronic.

In our culture, it is taboo to admit you do not have an answer. Leaders are supposed to establish credibility by showing that they are in control of the situation. Yet we cannot know all the consequences of our decisions. That is the nature of change and learning. Our lack of certainty is perhaps our greatest source of fear. We all have different coping strategies to deal with this, and it would be easy for these things to overwhelm us.

Or… our context and our apparent failure to work out what to do could be our call to action.

A problem, it is said, cannot be solved using the same thinking that created it, so we must examine our current conceptions of leadership before we act. The relationship between management and leadership deserves a little attention here because they are often treated as very different. Some view them as two separate domains. Others see being a leader as a sub-set of being a manager. Canadian academic Henry Mintzberg takes this latter view. From observation and interview of many senior managers he concluded they may perform up to 10 roles[1]:

Interpersonal

Figurehead: The ceremonial representative of the company
Leader: Visibly the one in charge and the visionary or guide towards 'what could be'
Liaison: The link between the organisation and the external world

Informational

Monitor: The keeper of a high-level view of what is going on
Disseminator: Transparent and regular sharer of information
Spokesperson: The recognised channel for information to relevant stakeholders and/or boss

Decisional

Entrepreneur: The initiator, innovator, and improver
Disturbance Handler: The sorter-out of disagreements and disputes
Resource Allocator: The one in charge of agreeing budgets and plans
Negotiator: An expert dealmaker, mainly internally

Does this match your own experience? You will see how only one of these roles overtly carries the label 'leader'. Is he very precise or very restricted? Perhaps you see leadership as much more than a management role. As we shall see throughout the book, defining what a leader is fraught with issues and pitfalls, and needs great care. Our point of view will greatly determine our answer. My view is like Mintzberg's: leadership is the intelligent interpretation of a rich menu of interrelationships and possibilities

---

[1] Mintzberg, H. (2004). *Mintzberg on Management*. Upper Saddle River, NJ: Prentice Hall.

or choices. As the main subject matter of this book it will include, but not be limited to, decision-making, sense-making, and meaning-making.

Two Paradigms of Leadership

A paradigm is a prevailing and widely accepted set of assumptions that have become unnecessary to question or explain to make life decisions. Paradigms are worldviews.

Our current paradigm for studying and understanding says that *leadership starts from the leader*. First the person, then you can have leadership. This has given us a powerful cultural narrative of the leader riding into town and heroically punching a leadership-shaped hole into the space around them. Having completed their mission, the leader leaves to perform the same miracle somewhere else. The bulk of current leadership theories conform to (or confirm) this idea or study the phenomenon from this perspective.

Societies tend to stability and encourage constant structures. Every organisation has programmed into it the imperative that, all other things being equal, it is better to exist than not. This may sound trivial, but it is vital and very powerful because it is a social truth, not an induvial one. At the same time, life is chaotic and outcomes unpredictable, so the stability organisations seekto mains is constantly under threat. At the same time, that organisational determination to continue existing as an entity has consequences on the environment that add to the uncertainty. It is part of organisational reality that things will happen. An alternative paradigm to the one above would turn everything on its head. What if *leadership all starts from the context*? First the situation, and *then* you can have the person. Change (and occasionally crisis) in the external environment equals a leadership-shaped hole, and that contextual need then calls or pulls people in. By being pulled in, these people (temporarily) become leaders.

These are two fundamentally different propositions.

Defining the Integrated Leader

Leadership is a concept as old as our species, found in every society across time and place. As a social species, we gravitate to one form of leadership or another as a matter of course, and as we do, we always dance around its meaning. What *does* leadership mean? For a start, it is an intriguing mix of concrete and abstract. On the one hand, an organisation's leadership is a flesh and blood collection of individuals who control or influence what happens and who move others towards a goal or outcome that might otherwise not take shape. On the other, leadership is an idea or notion; a desire and an attitude with no form because it is the intangible relationship between people. It is aspirational.

To be a leader is sometimes to guide others on a journey through already charted lands. At other times it is to be an explorer discovering, perhaps alone, what no one has yet seen. Leadership is acting collectively or singularly to influence the experience of events. We may need leaders to be guides or explorers in the tangible, measurable world of events, or the intangible, immeasurable realm of the imagination. The central idea is that leadership is an integrating activity, and therefore leaders must themselves be integrated.

The Oxford English Dictionary defines the word 'integrated' as something, or someone, entire and complete. Its Latin root, *integrāre,* means to make whole; in Anglo-Saxon, the word 'whole' shares its ancestry with 'heal', 'holy', and 'health'. An Integrated Leader is someone who unites the person-in-the-world with the world-in-the-person in a way that leads to health and well-being. There are four aspects that an Integrated Leader tries their best to pay attention to:

Noticing: Observing the world as it is, without judgement, without filters or conditioning, and without expectation. This is awareness, and none of it is easy to do, as noticing must eventually be done without the thought of doing it.

Accepting: Agreeing that things are as they are should be followed by *accepting* that things are as they are. Even when we manage to see unfiltered, we often immediately invest our energy in imposing feelings about it. Agreeing *to* is not the same as agreeing *with*, of course, but nor is the same as disagreeing with. Acceptance is liberation.

Engaging: A person liberated from addiction to judgement (relatively, we are only human) can listen with intelligence. Leadership is an act of enquiry as much as it is about decision-making. The way to engage with how things are is with fully present curiosity and humility. Engagement is intention.

Acting: In the same movement, leadership is behaving earnestly and with integrity. To act completely in tune with the way the world is and not in conflict with it. In this sense, acting is participation. It is also a way of preserving flexibility, defined as 'the potential for change, held in reserve'.

The Integrated Leader is a person who has fully explored, through a combination of experience and reflection, all four aspects of self-awareness and identity.

However, this is not where most managers start on their journey to become leaders. Nor is it where most existing leaders start in their quest to be better ones. Conventionally, organisational leadership has dealt mostly with questions concerning i) what resources are available and how they are converted into value and ii) what rules apply to growth of what the organisation does. That is leadership of the parts, not the whole, and it can end up in decisions that might have positive short-term effects for an organisation, but must have detrimental long-term outcomes for the health of the environment the business requires.

You will face many challenges in your career that require wisdom. Past success is no guarantee of wisdom; your track record may even be what is leading you away from it. Equally, despite the mantra that we learn most from our mistakes, past failure carries no inherent wisdom. A transition in thinking as a foundation for lifelong management learning is what this book is about.

The Structure of the Book

Management learning is the connection between personal development, professional practice, and knowledge of how organisations and businesses operate. You cannot achieve advancement in one without advancement in the other. As managers work to improve their practice, direct their careers, and discover their passion and purpose, they reveal new self-reflection levels and tap into new reserves of resilience and creativity within themselves. The three parts of this book offer a foundation of ideas to play with as you go about your business. They are an invitation to play in that you will find few, if any, solutions, instructions, or recipes. What you will find, however, are ideas that challenge you to think. We begin with a set of principles that encapsulate the spirit of the Integrated Leader.

Chapter 0   The Integrated Leader's Manifesto
The manifesto has 11 statements of presence and transformation for any mid-career managers who have chosen to challenge their stuckness. Each statement is later reflected on between the chapters.

The 11 main chapters are organised into three parts:

Part 1:   Getting in Your Own Way
There are many people around us who want to tell us what we should think but few who challenge us on how we think. Learning must always interrupt core assumptions. This first part of the book establishes a framework for personal development that can be applied to any aspect of life, career, job, or task. These are the underpinnings we build on in our knowledge and understanding. We will cover awareness, learning, and knowledge, and define integration and leadership, but the three main elements are a beginner's mindset, punctuation/categorisation, and difference.

Part 2: Getting Out of Your Own Way

The five chapters in this part explore the main barriers and restraints to becoming an Integrated Leader. We begin by opening the framework for awareness from Part 1 to the taken-for-granted assumptions in current leadership theory. The question of purpose and meaning as they apply to you and your development is also examined. Some of the greatest restraints in leadership are generated externally by elements of social life that are not aligned with health and well-being. Other obstacles are limits we generate for ourselves, perhaps as narratives or stories, perhaps as mindsets or attitudes that restrain growth. Part 2 covers many aspects of selfhood, including lifelong learning, and returns to the central message of personal development, which is health and well-being.

Part 3: Don't Forget You're Change

This part looks at three aspects of current experience as they involve the future and future leadership responses. Integrated leadership is about implementing change and remaining resourced in life to meet what comes to you over time. It covers re-framing strategies, re-orientation to personal and professional narratives, liminal identities, transformation, and tactics for using self-awareness to explore the world with freshness and spontaneity. This section of the book's message is that 'change' is not only what the world is making happen in you, but also what you are making happen in the world. You are change.

As a book, the Integrated Leader cannot avoid having a point of view. As the writer of the book, no doubt its point of view carries with it my own. I have tried to include and be transparent about any assumptions I'm using, and for further orientation to how I see things, I have included a glossary of terms and ideas at the end. These are typical of the ideas that have been valuable in my own personal and professional development. You may jump to this list and read it first if you are curious, or read them when you get there. I encourage you to find your own way.

Chapter 0

The Integrated Leader's Manifesto

What the superior person seeks is within themself, what the inferior person seeks is in others. The superior person agrees with others without being an echo. The small person echoes without being in agreement.

Confucius, The Analects

Why a Manifesto

Leaders are frequently constrained by external convention and restrained by internal, self-limiting beliefs. These are connected but we don't often realise it. Sorting out the useful from the ineffectual, the good from the bad, and the healthy from the unhealthy is difficult enough, and seeing how the external and the internal are the same thing is no small task. The Integrated Leader is one who is open to such possibilities.

Integration in leadership is, I think, a threshold concept. This means that once it's understood, everything changes. The difficult part is that you must find out for yourself from within. Reflection, and some hard work, is required.

The Story of the Integrated Leader's Manifesto

In 2017, Diana Naya, an experienced yoga teacher based in Ibiza, showed me a document she had written. It was a manifesto[1] of principles and ideas for teachers and practitioners of yoga. It was an offer for development. I was struck by how many of the phrases and ideas in Diana's manifesto were right on the nose for business leaders and managers, too. From my own experience, I knew that these ideas could speak profoundly to mid-career managers who have chosen to challenge their stuckness and act to improve their practice, direct their careers, or rediscover their passion and purpose.

I asked Diana if she would prepare a version that could be used with the Executive Master of Business Administration programme, and we discussed what would need to change, and how this might best be organised within the principles of personal development I had been developing in my course. The text in this Integrated Leader's Manifesto is the result. Diana has given permission to publish and share the Integrated Leader's Manifesto. It has 11 statements that address various aspects of personal or professional transformation at a deep level. The purpose of the Integrated Leader's Manifesto is to present a fresh perspective for you to react to. Each is a principled position that, if accepted, may then be used as a presupposition for dealing with the world as it unfolds and comes towards you.

The manifesto covers four radiating contexts of leadership — *self, self with others, self with an organisation,* and *self with a community.* Each section stands on its own as well as part of a collective. For now, I invite you to read and highlight any parts that stand out for you, either because they resonate well or because in some way, they interrupt your flow and established worldview.

---

[1] A manifesto is a public declaration or explanation issued by a person or group. It is often used to express a point of view or theory on life. The word has roots in the Italian noun *manifest*, which was the list and declaration of the cargo carried by a ship or other transportation.

Leading Self

- 'I'm willing to recognize that my power as a leader does not come from me, but *through* me.'
- 'I strive for learning, not perfection (perfectionism is by definition unobtainable and meaningless). I know that there are many blind spots in my experience and knowledge. Therefore, I keep my humility, honouring the diversity of the wisdom of others. The alternative to perfectionism is awareness.'
- 'Keeping up to date in my knowledge and skills through inquiry and study is my obligation. It is not a choice, but a responsibility I have. I'm happy to revise my practice and assumptions every day. I'm happy to listen to others, and at the same time I'm grounded in my convictions and values.'
- 'Becoming a transformative and integrated leader might be a slow process; I am willing to honour this rhythm.'

Leading Self with Others

- 'Judging others will not help them and will interfere in my ability to manage and lead. As a leader, I therefore seek awareness of my own emotions in every moment. This awareness emphasises my capacity to support others in transition. We all have fears, doubts, and weak areas. In our vulnerability lies our power for transformation.'
- 'Each person takes 100 percent responsibility for their skilfulness, practice, and professional development. Equally, we share in a desire for learning, so we help those around us to find their own resources. Every team member has a right to freedom and decision-making in their evolution and practice, and I am happy to accept them just as they are.'

Leading Self with the Organisation

- 'Humility and tolerance are necessary for the health of my organisation. There is no human hierarchy — only different levels of experience and knowledge. An organisation is a creative space, not a space of followers. Each person has the intelligence and capacity to make their own decisions, and at the same time remember that their behaviour affects the whole. Therefore, we always act with responsibility and integrity.'

- 'The organisation does not absorb individuals or own their personal paths and development — it supports people refining themselves through interaction with peers. An organisation is a community with its own culture. It represents that culture with its actions. What culture do we want to create?'

- 'Creating a new culture requires time, dedication, intention, and patience. New habits and behaviours are necessary for personal development to be born.'

Leading Self with the Community

- 'Leaders have the power to transform and affect the world. I become a leader when I remind myself and others each day that the goal of collective transformation is a priority and more important than individual goals of personal success. True success is the success of the community.'

- 'Willingness and attitude are the roots of our strength as a community. All members need time to reflect on the right balance of freedom and commitment. Spiritual maturity will give us the courage to move forwards and grow. Every organisation works better in thought, word, and action when there is truthfulness.'[2]

Which ones did you pick out? Remember, for each one, the next task is to ask yourself:

If this is true, what do I need to stop, start, or improve in my practice?

---

[2]Diana Naya's Manifesto Samyama original version can be found at: www.samyamayogaibiza.com/blog/manifestosamyama (with permission).

The manifesto is a resource and starting point. It requires reflection and intention as self-understanding grows and it can be amended or added to in line with experience. Eventually, you will aim to reflect on all aspects and synthesise your ideas to clarify and integrate this with your practice.

In the spaces between the next 11 chapters, you will find my reflections on each manifesto statement. These reflections are meditations, not instructions; thoughts, not tools. You should take them as prompts in a dialogue for you to develop in whatever way is healthy for you.

Part 1

Getting in Your Own Way

Wisdom is seeking wisdom.
Dogen

Either as a leader or follower, it is likely that you already know that some ideas are hard to put across not because they are complicated or complex, but because they are unfamiliar. Every radically different idea that re-shapes how we think and what we do starts as opposition by challenging how we think and see. If our ignorance of how we make sense of the world is the problem (and this book is saying that it is), then we must first interrupt the flow of our unspoken or hidden assumptions. We must get in our own way, for a bit. The three chapters in this part lay the foundation of how to stop and think about how you think.

Why is it a good idea to intervene and interrupt the flow? After all, it is probably a golden rule for a leader that they do not impose personal change on someone else. When it comes to other people, non-interference means leaving other people's delusions with them to deal with. True personal development must come from within and while you can lead a person to change, you cannot make them think. No one will become self-aware unless and until they are ready. After all, when someone is asleep, would they like to be disturbed from their peaceful slumber?

When it comes to yourself, however, non-interference is effectively the same thing as living a life of self-delusion. If you are content with that, then there is no need to do anything. On the other hand, the impulse for personal development arises from within. A deep curiosity and interest in yourself is not a prerequisite for personal development, it *is* personal development. Most of us do not tap into this inner curiosity very often, preferring instead to construct a façade of opinions about ourselves based on the opinions of others. If you do, however, feel like going your own way, you can begin by consciously getting in your own way. Introducing a few simple patterns of interference to your routine is a preliminary step. Enjoy waking up. We are full of plans, so one such pattern of interference is to have no expectations.

Chapter 1

The Beginner's Mind

In the beginner's mind there are many possibilities, but in the expert's there are few.

Shunryu Suzuki[1]

Learning requires questions and questions imply doubt. Integrated Leadership is therefore about granting yourself the freedom to doubt what you think you know. We go through life gathering knowledge with little understanding of the nature of knowledge, and the relationship between knowing, not-knowing, and learning.

Beginner's mind, a phrase from Zen Buddhism,[2] conveys a truth about learning found in just about every philosophical tradition in the world. A well-known story illustrates this principle and tells of a Zen master who is visited by a venerated and learned scholar, an expert in a great many fields. The scholar offers to bring his vast knowledge to the search for enlightenment. The master suggests they should discuss the matter over some tea. When the tea arrives, the master begins pouring the professor a cup. But when the tea reaches the top he does not stop pouring. It overflows, covering the table and spilling on to the floor. The professor is startled.

---

[1]Suzuki, S. (1970). *Zen Mind, Beginner's Mind*, New York, NY: Weatherhill (1986 reprint, p. 21).

[2]*Shoshin* in Japanese.

19

'You are spilling the tea. Can't you see the cup is full?'

The master smiles, 'You are like this teacup,' he says, 'so full that nothing more can be added. Come back to me when the cup is empty. Come back to me with an empty mind.'

A similar idea can be found in Western science. In 1955, the Nobel prize winner physicist Richard Feynman said,

> 'The scientist has a lot of experience with ignorance and doubt and uncertainty, and this experience is of very great importance, I think. When a scientist doesn't know the answer to a problem, he is ignorant. When he has a hunch as to what the result is, he is uncertain. And when he is pretty darn sure of what the result is going to be, he is still in some doubt. We have found it of paramount importance that in order to progress we must recognize our ignorance and leave room for doubt.'[3] (p. 14)

We can never *really* know what course of action will lead to better, and which will lead to worse consequences. It is awareness of this that makes the difference. Everyone has experienced beginner's mind at some point in their lives, even if only in childhood. That we lose this or forget it says something quite serious about what we think counts for qualification to work in an organisation at any level of responsibility or authority. A beginner's mind means granting yourself enough freedom from your conditioning to see the big questions of life in the small, mundane details. It is a 'don't know' mindset that uses doubt as its guide for finding out.

Our desire for answers is strong. To desire a thing is to be attached to it.[4] To know this intellectually is one thing, and it is another to be truly free from the search for certainty and control. John Little's *Bruce Lee: Artist of Life* is a collection of the thoughts and notes of the famous San Francisco born and Hong Kong raised martial artist, actor, and philosopher. Lee died aged 33, but we can

---

[3] Feynman, R. (1955). The value of science. *Engineering and Science, 19*(3), 13–15.
[4] Equally, the desire not to be attached to it is an attachment.

see how he had a remarkable eye for the simple essence of living in this extract called *The Six Diseases*:

1. 'The desire for victory.
2. The desire to resort to technical cunning.
3. The desire to display all that you have learned.
4. The desire to overawe the enemy.
5. The desire to play a passive role.
6. The desire to get rid of whatever disease you are likely to be infected with.'[5]

Leadership often expresses desires, wishes, goals, and outcomes. The most common idea is that leaders desire to influence others to follow. To be attached to influencing others is to set up a dangerous dynamic in the workplace. Can this be avoided? How can experienced leaders fulfil the potential of leadership without falling into traps of their thinking? The beginner's mind is the attitude that gets you there — **if** you can see past your web of assumptions.

Assumptions and Presuppositions

An assumption is anything learnt or absorbed in the past which remains unstated, unquestioned, and accepted as true in the present, and which is used to form opinions, make decisions, or undertake actions. Assumptions are neither intrinsically good nor bad; they become so only from context. Many are important to the flow of communication and can be useful short-cuts to avoid long, unnecessary explanations of context from scratch. We routinely use or are given thousands every day, most of which are hidden cues that can safely be left unexamined. Heuristics, or rules of thumb, transmit earlier learning and save us from constantly

---

[5] Little, J. (1999). *Bruce Lee: Artist of Life*, North Clarendon, VT: Tuttle Publishing (p. 196).

reinventing the wheel. There are, however, two situations in which unexamined assumptions do need to be surfaced and questioned:

1. Where people are speaking at cross-purposes because each is relying on underlying, unspoken, and taken-for-granted assumptions that conflict. Such assumptions will inevitably blind one person to the other without either knowing why.
2. Where the need or the aim is one of learning and change. Such a need will be a product of the context; it will matter in some situations that we are precise in our assumptions. Here, unspoken assumptions act as resisters and blind people to new thinking and development.

The economist Daniel Kahneman suggests in his book *Thinking Fast and Slow* that our brains have evolved two types of thinking ability. One is quick, convenient, fast-thinking, and sense-making, which he calls System 1. The other, labelled System 2, is slower, rational, and more resource-intensive. Kahneman says we tend to prefer System 1, even when the slower way could produce much better results both for the person and the organisation. When everything needs to be done yesterday, the easy and quick answer will likely be favoured even though application of the wrong thinking system to a context leads to thinking biases and errors which can be disastrous. Kahneman covers several common biases as applied to the psychology of economic decision-making.

A *presupposition*[6] is a consciously identified assumption used as a preliminary best-guess for further conjecture. Presuppositions are often well-thought-through and coherent in their structure, and they should evolve as new information comes to light and new knowledge is gained. In *Mind and Nature: A Necessary Unity*, the scientist and anthropologist Gregory Bateson wrote:

> 'Science, like art, religion, commerce, warfare, and even sleep, is based on presuppositions. It differs, however, from most other branches of human activity in that not only are the pathways of

---

[6] A presupposition is the assumption of a pertinent and pre-existing truth. A good presupposition creates questions and enquiry.

scientific thought determined by the presuppositions of the scientists, but their goals are the testing and revision of old presuppositions and the creation of new.'[7] (p. 25)

Note the double level of presupposition here. The object of our interest and curiosity is full of presuppositions, and so are the questions we bring to it. What we see is predetermined to an extent by how we already know and see the world. Being conscious of what you are doing as a manager, leader, researcher, or adult learner is called *reflexivity*. Reflexivity is the capacity to turn and look at yourself and it is of supreme importance for breaking self-limiting or even self-destructive patterns of thinking and acting.

As mentioned, presuppositions can be examined and challenged. For example, it has long been presupposed by many large organisations in free-market economies that economic performance underpins every other consideration. The manager must return value by seeing what is (a) permissible by law, (b) ethical, and then (c) a net positive contribution to society, in that order, and an organisation may be designed expressly to fulfil these. An unintended consequence of this has been that, despite what they say publicly, many organisations only help make a better world if they must, and only after their managers have fulfilled the fiduciary duty to the shareholders. There are many signs this is not sustainable. Presuppositions can be set to work designing all sorts of experiments and enquiry of leadership (remembering the mindset of the beginner's mind). For example, here are six that the Integrated Leader could use to form working hypotheses:

1. A business is as sustainable as its environment. Destruction of its habitat is destruction of itself as a business.
2. Human activity, including business activity, adversely affects the capacity of the natural environment to renew and maintain itself as a resource.
3. Human activity, including business activity, can restore the capacity of natural environments to renew and maintain themselves as resources.

---

[7] Bateson, G. (1988). *Mind and Nature: A Necessary Unity*, New York, NY: Bantam.

4. Leadership is a universal social phenomenon present in some form without exception in every society.
5. There are no fundamental laws or axioms of leadership, although there have been many theories.
6. *All* divisions in nature are human-made. Nature contains no such categories in and of itself.

This list is generated using presuppositions developed in the arguments presented in this book. While these are not definitive or exhaustive, they do allow us to form further questions about how we see the world, and therefore what interference with our world view might lead to new insights. Here are a few such questions:

➢ In your outlook and thinking, do you dwell exclusively in the past, live only for the future, or thrive best in the possibilities of the present moment?
➢ At work, should you delay acting on a problem until it is fully understood?
➢ Do you restrict and exclude certain elements or give everyone a voice and everything a place?
➢ Do you embrace or resist change?
➢ Do you use your authority primarily in service of the health and well-being of the system, or primarily in service of yourself?
➢ Where is your self-esteem located? Within your control or reliant on validation by others?

There is no need for you to have answers to these now. Responses will arise in their own time and other questions will follow. This is part of personal development, which is defined as:

> 'the identification and removal of those restraints that limit the likelihood of sustainable individual, organisational, social, and environmental health and well-being.'[8]

---

[8] Dalton, C. (2018). "Reflection is embedded in my brain forever now!": Personal development as a core module on an Executive MBA. *Reflective Practice*, 19(3), 399–411.

The key part is the phrase 'health and well-being'. Three related ideas help illustrate what is meant by limiting restraints to health and well-being: absence, awareness, and ignorance.

Absence, Awareness, and Ignorance

Times of uncertainty call leadership into being. Uncertainty suggests there are elements which are not present and need to be. Therefore, in one way or another, leadership deals in and represents absences. When things are going well and running smoothly, we tend to think that there is no great demand for leadership. When the imperfections of an organisation do not seem to be interfering with outcomes, leadership takes a back seat to day-to-day management of the status quo. Leadership is not synonymous with change, but the higher a person rises in an organisational pyramid, the closer they come to the type of decision that will result in, or result from, change. For the most part, leadership is grounded in knowledge, but there are three contrasting ways this may play out, as follows:

> *I know,* and therefore all my choices go unfiltered without me questioning assumptions or seeing my biases and conditioning. This is probably how most people function.[9]
>
> *I know that I don't know,* and therefore I have at least an added choice of examining what I do know through increased awareness of my conditioning.
>
> *I don't know (as my default start point),* and therefore I am not using my conditioning to filter my choices. I am not seeking to confirm what I do know; I am ready to see what happens and trust that the simplicity of not knowing will meet the complexity of the leadership-shaped hole around me. From that meeting, we will find what needs to be done.

---

[9] The corollary of this must be *I don't know that I don't know,* which could be an insightful opening in personal development if you knew that you don't know that you don't know. Which is rarely the case, sadly.

There are many ambiguous contexts where leaders will encounter instability and risk. Different industries or sectors, varying market needs, and disparities of size, shape, and stage or maturity of organisations make us look for evaluations of good leadership versus bad leadership. In trying to work this out, we start with the particular case and then study its characteristics to see how it fits in a generalised set. However, we can generalise only to the extent that one example is alike in some way to some other example or group of examples (that one case in some way formally maps on to others). We may think we are building up an accurate, global picture based on local evidence, but both our observations and our generalisations may be more biased than we admit.

What sort of a leader was American President John F. Kennedy? As he is a major historical figure you probably already have an opinion on that. Where did that opinion come from? How did you form a judgement? How much do you know with confidence and certainty, and how much of what you *think* you know would need to be checked for accuracy? What is the minimum any person would need to know to answer the question? How much can ever be known, particularly now nearly 60 years after his death? If you still have the same opinion, you must ask yourself how. Leaders and followers can find themselves deeply entangled in webs of things half-known, facts not there, words never actually said, deeds not done, or events not fully understood. This is not surprising, and probably not completely curable. We all operate in our day-to-day lives with short-cuts and just enough information for it not to matter (usually) whether we fully understand everything to get things done. It is a different story when the stakes are higher, as they should be in questions of leadership. If absence is part of the equation, what is wanted is an understanding of the nature of absence itself. The missing link must be something to do with a manager or leader's awareness of their conditioning. Without awareness, we will remain prisoners of our thinking. At the same time, it is dangerous to try too hard to focus on the absence of awareness because that absence will become another source of stress. Awareness of absence needs to be understood and valued as a pre-condition for learning and change.

There are several definitions of awareness in common circulation. One equates it to a form of 'conscious seeing', which is a subjective report of paying attention (i.e. whatever is held in the focus of the mind's eye; a thought). This implies that awareness cannot be objectively observable. If I say I am aware of something, then that is what awareness is. Another definition equates it to 'conscious knowing', which is an objective measure of decision-making (i.e. where a better than random outcome of a decision results *because* one knows things). Awareness in this case would be inferred as objective through what I can do. Here it is implied that awareness is the attainment of an answer, a solution, or new knowledge of some sort. In each case, awareness suggests that a threshold has been crossed, but both explanations have some problems, as we will see in Chapter 3.

Perhaps there is another way of looking at this, starting in the Old English root of our modern word 'aware', *gewær*. This carried a sense of being on your guard or cautious (the same root gave us *wary* and *beware*). There is a cutting edge to awareness that is a kind of alertness or watchfulness.[10] Awareness is wakefulness, when all our senses are present, reaching out to touch the world around in as open a way as possible. But awareness in itself contains no knowledge and awareness says nothing about whether what we think the world is like is what the world is, *per se*. Awareness is not an end; it is a stance we take so that we then are better able to see things as they are.[11]

The antithesis of awareness is ignorance. Ignorance can be of several types.

---

[10] Edges are important in learning and growth and this view is useful as an antidote to assumption-fuelled knowing, and vaccination to the formation of assumptions we might come to forget we are making later.

[11] It is a separate matter as to whether awareness needs a why alongside a how and a what. Does it serve a particular function?

1. *Innocent ignorance* is the state that novices, children, or newcomers have regarding any circumstance not encountered before. There is no pre-set perspective taken and no prior basis of knowing. Everything is entirely novel. This is the beginner's mind and applies not only to events that can be experienced and processed by our brains, but also to things which are not open to direct experience, such as consciousness.[12] Innocent ignorance is a sort of 'before' or precursor to awareness and is quite straightforward. It is more than not knowing where you are going when you start a journey, it is not even knowing that you have started one!

2. *Wilful ignorance*, the second kind, is more problematic. Wilful means that a person is choosing not to know or choosing to deny that they know, see, or already understand. This may be a self-deception or a deliberate tactic. An example of the latter happened during the Battle of Copenhagen in 1801, in which Admiral Nelson is reported to have ignored a signal for him to retreat by saying 'I have only one eye — I have a right to be blind sometimes', adding while holding the telescope to his missing eye, 'I really do not see the signal.' Less heroically, wilful ignorance may be practised by people in positions of authority or power to achieve their agenda.[13] A more benign form of wilful ignorance — and perhaps this is the most common — is a sort of self-deception that stops us from seeing and understanding ourselves when we suspect the consequences of finding out may bring about some uncomfortable changes. Put another way, the reason we want something is the reason we do not have it. After all, 'ignorance is bliss'.

    The path out of these two types of ignorance is curiosity. Curiosity is a light that can be shone in any direction, into any dark corner. Curiosity illuminates the intrapersonal (the introspective and private inner world) and the interpersonal (the

---

[12] You really can't step outside consciousness to understand consciousness, just as you can't touch the end of your finger with that finger.

[13] See Margaret Heffernan's 2012 book, *Wilful Blindness: Why We Ignore the Obvious* (Simon & Schuster).

public web of connections and relations between persons). Our ability to self-examine, to contemplate our thoughts *through* thought, to ask who we are and what we might be, and to express ourselves to others and understand their point of view, is what makes us human. You add to this, acceptance, which is the willingness to take what you find on its own merits.

3. *Aware ignorance* is the enlightened position some people realise once they have worked out that what they know is nothing at all. This point is close to our vicarious understanding of the method of the Greek philosopher Socrates, but it has been recognised by many other scientists and philosophers over the centuries since. This sort of awareness is not a denial of previous experience, merely a recognition that a person is not held in check by it in the present.

    It is in this type of ignorance that we find the edginess in awareness mentioned earlier because it consists of, and values, wariness and doubt. Knowing that you do not know is not a weakness, it is precisely the whole point and an attitude which is the learning edge for most innovations, inventions, and discoveries.

Awareness is the understanding of our ignorance. Applying the presuppositions first met in the Introduction, awareness has four aspects.

1. Acknowledging that you see the world not as it is, but as you are.
2. Agreeing to the world **as it is** and having no expectations that it should be any other way.
3. Admitting and accepting that you resist change; that you are who you are, baggage, fallibility, and warts and all. Awareness cannot be imposed from outside.
4. Acting in tune with this, dealing with what you can control.

The knock-on effects of awareness can be felt in almost any sphere of life, business, personal or social, and this is the space where the Integrated Leader excels. Personal development unfolds in richness and depth with self-awareness — the more you look at awareness, the more awareness you find.

If this sounds too simple, consider how often you really, honestly stop and think about how you think. It is very hard to do. Management as a process is fine-tuned for operational excellence and the reward of results, but it is also geared towards eliminating or even discounting doubt. We might call this a bias against not knowing. We respond to calls for certainty by delving into what we know and we equate the leader function with control and certainty. In leadership studies, *control* is always present as an assumption (actually, as a metaphor), while confusion or uncertainty is treated as noise to be reduced rather than the essence of the kind of exploration of the unknown that many agree defines a leader. Beginner's mind means starting from where you are (where else is there?), internally positioning it as 'this is all brand new to me'. However, this is not to take a naïve position: it's the awareness that you will still be bringing bias to how you frame and ask the question.

Reflecting on the Integrated Leader's Manifesto (Leading Self)

#1

'I'm willing to recognize that my power as a leader does not come *from* me, but *through* me.'

'Leader' is a role and label often assigned to an individual. Does this mean that leadership is a property of that person (in their character, behaviour, or skills)? If you believe so — and it may feel like common sense — then it will follow that a leader takes 'leadershipness' with them whenever and wherever they go. Companies hire (and fire) people on this basis, in the belief that they will bring good leadership with them, or perhaps take bad leadership away. This is a seductive and pervasive idea and it is not difficult to find innumerable examples in the media or in corporate folklore where the power in a position is equated with the person holding it (and vice versa).

If you believe that power as a leader radiates from you, then there will be some consequences. First, you are defining power in terms of interpersonal influence and control, and it follows that if it is you that has the power, there is intrinsic inequality because everyone else is dependent on you. It follows that improvements in leadership are tied to your ego. Each can cause quite a serious derailment for the person identified as leader, and even more serious disaffection, detachment, and defeat on the part of everyone else in the organisational system.

When power is derived from being the one in control, and is identified with ego, then it is very brittle under pressure. When over-exerted, it becomes tyrannical. Theorists see this but struggle to break away from the prevailing idea that leadership = leader. Although Jim Collins's 'Level 5 leader' and Robert Greenleaf's 'Servant Leader' attempt to mitigate the worst outcomes of power as embodied in the person of the leader, both approaches still start from a premise in the existing paradigm that says study the leader and you're studying leadership.

Is it so, or are we just conditioned to see it this way?

This manifesto statement presupposes that the system creates a field, or a 'leader-shaped' space. This field calls for someone to fill it. The person who steps in needs certain talents to do so, but they are what they are because this is what the organisation requires (whether in a healthy or unhealthy way). So, when we say that leadership comes through a person, something else is going on. Whatever leadership is, it isn't intrinsically you — or any particular person — but an aspect of a system of relational interactions between many players. In this way, we can all be playing different parts, and all parts are equal in terms of importance to the whole. The leader cannot take power with them when they leave — they were custodians, guardians, or stewards of something that flows through the business. That doesn't make them any less important, but it does create the requirement that they acknowledge their place, and every other person's place, in the system.

This is about stewardship. Leaders are holding something in trust — whether this is the vision of the founder, the mission of the organisation, or the respect towards all those who have agreed to join and make these things happen. It must now include the idea of the fate and state of the environment for sustainable business.

A leader does not become powerful because they well know how to acquire power, but because they know how to let go of it well.

Chapter 2

Punctuation

Cold! If the thermometer had been an inch longer, we'd all have frozen to death.

Mark Twain

Sense-Making and Meaning-Making: What's the Difference?

This is about how we think. It explores how we make sense of our environment, each other, and ourselves. Sense-making is a necessary prior step for attributing meaning and deciding what to do about the problems of life. The goal here is to raise your awareness of what is going on in your mind before you impose or accept meaning.

Every human being has the capacity, part innate or evolved and part acquired or learnt, to make sense of the world around them, to divine existing patterns and make coherent new ones. This ability is essential for survival and therefore not a surprise, and although there are many *ways* of sense-making found among and between different communities, there are also standard conventions. An example of such sense-making is naming, or the bringing of 'things' into existence as nouns. This appears to be a universal — every society and language on Earth names. It is hard to say anything exists until we give it a name. Names form clusters, and then systems of clusters, and while this complicated web of conventions has been a successful method for social and economic progress, it carries a few vitally important drawbacks and implications.

Sense-making is about perception of pattern and order, while meaning-making is about perception of the *consequences* of pattern and order, as they affect us (e.g. how a pattern in the past might now influence what I do in the present).

Meaning is about value, purpose, and intention. There are varying views on how meaning-making functions as a process, the most common of which is a family of theories of underlying structures in social discourse and dialogue. Erving Goffman, a Canadian sociologist, put forward the idea that meaning emerges from the network of our interactions with others.[1] Selfhood is a little bit like a theatre performance that is always adjusting itself to fit how an audience would like to watch it, and meaning is a kind of dance of agreement with others on those things which have meaning (this feels a little bit circular but seems to work in day-to-day life). Meaning is the perception, among the bewildering total of all possible data, of an order that has consequences for us. The universe need not have an intrinsic meaning for humans still to detect and find meaning within it. Goffman later added the idea of 'conceptual frames',[2] which we use to organise our experiences by putting boundaries around them. We are then imposing guidelines or rules, derived from our evolved capacity for sense-making, that hold for a context. He saw several different types of primary frames, but the two most important were *natural* and *social*. Natural primary frameworks impose meaning on our experience of naturally occurring phenomena (i.e. things which happen independently of us and which, in and of themselves, have no intrinsic meaning.) Social primary frameworks, on the other hand, explain and guide our conduct with each other in contexts of our own

---

[1] For more on this, see Goffman, E. (1990). *The Presentation of Self in Everyday Life*, New Edition, New York, NY: Penguin.

[2] Goffman, E. (1986). *Frame Analysis: An Essay on the Organization of Experience*, Boston, MA: Northeastern University Press.

making. Through these, we co-construct what it means to be human. And this is where the fun starts.

Punctuation

Which came first, the chicken or the egg?

For reasons deeply embedded in our cultural, scientific, and education systems, even though we have trouble coming up with an answer, the question is valid. For us, it makes a difference to divide the chicken from the egg (or the egg from the chicken). For the egg and the chicken, however, it does not. The chicken is content just 'chickening', the egg happy 'egging', with no nouns required, and without concern as to which follows what. Nature works in this unpunctuated way, human discourse does not. Nature might not be arranged in discrete parts, but our understanding of it usually is. In this book, any system of cutting up an undifferentiated world into differentiated pieces is called 'punctuation'.[3] Punctuation (the word) derives from a technique developed over a thousand years ago by scholars and scribes in western Asia. Religious texts, which we assume began as oral traditions memorised and passed down, were transcribed in written form in an unbroken continuous text on scrolls that came with no agreed system to indicate where there might be a beginning, middle, or end. This made it difficult to keep track of place when reciting, and so, using a pointed implement, holes were pricked (punctured, in fact[4]) in the document, indicating breaks and pauses. In a diverse region of travel and trade with few linguistic conventions, this was a major innovation and an early example of standardisation. As time went on and as writing became widespread, more sophisticated systems of punctuation were developed. This gave us sentences, paragraphs, vowel variations, and indicators for readers and speakers on how the written word

---

[3] This is a mental process. As far as we know, we are the only species that does this. The rest of nature gets by without such an abstraction.

[4] Punctual, punch, point, and punctilious all share the same root idea.

should be comprehended. Punctuation is ingenious and useful, and a human invention. Punctuation is therefore an excellent metaphor to communicate any system of signs that differentiates one thing from another.

We are a species in co-evolution with our environment and like every other family of living organisms, it is a truism to say that we are fine-tuned to interact with the world. In truth, we 'go with' our environment, but we have also evolved to make sense of that environment through sensory discrimination, which is a form of separation. Part of the human experience is a sensory position that evokes a feeling of removal from what surrounds us. In other words, evolution includes our mental capacity for self-consciousness,[5] which brings with it the question of the meaning of existence. For that sensation of self to be experienced, some sort of punctuation, some kind of system of distinguishing, is always needed. We are gregarious and resourceful, and these go with highly developed talents for communication and invention. Equally, we are fallible in our understanding of each other and of the world we live in. In sum, we are capable of understanding, of error, and of learning. Largely, we are ignorant of how we do any of these things. Much of the time this does not matter in day-to-day life, and when we speak to others who are using the same system, we do not really see what punctuation is being used, nor do we need to. It remains below the surface and we can still follow each other's meaning. Leadership, as we usually mean it, is not about the everyday.

Punctuation is the imposition by us of agreed conventions to organise experience into chunks that we can deal with. Layer upon layer of our descriptions of the world, our rules, our guidelines, our agreements, our boundaries, systems of communication, ways of seeing, saying, and making sense. In the next chapter, we will

---

[5] We strongly suspect self-consciousness is unique to us as a species. Even if it is so, that capacity emerged from (and goes with) an innate facility for interacting with our environment that is shared with every other mammal and many other species.

look at the basis for this, but for now the following are some examples we are all familiar with:

> *time; money; the periodic table;*
> *the Schengen area; rules in sport;*
> *Sundays in Ireland; Saturdays in Tel Aviv, Fridays in Egypt;*
> *Inside/outside; part/whole; ego/id/superego;*
> *academic disciplines; life stages; race;*
> *an edited feature film;*
> *mental health (+ mental ill-health).*

They may feel solid and comprehensive, and even fundamentally true, yet each is an abstraction. Each contains a selection, codification, and simplification of the total data available in events. Our punctuation frames our experience, and it can be taken as a working hypothesis that the contents of your thoughts, your outlook, and many of your most fervent beliefs are framed by whatever systems and conventions of punctuation you grew up in and are part of now in life. Punctuation is not just what you think, but *how* you think. Self-awareness is another way of saying that we can examine our punctuation, and once examined, it can be understood. Better understanding should lead to better awareness, more choice, and freedom. This awareness of categories and boundaries, of the nature of divisions and wholes, and of meaning-making can reveal the vast and mostly unspoken set of assumptions and agreements that operate to allow (or prevent) groups, organisations, communities, and societies to flourish, learn, invent, and change.

Don't Judge, See

Some forms of punctuation are so basic that they are deeply grounded in nature, and because of that, they are robust parts of our being. That I am a son or a daughter, or that I am (if it is the case) a mother or a father, for example, represents biological and genetic elements that are 'just so' parts of the natural order. And these would remain just so regardless of what I think, and regardless of shifting social conventions that might label them one role or another. Similarly, that most rudimentary example of punctuation, the division between day and night, exists as a reality beyond our invention as a species. There are links between 'clock' genes and the ill-health or stress experienced by people who have their 24-hour rhythm disrupted by, for example, prolonged periods of night shift work, long-haul travel, or too much time working in rooms without natural daylight. According to recent research, psychological disorders and metabolic illnesses are linked to how much natural light we are exposed to. A 2018 study by Jeanne Meister in the *Harvard Business Review* highlighted how access to natural light is not just a priority for workplace wellness among office employees but is also linked with bottom-line productivity.[6] This is a clue that punctuation matters in awareness.

While some forms of punctuation are obvious and easy to see when they are pointed out, many others are hidden or submerged in assumptions. Consider the following questions:

Is the purpose of business to make a profit?
What is a management decision?
What is a leadership decision?
Is there anything in leadership that cannot be measured?
When everyone leaves the organisation to go home, in what sense does the organisation still exist?
What would it take for an organisation not to exist anymore?
If no-one who works for IBM today was working there when it was founded in 1911 and nothing it sells now was sold by it then, is it the same organisation? How?

It may not immediately seem that these are all connected, but they are. To understand the nature of that connection requires you, sooner or later, to say something about philosophy.[7] Before that, we can consider the changing face of work.

---

[6] Meister, J. C. (2018). The #1 Office Perk? Natural Light, *Harvard Business Review*.
[7] I like to call this the f-word in management education.

The Nature of Work

It is possible to get through an entire business career and achieve high status armed only with the pragmatic and cumulative know-how that comes with years of practising the craft. Experience is the royal road to management. This may be a good and default description of what a manager is. Without experience, there can be no substance in management and leadership and no theory of management can have any point except in the light of experience. Management's theories and models can be studied from a book, as well as in education, but its forms, skills, and practices are developed and tested and incrementally improved upon on the shop floor, as it were. Indeed, some organisations still take great care in developing and training employees into supervisory positions and then on into management or leadership roles on the principle that you start at the bottom, learn the ropes, and get your hands dirty understanding the business before you run it.

The days of lengthy apprenticeships guided and supported by experienced mentors are now something of a rarity. The employment market is hungry for people who can insert themselves into various levels of authority and responsibility, already armed with the right tools and already saying the right things. In some places, young people are encouraged to move from an undergraduate business degree to a Master of Business Administration with virtually no space between to learn their craft. Accordingly, the typical attitude to career in the 21st century is now one of a willingness (perhaps an ambition) to demonstrate worth by aggressive and frequent jumps from one organisation to another. Job-hopping became a mainstream tactic for career development when companies took to stripping layers of management from corporate hierarchies in the 1980s and 1990s. Contemporary ideas of how a career should be managed are always influenced by what the generation establishing its presence in the workplace (currently it is millennials, or Generation Y) are thinking, and by the older generation's ideas of what the incoming generation is thinking.[8] The scale of modern industry long abandoned the local, artisan manager. The scope of change in society, the shape of economics, and the pace of technology have all transformed how we might define what a manager is, and therefore what a business leader should be. The world of work, quite understandably, is constantly shifting, with the only constant perhaps being how bad we are at predicting what the future is going to look like. Business schools are great at the retransmission of theoretical frameworks and models that have been developed in the past, and often creative in *re*-presenting these as pragmatic applications to the world we're in now, but they are much worse at predicting what the future will be.

To illustrate the general point further, let us take another concept often placed at the heart of leadership, change. There is a lot written about change in management, but to best understand change we may start with its corollary, the existing situation, or the status quo. Broadly speaking, there are two views about the nature of the status quo in work and organisational culture:

1. The status quo is never static and is constantly and incrementally in the process of adaptation. Status quo never stays still; it only appears that way because we measure it at given points in time. Organisations are fundamentally fluid. Things will generally be changing and in flux *unless* held in place and not allowed to.
2. The status quo is always static and equilibrium is the default. Whenever we see change, it is because the status quo is forced to move, to look for a new equilibrium. Organisations are fundamentally stable. Change is resisted by an organisation until either it fails or is forced to move. Things will stay still and the same *unless* they are forced not to.[9]

---

[8] Hamoiri, M. (2010). Managing Yourself: Job-Hopping to the Top and Other Career Fallacies, *Harvard Business Review*.

[9] For a diversion on the same theme, consider that the height of Mount Everest is thought to be growing at about 4 millimetres per year. When Edmund Hillary and Tenzing Norgay reached the summit in 1953, it was 26.8 centimetres lower than today.

Which is correct? The business consequences are different in each case. A leader who held that change is the constant would not set up the same goals and measurements, or demand the same sort of followership, as one who held that change was the necessary step to get to the next fixed state.

How do you even go about answering that? Do you uncritically take it from others as to which view of change is correct, relying on the maxim of follow the crowd (i.e. right or wrong, imitate what everyone is doing)? That is expedient and might provide a quick fix. Or do you examine the basis of each claim and investigate their premises, and then see what makes sense?

When it is at its most potent, leadership is supposed to be about challenging the status quo and bringing about change that better fits with intended goals. Leadership should be about creating new possibilities, and if this eschews old ways of thinking or doing, then to succeed it needs rigour and depth in enquiry. In business, the usual pattern is for people to act to obtain a goal, and what organisations do is marshal the actions of many people toward that end. Every deliberate action (or deliberate absence of action) is the result of a decision, which will have been based on a judgement. But here is the thing, that judgement (meaning-making) was embedded in whatever guiding beliefs or principles the people were using for sense-making. Normally we pay little or no attention to the grounds upon which our decisions to act are made. How can a true and profound change in an organisation happen if everyone, leadership, employees, and stakeholders, restrict their creativity only to the level of the implementation of a decision, and not the thinking it was based on? People will be responding only from their conditioning, and their conditioning may be the problem. These are familiar questions, but now we must preface them with the proposition that the leader needs to understand the nature of change before they start to practice it. To appreciate the nature of something (its essence) is to enquire more deeply into what defines it than most of us are used to. This is a philosophical question.

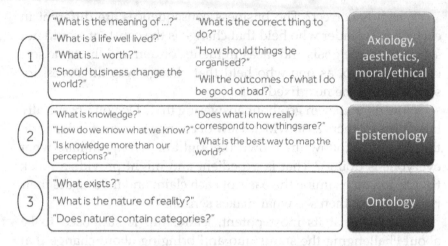

Figure 2.1. Three types of philosophical questions.

The Integrated Leader's Guide to Philosophy

I have found that the best way into this is to offer a brief introduction to three types of questions in philosophy, as shown in Figure 2.1

Each group corresponds to a different category of philosophical questions, namely axiology, epistemology, and ontology. These are not terms used much in day-to-day business (and I am not recommending you start!), so they need some expansion and explanation. Let us start with Group 1.

Axiology

Axiological questions are about agreeing on or demonstrating meaning, assessing value and worth, and making moral judgements and ethical decisions. This includes questions found in aesthetics, which is the appreciation of beauty, art, and the sensorial appearance of things. Because it is home to questions of 'should', axiology is a very crowded category when it comes to management theory and Group 1 is full of many of the questions you meet or generate first-hand as a leader. Try these for size:

What would be a better way of doing what we do?
What makes a good leader?
Should a leader be a good person?
Are we proud of what we do? Is it worthwhile?
What is a leader to do in our organisation?
What is the true impact of what I do?

These are about value and are representative of innumerable management trainings, leadership development seminars, and corporate team building events. Whatever responses come to mind, notice what evidence you are using to support your thought process. Nearly every business theory, model, or framework is about meaning, judgement, and how to act. That is not surprising, of course. Management, business, economics, and leadership are goal and decision-oriented social concepts, concerned with defining the correct or most favourable course of action. Although leaders are sometimes encouraged to think critically not just about what they do but about the theories they are applying in doing it, this is easier said than done. In practice, when time is short, resources limited, and calls for long-term survival are smokescreens for short-term wins, many people are lured by novel and easy-to-understand solutions. Serious questioning of where a new theory or solution comes from gets ditched, often because the risk is low in the short term. Leaders can often sneak away (or be swept away) before the consequences of their actions are fully realised. After all, someone else in the leadership industry will surely come up with a better model if the current fad does not work. Avalanche after avalanche of 'new and improved' remedies, plans, and recipes aimed at organisations fill stacks of books, magazines, and countless websites, and yet over time we never see real progress (just a never-ending churn of claims and counterclaims). The same questions remain.[10] Not only that, but the situation can often be made worse through the nature of social theory. What people believe about leadership and management affects how theory develops. In social

---

[10] The current book cannot be entirely free of this stain.

science, theories can become agents of change of social reality in a way that in the natural sciences they cannot. The effect of a bad management theory is that it may drive away the good. Applied to business and management, axiology forms subject domains such as human resource management, marketing, strategy, and leadership. Applied to the personal, axiology deals with the specifics of mind-set, attitudes, values, and beliefs. This is the domain of the pundit, and where we enter the world of the psychometric test.

Psychometrics is a general term applied to standardised assessments that measure a range of psychological attributes, aptitudes, personality traits, behaviours, styles, preferences, and abilities. They may be used for personal reflection or evaluation as part of a selection or training process. The list of tests available is long and grows exponentially in proportion to the demand for leaders.[11] Some of the better-known include:

- Myers–Briggs Temperament Indicator (MBTI)
- DISC assessment
- Honey & Mumford Learning Styles Inventory
- Graduate Management Admission Test (GMAT)
- 16 Personality Factor (16PF) Questionnaire
- Big 5 Personality Traits
- Fundamental Interpersonal Relations Orientation-Behavior (FIRO-B)

Many have been around for quite some time, which either means they can claim legitimate value as well as longevity, or they are pseudoscience and just very hard to get rid of. Some are fun to do and one or two will get you thinking, but none make any sense except in reference to other people or, occasionally, to an abstract idea. If you feel the need to find out what psychometrics reveal to you about yourself, then dive in and explore as many as you can because

---

[11] There is an old joke that anyone who wants to see a psychiatrist should have their head examined. Whether you think these tests will tell you something, or whether you believe that they will not, you're probably right.

patrolling the frontiers between all these ideas can be educational. But note whether your test results and the labels they use then become short-hand to represent yourself to others and shortcuts used by you in categorising others quickly and efficiently. There are two major pitfalls to this approach (this punctuation):

i. When the tool in your hand is called a hammer, everything else tends to start to look like a nail. The labels are pervasive and a day or two's exposure to a Myers–Briggs Type Indicator training, for example, often has everyone in the room labelling everything and everyone in those terms.

ii. There is nothing to be learnt through a psychometric lens that could not be or is not already accessible to you without them. In other words, they reveal primarily themselves, and perhaps they convey some of the theory behind them. No psychometric has a complete answer to the question 'who am I?'. You may go on an exciting detour, but you eventually end up right back where you started, unmoved.

While we could hardly maintain a functioning society without social and psychological theories, a critical eye is needed if we are not to become lost in the vastness of so many variations on themes. Leaders who naively accept the latest trend without checking to see what assumptions it hides, obscures, or justifies, may experience a series of unintended consequences that exacerbate their strategic problems. Worse, they may even endorse working practices that have a decidedly unethical side to them. For example, when there is an apparent conflict between the health and well-being of employees and the imperative for lucrative results for shareholders, the choice of narrative for justification of what gets priority really starts to matter, and the potential for internal conflict and entanglement can grow exponentially.

The views of others are undoubtedly useful for triangulation, but this usefulness should come from how their ideas challenge yours. Rigid adherence to someone else's ideas does not result in freedom for you. If you live your life and conduct your career only in terms of the type of philosophical questions asked in Group 1, and never look beyond imitation to underlying questions, then you will live in the limitations of your thinking.

The Integrated Leader seeks to understand the world more fully, and more critically, than is often the mainstream. How to judge which theories of 'what should we do?' and which of 'who am I?' are stronger and which are weaker? Do you take someone else's word for it, or can you find out for yourself? And how do you do that? The answer to the last question is knowing more about how **you** think, and this brings us to Group 2 and the question of knowledge. Meet epistemology.

Epistemology

Epistemology is the branch of philosophy that deals with two things; first, the nature of what we know and how we know it.[12] Second, it refers to the study of what we know and how we know it (we can look at our epistemology, although we are using epistemology to do so). It answers questions such as how we separate the world into things, what counts as boundaries between one thing and another, and on what basis we can find common ground to communicate and make sense. It deals with the formation of primary and foundational ideas upon which we then act.

Epistemology is how we perceive the range of data that we do, and how we convert that into meaningful information (and it is also the description of this: always at two levels).

Data and information are not quite the same. Let us be precise about each:

> *Data:* though we usually think of data[13] as a mass-noun meaning numerical items or quantities used in analysis or research (and as

---

[12] This is where current advances in genetics, neuroscience and a host of other disciplines is relevant to the general subject of learning, although specific relevance to management and leadership theory (axiology) is still far too speculative.
[13] The plural of the singular, datum.

whatever we have stored digitally), originally it meant 'that which is present'. Data represent the full *potential* of what our senses can perceive (or measure) and this includes anything with the potential to be 'noticed' by the mind. Potential data surrounds us because our nervous system is synonymous with being in touch with the world. There is always far more data around us than we can use and like any raw material it needs processing.

Information: is a sub-set of data. Data that is perceived *and* punctuated may become information if it makes a difference. Data not attended to in consciousness, for example, makes no difference and remains unpunctuated.

Difference here does not mean disagreement. Difference expresses an elementary idea and is the basic building block of every aspect of human knowing. The only way we detect information from data is through difference, a biological reality we share with every living system. An ecosystem requires information for its cohesion, and the complex system of responses and relationships that maintain and sustain any system (whether a planet's climate or an executive board of a multinational company) is expressing something about its epistemology in this way. Difference is a concept with three fundamental properties — relationship, zero-dimension, and generativity — and is such an important point for the integrated leader that we will devote the whole of the next chapter to it.

So, epistemology deals with knowing and knowledge. The intellectual tradition most usually associated with our modern understanding of knowing and knowledge derives from the Greek philosopher Aristotle, for whom knowledge had three aspects.

1. *Episteme:* knowledge of that which is universal, invariable, and not tied to any context. This is the knowledge aimed for in axioms and general laws. We now think of this as the embodiment of the scientific method and to the rigorous pursuit of fundamentals (very close to any academic's heart).
2. *Phronesis:* knowledge from the use of rationality and reason, to be purposive and achieve goals and ends, and to predict.

Phronesis is knowledge that is practical and context-dependent. In our time, we might label this intelligence and see it as the basis for knowing the most prudent way to act in each situation. This is quite closely related to another Greek term, *techné*, or the 'know-how' principles of crafting, organising, and producing (very close to any manager's heart).

3. *Sophia*: wisdom. Sophia is more than intelligence and creativity; it is the derivation of meaning for choice. This is knowledge based on (and gained through) introspection and reflection on universals. Wisdom is finding one's place in nature. There is something here about looking at what transcends many apparently separate and different modes of thought (very close to my heart).

Wisdom is a word used in a common-sense way (e.g. knowing what to do and what not to do), but it needs a little more precision in its definition for this chapter. One that speaks nicely to personal development and the Integrated Leader comes from Carolyn Aldwin, writing in 2009:

> 'Wisdom is a practice that reflects the developmental process by which individuals increase in self-knowledge, self-integration, nonattachment, self-transcendence, and compassion, as well as a deeper understanding of life. This practice involves better self-regulation and ethical choices, resulting in greater good for oneself and others.'[14]

There is a lot in there to get to grips with, including a few elements that are very difficult to measure in terms that you could apply in business and management. In the context of mapping lifespan development (see Chapter 7), we find the psychologists Erik and Joan Erikson defining wisdom more poetically (or more starkly, depending on your view) as:

---

[14] Aldwin, C. M. (2009). Gender and Wisdom: A Brief Overview. *Research in Human Development*, 6(1): 1–8, DOI: 10.1080/15427600902779347 (with permission).

'informed and detached concern with life itself in the face of death itself.'[15]

This definition shows us an aspect of knowing that is unique to humans. Awareness of mortality is awareness of the inevitability of the most defining act of punctuation we can imagine — death. One could spend decades in contemplation of that and be no closer to truth. At the other end of the spectrum, there must surely be an epistemology we cannot be conscious of, namely knowing at the biological level. Somehow your body 'knows' how to breathe without you thinking of it, your brain knows how to think without thinking to do so, and your body knows to regenerate itself after illness or injury. Breath, brain function, and immune system are as much a part of you as your sense of self-identity, but we often do not process ourselves that way. Between genetics and philosophical self-awareness (consciousness), it is epistemology that must be the connection.

A Word (or Three) on Consciousness

We are all conscious, so you would think we would intuitively know what it is. We do not. That said, it is worth visiting consciousness before moving on, even though any attempt to shed light on it is doomed. Some people spend their entire careers studying consciousness and try to come up with an answer as to what it is. They invariably fail, or fail to convince, and the consensus among those in the know is that, frankly, no-one can ever really be in the know about this thing. For sure this is partly because consciousness is a suitcase concept, stuffed full of so many different things that it will mean different things to different people. It is something so basic and so fluid that every branch of science will conclude something different about it. Consciousness has too

---

[15] Erikson, E. H. (1997). *The Life Cycle Completed.* Extended version with new chapters on the ninth stage of development by Joan M. Erikson. New York, NY: W. W. Norton. (p. 61).

many aspects to make sense of as one thing. At the same time, we must acknowledge that thinking about consciousness can only be done with consciousness and, rather as a mirror cannot reflect its own surface, we cannot find out what consciousness is this way. We cannot use something more than our consciousness, as being conscious is the defining characteristic of being human. We end up studying the *idea* of consciousness, which usually gets stated as the state of mental awareness of thought, feeling, and self-agency. This is circular, which is hardly surprising, for reasons stated earlier.

Given a logical impasse, we resort to defining consciousness by what it is not, and that immediately embroils us in the baffling relationship between the conscious and the unconscious. Are they separate? Are they different? Can you have one without the other? Is the conscious a sub-set of the unconscious, or vice versa? Can either be measured? Can attention move from one to the other without one becoming the other?[16] The debate about consciousness has been fierce, the confusion unending, and resolution absent. There is, however, general scientific and philosophical agreement on consciousness being mental activity, and an emergent property of the functioning of our brains. Mind is embodied.[17] However, this does not really get us too far because many humans are still content with a split, for identity purposes, between some things my brain does which equal an 'I' that is doing the thinking, and others that equal a 'me' to which this thinking is applied. Only a tiny fraction of what my brain and body are doing is categorised by me as 'I'. I am content to believe that I am moving my eyes, or that I am chewing my food, but not that I am growing my hair, or digesting my food, and so on. And yet my brain must be such that it is ('I'?) processing simultaneously *every* aspect of what I am doing and thinking.

---

[16] We will never really know. This is analogous to seeing whether the light in the fridge goes off when you close the door.

[17] In fact, it would be more accurate to say that mind is immanent in the material. Whether or not there is an immaterial, metaphysical identity (soul?) is not resolved by this, at least among those who believe that there is such a thing.

You can hunt for consciousness in quantitative or qualitative measurement, via psychology or neurology, in observation of behaviour, or from evidence in experiments. There is plenty of interesting data but very little information. Just more questions. Can the subjective ever study and explain itself? Or do we leave the phenomenon as the best explanation of itself? Our search to understand consciousness feels like another example of the Indian fable of the men, blind from birth, who were summoned by a wise king, out to make a point to his philosophical advisors whom he saw as intellectually and figuratively blind. The king presented each blind man with a different part of an elephant, saying 'such is an elephant'. From their fragment, each then declared that they knew what an elephant was like. Of course, each description was of something else. In the fable, the blind men began to fight among themselves, because each thought their view was the whole truth.

Perhaps what we are trying to describe is an ocean, and what we experience as consciousness is just the surface of the sea. An ocean consists of one thing, water and all water in the ocean connects as one. Only a fraction of the water in the ocean is its surface, however. 'Below the surface' to us appears another world, remote, mysterious, full of deep currents. Little or no light from the surface reaches the depths and close to the surface there is plenty of activity and some vibrant ecologies. Were we to raise a bucket of 'deep' from the bottom and place it at the surface, it would become surfaced. Conversely, were we to drag a bucket of 'surface' down, it would become the deep, but in all cases it is still water and still the ocean. Consciousness and unconscious are two words for two aspects of one thing, not two things. The concept of consciousness may have so little explanatory use that we may safely dispense with it as relevant for learning. It may not even be useful for understanding self-awareness. That does not mean it stops being important, fascinating, or a generative source of creativity and innovation, but it might be the insight we need to free us from the age-old search for ourselves in consciousness. Would that be a huge step toward integration as a leader?

There is yet one more level of philosophical questions to consider. The most robust theories will seek alignment from the top to the bottom. So what is lurking at the bottom of philosophy? Meet ontology.

Ontology

Ontological questions are those that ask 'what exists, independent of us and our thoughts?'. Reality is one word for that, nature might be another. Reality is beyond punctuation, but punctuation eventually relies on reality for its potency. Ontologically speaking, there are no beginnings, middles, or ends, and there is no such thing as an experience because that requires an experiencer, a knower. The universe just is, and the long debate in philosophy (you would not expect this to have been a recent argument) has been whether anything at all can be said about reality. And if so, what? The German poet Rainer Rilke, writing in a letter to a young friend, captures this conundrum:

> 'Things are not all as graspable and sayable as on the whole we are led to believe; most events are unsayable, occur in a space that no words have ever penetrated.'[18]

We can try to describe reality, but its essence retreats from our words. One view is that it is literally senseless to ask questions about the nature of reality beyond our knowledge because they cannot be asked in a way that does not use epistemology, and epistemology draws only from sense-data. Other data might exist, but they will always be inaccessible. Another view says that ontological questions, again, are literally meaningless without reference to axiology, and that reality has no moral aspect.[19]

---

[18] Rilke, R. (2014). *Letters to a Young Poet*, London, United Kingdom: Penguin Modern Classics.

[19] This doesn't prevent people from arguing that you can ask, and that reality is a manifestation of a moral force. However, this is beyond the scope and limitations of this book.

When we ask about what exists, we are seeking the most basic level of classification possible. What category does *everything* belong to (assuming such a category exists)? What is bedrock and cannot be explained in terms of anything else? The content of that category is the answer to the question 'what exists?' and it is non-negotiable; what exists is what exists, whether you believe you can say something about it or not.[20] My view is that whatever else it is, this undifferentiated, unpunctuated, and ineffable reality is not necessarily chaotic, nor beyond a sincere attempt at comprehension. For a start, it must contain regularities such that the events of the universe proceed as they do, including those that have resulted in this solar system, and life on this planet as we experience it. That which we call evolution would be 'real' in this sense, and so would a species with a capacity to perceive it as such — us. But the nature of reality is unlikely to have merely material dimension, as the science of quantum physics is now suggesting. What constitutes reality is, for want of a better way of saying it, information, and pattern.

I don't think this is irrelevant to leadership, although you don't need to contemplate the deep nature of reality each time you decide on allocations for next year's budget, or ponder whether artificial intelligence is going to seriously affect your business in five years. However, even the most prosaic company

---

[20] There have been two major schools of thought on ontology. Realists say there is a world 'out there' independent of our knowledge of it. All realists agree on that, but there are sub-types. Positivists believe direct experience (sense-data) carries evidence of reality, and we can hypothesise and conduct experiments to find laws which objectively are the same thing as reality. Critical Realists argue that while thought is constituent of reality, our understanding of reality is necessarily partial. We can infer independent, generative mechanisms that result in the world we see, otherwise we would not be here, but our knowledge is fallible. The other ontological school is that of the Idealists. Strong idealist ontologies accept knowledge of the nature of the world *only* as a set of culturally negotiated and interpreted meanings. The most that we can do is to document the differences between cases. In place of law-like empirical regularities, the hermeneutic (interpretive/linguistic) tradition in social science can generate law-like rules only about its own conceptualisations.

decision-making has a context and can become a context as it radiates out in time into other spheres. In addition, you are a finite human being and your life, as with everyone's life, calls out for a frame for meaning. Ontology deals with everything that is so. Picking an argument with reality is picking a fight you can never win.

Finally

So, when we are looking at the questions you should ask as a leader, and the questions you should ask of a leader, it is critical to start with an open mind and critical faculty to see how you have constructed the world.

It is the job of the leader to understand fully the purpose of business, to make decisions that will have wisdom and longevity, and above all to make decisions about organisational health and well-being that are genuinely in tune with the way the world is. The consequences and repercussions of poor leadership decisions, arrived at uncritically and implemented unthinkingly, will cascade into all aspects of work and life. It means nothing if an organisation has an inspirational mission statement on its website, a sparkling vision statement on display in its headquarters, and state-of-the-art training programme for every employee if what it is proposing to do is out of step with reality.

This chapter has been built on a premise that your personal development is the relationship between you and your conditioning, and that your conditioning is a complex and multi-layered question. It is necessary to understand your conditioning (punctuation), and even more important to understand how and why you are attached to it. The Integrated Leader is someone who has begun this and has become committed to showing others where the relationship they have with their conditioning might now be a barrier, limitation, or restraint to sustainable health and well-being (of the organisation, but there are other levels). When all sides see that they live through conditioning, and that conditioning is just punctuation, then everyone can begin changing the rules of their conditioning to live better. The Integrated Leader is interested in such mutual development as an exchange between equals. We find ourselves more honestly when we meet the stranger who most differs from us.

The Integrated Leader's Manifesto (Leading Self)
#2

'I strive for learning, not perfection (perfectionism is, by definition, unobtainable, and meaningless). I know that there are many
blind spots in my experience and knowledge. Therefore, I keep
my humility, honouring the diversity of the wisdom of others.
The alternative to perfectionism is awareness.'

*Perfection signifies being in a state of completeness. There are two cases
where perfection could have meaning:*

1. *When a thing is in and of itself complete, whole, and finished, independent of anything else or in comparison to anything else. Perfection
   thus exists as a conceptual state and an abstraction found, in theory,
   in reference only to itself;*
2. *When a thing possesses every quality from a set of qualities within
   a given set of boundaries, as for example when the gymnast puts in a
   faultless performance and gets the maximum score. Perfection is a
   theoretical position used for improvement in closed systems[21] that
   operate with pre-set and agreed rules.*

Elsewhere?
*Is it reasonable for a person to wish for perfection either in their
knowledge (learning) or in their output (experience and performance)?
The goal of the perfectionist is to be free from defect, flawless, or without
fault, and therefore free from error. It is difficult to see how it fits with
learning, which needs mistakes and failure, and is only feasible in business in processes or systems that don't have an element of the unknown
or the random. Unless you can create one of these two categories above,
then perfectionism is setting yourself up for disappointment.*

*Perfectionism is a negative starting point for personal development
because human learning happens in an open system. Perfectionism is a*

---

[21] The Toyota Production System (TPS) would be a good example.

scourge in management practice, where the time for self-reflection is already limited and where there is relentless pressure to deliver results to please the levels above ('do more, do better'). Trying to live up to that urge from others to improve performance, when turned on the self ('be more, be better'), is a commandment that can lead to stress and burn out.

The good news is that learning is something we all have access to, by virtue of our innate physiology and mental capacity. If we have blocked, forgotten, or denied that inborn capacity to adapt, then we may perceive that we do not have the flexibility to change. The absence of this flexibility is going to be a source of stress. A belief that we must strive for perfection is a self-limiting belief.

Seeking perfection is not the same thing as learning. Studying and passing exams is not the same as learning. Effort and exertion are not the same as learning. Validation is not learning. Personal development can begin when you know for yourself, and can admit to others, that:

1. The capacity for adaptation and change is natural and immanent[22] in you
2. This capacity to adjust is accessible
3. Your perfectionism can be reframed without risk

Learning is realisation of insight that comes when we access our innate capacity for learning.

---

[22] Immanent = already present and operating.

Chapter 3

Difference

The old pond.
A frog leaps
in the water's sound

Haiku, by Basho (1644–1694)[1]

The Basis of Perception

What is the difference between management and leadership? Like the 'Old Faithful' geyser in Wyoming, this question seems to erupt with predictable regularity in any training for leaders. We could rehearse the usual responses, but an examination of the question is more worthy of effort than the imposition of any answer. You can describe management and you can describe leadership, but does it make sense contrasting one with the other? Is one a subset of the other? Are they overlapping but otherwise distinct categories? Or entirely separate realms? People usually dive in forgetting first to question those sorts of premises. As we shall see, any comparison implies a relationship, and a relationship of difference must be proven to make a difference.[2]

Humans make sense of the world through knowledge based on intuition (immediate apprehension), and reason based on

---

[1] This is perhaps the most famous haiku from the golden period of Japanese short poem wordplay in the 17th century. (Furu ike ya, kawazu tobikomu, mizu no oto).
[2] To one or other of the people asking, or to you. A third party is required for meaning.

perception, yet we rarely stop to think about the nature of perception as a phenomenon. We tend to take our capacity for sense-making and knowing for granted. All life may be said to be the creation of moment-to-moment perception. From simple organisms that react to external stimuli to sustain themselves in their environment, all the way to complex animals that include each other and themselves in their field of perception, how the senses respond to data from outside is the primary source of all information.

How do we know what someone else is feeling? We see their body and its expressions, we hear their voices, and we can even react with touch to learn more. In healthy humans,[3] the innate ability, physiologically and cognitively, to perceive is combined with a knack for social cohesion. Ideas as well as genes can be passed from one generation to the next. This has generated a technological boom that has elevated us to a level of dominance of our environment. This sense-making is the heartbeat of life, and every leader relies on it to fulfil their role, but it is a double-edged sword. We are now so dominant through our perception that we detect evident stresses on our own ecosystem's ability to sustain itself. To perceive is to discriminate. If we did not or could not discern, we would not perceive. We have evolved to detect change in our environment through our senses, from sense-data. Our ability to do this, however, is limited both by threshold sensitivity (for example, our eyes can detect only 0.0035% of the full electromagnetic spectrum), and the quality of our attention (we are easily attracted, and even more easily distracted). We may pick up on some cues of change but be blind (physiologically or mentally) to others. Very small variations in our surroundings may not be registered and, counter-intuitively, large-scale, or long-term changes may be difficult to detect or acknowledge. Staff in well-established and reputable companies may fail to see that, despite top customers remaining faithful and operations efficient and profitable, the world has moved on. The fact that there is no

---

[3] There are many medical conditions (e.g. face blindness) where one or more aspect of sensory perception or cognitive processing has been damaged or is missing. These tell us much about the nature of our total mental capacity to operate in the world.

new generation of customers waiting in the wings for its existing offer may be ignored; the organisation has failed to see the trend.[4] More tellingly, the industry that fails to notice (or deliberately ignores) the pollution, depletion, or destruction of the ability of its environment to re-generate has made the same error.

The previous chapter highlighted the richness and variety of our systems of punctuation, but that begs the question in that we must have formed the categories and hierarchies necessary for punctuation in the first place. How did we do that? Is there a basic unit from which all our sense-making is constructed? The answer is difference.

What's the Difference?

Difference is an abstract concept that is both straightforward and challenging to grasp. It is not rare, though. In fact, all living systems operate using difference as their primary and fundamental reality. We all experience difference because experience is a matter of sensory differences. Think of a radar on a ship, which is a relatively simple device that sends out a high-frequency radio signal in a rotating beam. The microwaves move outward until they touch a surface sufficiently solid enough to bounce some of the waves back to the antenna on the ship. Sensitive electronic equipment registers this particular data and converts it to visual information that the ship's crew can use, for example, to steer a course, avoid a collision, etc. News of *no* interference is, as far as the radar equipment is concerned, as necessary in the system as news of interference (an object). But for the radar user, only some of the total data is information. The extra element in the circuit is the sense-making system of the human being looking at it. A radar is a device to provide news of difference to human sense organs. We can use this analogy to start to understand not just how the human brain co-ordinates all the ways the body has for 'touching' the world around it (by sight, sound, touch, taste, and so on), but also how the mind processes and selects certain

---

[4]This is known as strategic drift.

data as information. This is the first of two extraordinary things about us; our capacity for punctuation — to recognise, conceptualise, and categorise the world. When we perceive something, we in effect outline 'this', and anything not within that line is conceptually 'that'. From this simple, general principle, we get an almost limitless potential of contrasts, such as 'me' and 'you', 'here' and 'there', 'is' and 'is not', 'this' and 'not this', 'leader' and 'follower'.

If that feels somewhat obvious, difference has two remarkable properties you may not have considered. To understand the nature of that, look first at Figure 3.1 and then try the following thought experiment.

Figure 3.1.   First thought experiment about difference.

First, imagine this two-dimensional shape as a three-dimensional sphere of uniform consistency and material. Now picture this ball expanding outward in size, rapidly and equally in every direction. Out, out it goes, to infinity, until all that is all there is. This infinite new universe has nothing in it, contains no features, and therefore no variation. It has no centre and no edge or boundary. There is no intrinsic 'here' because there is no 'there' for it to be in relation with. Next, in your mind, imagine yourself inside this universe. With nothing to move toward and nothing to move away from, the concept of direction or movement is senseless. There would be no way of moving and no way of telling if you were.

Because there is nothing other than you in this infinite, uniform universe, there is no sense data. The senses have nothing to sense. There is nothing to discriminate, discern, or differentiate. Can you think? Yes, but there is not much point because thinking cannot translate to action. Imagine now another person with you in this universe. From the perspective of one or other of you, a basic epistemology is established. Difference. There is now in theory, and in practice, a basis for 'this' and 'that' (or 'here' and 'there', and so on). Movement is now possible, but this is relative to the other object, the other person. There is still no objective way of agreeing who is moving toward or moving away from whom. Only when you imagine into the universe a *third* person do things become interesting, because while movement is still relative in terms of the infinite universe, there is now a rudimentary notion of a system. Two's company, but three is an epistemological leap forward because each player now has double dimension to work with. In nature, the power of two dimensions allows for the emergence of a third.

Figure 3.2 represents the advance from Figure 3.1 in terms of contrast. It may be recognised as a (incomplete[5]) *yinyang* symbol, the visual expression in Chinese philosophy of the fusion of opposites, of light and dark, and so on.

Figure 3.2.   Second thought experiment about difference.

---

[5] Yin-yang as a symbol is portrayed with a dot of white in the black and a dot of black in the white.

The s-shape expresses the dynamic flow of relationship of one side around the other. The next step is more problematic. What colour is the boundary between the light and dark in the figure? You may soon realise that there is no way of answering this unless you take a position. You must first select one to be the foreground and the other the background. Foreground and background go with each other such that you cannot meaningfully have one without the other, just as you cannot have an up without down, inside without outside, and life without death (see Chapter 7). Human relations are governed by agreements based on what position we take regarding difference.

Now we come to the two remarkable properties of difference.

1. A difference has no physical dimension. Differences between the light side and the dark side in Figure 3.2 are not a property of either.[6] Difference is an idea, and as such is not located in space or in time.
2. A concrete event can be triggered by an immaterial difference. This will feel counter-intuitive because we are accustomed to believing that events are caused by material things, and that a difference is a material thing. Indeed, much of the frenetic activity consuming a good chunk of a manager's time is directly or indirectly the result of that premise.

For example, the difference between China and the United States feels like a very real thing, as no doubt does any difference between your organisation and its main competitor(s). We may start to think that our differences are real and that they constitute who we are when no one else is around. But we forget that we are dealing with a perception only. Since difference is not a material thing, it cannot be quantified, only qualified.[7]

---

[6] Difference is a comparison, and the property of a comparison is not a property of elements being compared.

[7] The famous Rorschach inkblot test is a great example if you are struggling to ground this idea in your experience.

Difference is a fundamental and complex organising principle that we use every day at work, at home, and in our heads. It is also the way that ecological systems function.

Difference and Meaning-Making

Chapter 1 asked you to adopt a mindful stance to yourself and to learning. Chapter 2 tried to reveal the incredible network of interconnected categories in daily use. These were both talking about how sense-making happens. Sense-making is the prerequisite to action, and in management or leadership, action is purposeful, which is to say that it intends meaning. Leadership is therefore about meaning-making.

Would you say you work for a small company? Whether you say yes or whether you say no,[8] you will by now be aware that you are already drawing distinctions and agreeing to conventions. You are in the world of ideas and not the world merely of blind and unthinking physical forces. 'Big' and 'small' are discriminations of a relationship between one organisation (foreground, whatever its size) and another (background, whatever its size). This is the first important step in sense-making, and you will find that you have implicitly used the following question to answer:

"Compared to What?"

Next, do you work for a good company? Your answer might rely on comparison, a reference point, such as the question above (e.g. "it is better than where I used to work"), or it might be using a second fundamental sense-making question:

"According to Whom?"

Here, difference is immersed in a validation, a comparison of beliefs/opinions/approvals/permissions of one person with another. 'Small', 'big', 'good' and 'bad' are not intrinsic properties of any organisation, even though you may feel intuitively that somehow they may be. Comparisons and validations are part of

---

[8] Or even whether you say, 'it depends' (although you may be more on the right path. It depends.).

the constant and dynamic interplay going on in a society and between individuals, and without the ability to compare, we would lack the information we need to adjust ourselves to fit in or adjust others to achieve outcomes. In some professional contexts, for instance, validation is an important and rigorous step for the legal right to continue in business or ethical standards to pursue a profession. In many other cases, it is simply the norm to judge or hold an opinion based on what other people say. You do this all the time. This is your conditioning, and the point here is not that you should drop comparison or reject the idea of validation (this is very likely to make you unemployable!), but that you need to be aware that this is how you are forming those relationships and opinions. Most leaders' journeys into awareness start in comparisons and validation. This is not surprising as we co-evolve with our environment and what we experience mentally is differentiation. The takeaway here is that comparisons and validations are forms of punctuation and as such, they are based on conventions. Conventions can change.

In a few critical cases, however, defining things in terms of 'compared to what?' and 'according to whom?' has severe limitations and restraints on health and well-being. The most obvious is your self-esteem.

Meaning-making follows from sense-making. Meaning-making is about interpretation of consequences. This matters because the Integrated Leader's function is to assign meaning to rapidly changing and unpredictable contexts so that the organisation is preserved in a better state than it was before any intervention by them. Three quick examples will help illustrate how we use punctuation and difference to move from sense-making to meaning-making.

First, a simple one. On my desk is an apple and an orange. As discussed, any difference between the apple and the orange is not *in* the apple and not *in* the orange, or the physical space between them; if I move the apple, or eat it, the difference is unchanged. Very few of the potentially vast number of differences between the apple and the orange matter; they are differences that make no difference. To say that something matters is to say that contextually it is involved in another part of a given system behaving a particular way. If I eat the apple and it was mine, this probably has no meaning for you. If it was yours, and your lunch, and you are hungry, then its absence becomes information that could affect the relationship between us. Difference thus enters the circuit of interactions which is our communication.

Second, an allegorical example. The philosopher Ludwig Wittgenstein[10] used the duck–rabbit illustration as an example of how perception works. The ambiguity of the illusion, shown in Figure 3.3, revolved around the question of whether you perceive this as the head of a duck or the head of a rabbit.

Figure 3.3.   The duck-rabbit illusion.[9]

At first glance you may see neither, then see first only one or the other, then successively one after the other.[11] At the heart of this is an ambiguity of form in the image sufficient to compromise our ability to recognise and discriminate the cues of what a shape represents. When a sign carries a lot of unambiguous information, we say that it contains redundancies. Normally, our minds can quickly

[9] Jastrow, J. (1899). The mind's eye. *Popular Science Monthly, 54*, 299–312.

[10] Wittgenstein, L. (2009). *Philosophical Investigations*, Hoboken, NJ: Wiley-Blackwell (pp. 193–208).

[11] Though not both at the same time because 'knowing' is one thing and 'seeing' is another.

compute the most logical and likely set of possibilities in a situation. For example, languages that use the Latin alphabet appear written in fonts with widely differing designs for the letter 'a', yet we carry with us a learnt ability for recognition based on cues in context and basic letter shape. We read without needing to go over and examine all the information and eliminate all the impossible combinations. This is a bit like 'the educated guess' of gut feel in decision-making at work, which saves time and effort.[12] Whenever someone can guess with more than random certainty what the other side will be thinking in response to a particular event or intervention, they are using the same process. Generally speaking, management is about finding and maintaining as many situations where things are clear enough for messages about them to be unambiguous, but simple enough in how much information is needed to avoid the need to repeat efforts or lay out 100% of the data to move on. Optical illusions interfere with that pattern, often in a fun or non-serious way. Self-reflection can be a pattern interrupter.

The Integrated Leader tries to be open to identifying such fixed patterns. In an open system such as the strategic environment of an organisation or its environment, signals can be just as dualistic and vague as they are in an optical illusion. Whenever we are unable to discriminate or be sure, we must find the space to stop and think about what is going on. This is where it gets interesting, and what makes it a valuable point about the current situation for almost every organisation, group, community, and nation in the world. Where a pattern disappears or cannot be discerned, our epistemology will impose a new one. This point is rather beautifully shown in this *New Yorker* magazine cartoon by Paul Noth in Figure 3.4.

For me, this message is the parable of our times. The meaning of the duck–rabbit problem is not in the ambiguity of the original drawing (this is a game of sense-making), it is in the interpretation of consequences to create meaning from that. We impose an ideological foreground, which can lead to dogma. Which side becomes foreground and which background is probably a matter of whatever lenses are our conditioning. The problem is *how* we are seeing,

---

[12]Sudoko is an extreme version of this as a past-time.

*"There can be no peace until they renounce their
Rabbit God and accept our Duck God."*

Figure 3.4. The social consequences of a duck-rabbit phenomenon.[13]

not *what* we are seeing. Whether I perceive a duck or a rabbit is a product of my sense-making. Whether that matters, becomes a good thing or a bad thing, may be cause for a new belief or grounds for action (and so on), that is meaning-making. Sense-making is the complex process of registering difference. Meaning-making is the web of relationships of socially constructed comparisons or socially available validations (your or someone else's authority or opinion).[13]

Lastly, a business case. The tobacco industry was until recently one of the most powerful business groupings in the world. It now faces an existential crisis. Its success and its likely downfall are

---

[13] With permission.

good examples of organisational rigidity in systemic contexts. Both the up and the down show how organisations can become fixated on finding meaning measured in profit and influence, without necessarily satisfying a real need or acting in the best interests of society. Tobacco is a native plant in the Americas and early cultivation was linked with several perceived medicinal and chemical uses, including as a poison. It was exported as a product as a key part of European colonisation and expansion from the 16th century onward. Tobacco growing was an intrinsic element in the triangular trade of slaves, goods, and raw materials between Europe, Africa, and the colonies of the new world. By the first part of the 19th century, its use was in decline, the smoking of its leaves, rare, and ill-health from side-effects, well documented and widely condemned. It might have gone the way of many similar questionable products from that period had it not been for the rapid expansion of the joint-stock corporation via a boom in the number of stock markets (led by the United States) in the late 1800s and early 1900s. For the first time in history, a firm could use vast amounts of capital to fund growth, mainly of consumer goods. Recognising the Great War and troop mobilisation as market opportunities, the tobacco industry established cigarette smoking as a mass-market phenomenon among men. In the decades that followed, the same companies rapidly expanded with new brands, especially targeting women smokers. By the advent of the next era of marketing after the Second World War, the range of claims for cigarette smoking as beneficial to health and well-being went far beyond what was evidence-based or reasonable. Without adequate scrutiny of their meaning-making premises, the industry aggressively sought to suppress any move to counter their narrative. In the 1950s, smoking was sold as healthy, relaxing, and sophisticated. In the 1960s, as aspirational and exciting in keeping with modern lifestyle. In the 1970s, as sophisticated and ethically managed, the overwhelming medical and public health case against smoking only just beginning to tip into public opinion, legislation, and litigation in the world's developed economies, prompting many tobacco companies to diversify at home while marketing aggressively to new smokers in developing economies. At every step, interpretation has shaped meaning and underlying patterns of sense-making left unexamined. Where the tobacco industry defended itself on the grounds of making a legitimate product with a natural demand, every element of this narrative has now been shown as false. The issue is much broader than seeking to blame corporates or executives without looking at the broader context of the purpose and ethics of business. In all of this, the same fundamentals of punctuation, difference, and interplay of levels of philosophical question have been crucial, sometimes by their absence from the debate.

Difference in the Corporate World

Classically, the purpose of leadership and management is to find more efficient and effective ways of organising resources and the activities of others. Leadership must first frame problems to solve them. But what if we have misunderstood how this happens? What if we have made an epistemological error? If so, then we will not be seeing things clearly now. For over 200 years, effective management has been predicated on the ability of managers and leaders to draw distinctions in and impose boundaries on the world around them.

Error may occur when we treat the intangible idea as if it were a tangible thing. This mistake is called reification.[14] None of the ways in which PepsiCo and the Coca-Cola Company are the same and none of the ways in which they are different are properties of either, yet what do they (and countless other examples of firms in oligopolies) nearly always use to define themselves? Each other. This premise is required for any application of a framework such as Michael Porter's Five Forces. This is too narrow for our times because it becomes like the duck–rabbit armies in the cartoon, and tells us nothing about the broader picture. Try this. How are the National Health Service (NHS) and British American Tobacco the

---

[14] Reification is treating an abstract idea as if it were a material thing. 'The market', 'the ego', 'IQ', and 'marriage' might all make suitable examples. The philosopher Alfred North Whitehead called this the fallacy of misplaced concreteness.

same? How are they different? How is the NHS the same as or different from the Coca-Cola Company? It is a little easier once we cleave the comparisons to see the nature of our comparing.[15]

Difference in the corporate environment plays out most explicitly in the arena of strategy. Strategy textbooks in business schools stress that finding and sustaining a profitable (or at least a value-creating) proposition is the duty of the leader. Except in rare cases, authors contextualise strategic theories, models, and frameworks so that we feel that the single organisation unit is foreground, and everything else is background. Within the organisation, two relationships are then elevated to foreground: the one with customers and the one with shareholders. Other relationships, such as those with employees, legislators, and competitors may be talked about, but when push comes to shove and strategic decisions need to be made, these are separate items of lesser importance. They become background, useful mainly to contrast the foreground relationships. Strategy may be about what an organisation thinks it must do to survive, but with this thinking, health and well-being become one-dimensional, isolated, and short-term. The view of leadership that is consistent with this operates on four presuppositions:

➢ The ultimate aim of a business is to keep growing into the future.
➢ Sustainability equals the survival of the fittest as measured by profitability, shareholder return, and the continuation of the organisation over time.

---

[15] Difference is a quality present when two things are different. Sameness is a quality present when two things are the same. Same and different are opposites but like all opposites they are eternally yoked. There are two important ways that 'different' and 'same' are connected: 1. They can each mean something complete, but only in relation to the other. They are independent of and interdependent with their opposite. Opposites such as same/different, good/bad are called apposite because they create a useful dimension with each other. 2. To stretch that division between opposites produces a tension. Opposites are reciprocal. That is to say, the result of the tension inherent in the polarity of same and different is creative and produces a dialectic movement.

➢ Organisational health and well-being are relative, not absolute, and value is measured by comparison with those you are competing with for the same customers.

➢ Sustainability in business is a zero-sum game (strategy is always 'more than/less than').

The Integrated Leader might modify these to[16]:

➢ The ultimate aim of a business is to contribute something of net value to how the world is today.

➢ Sustainability equals survival of the organisation and its environment/ecology, which includes suppliers, customers, and the idea of the health and well-being of its competitors.

➢ Organisational health and well-being is absolute, not relative, and value is measured only by comparison with *your* performance.

➢ Sustainability must be win–win, or it is not sustainability. Strategies based on win–lose are unsustainable.

Is my business school different from other business schools? Yes, I certainly think so. It has its own identity and a lot of features that others do not or cannot have (and vice versa). Does that matter? It should not (although if a business school struggles with self-esteem, it may become the only thing that matters). That which might appeal to a manager or leader in their studies at my school ought to be evident in and of itself. If the same good thing(s) can be found in another school, then that is an indicator of a healthy eco-system and ought to be celebrated, not guarded jealously as a trade secret. Any distinctive feature can become a comparison, and we all easily fall into the trap of defining ourselves vis-à-vis others, but without those others, we would not have a definable business in the first place. We need the contrast and comparison as a basis of detachment and broadcast of an image to people who are looking around and comparing. Equally, is my business school the same as

---

[16]This is proposal, not an instruction. You may have a different interpretation.

other business schools? I certainly hope so. Without similarity, we would not be able to communicate easily what we do, and without validation of what we do many managers and leaders would miss an important factor for them in deciding where they should go to study. Difference and similarity are both useful in calibrating ourselves to the world and getting things done. They perform a function, but when an organisation starts believing that the difference or the similarity is real in the sense that it describes a property they have, they run the risk of devoting all their resources to measuring, maintaining, and making everyone subservient to a relationship. How much more challenging and beneficial it would be to look within to define and decide that which is essential.

Difference and Personal Change

As a general phenomenon, difference is neutral. Difference may generate innovation, creativity, synergy, and progress, and just as easily lead to conflict, demolition, entropy and friction. Sensitivity to the source and nature of the role difference plays in life can help you re-evaluate your perceptions of professional and personal development. If you are wondering how, consider this series of heuristic self-questions:

➢   As a leader, do I see the world as it really is, or am I just seeing an image of the world as it appears through my conditioning? How would I tell?
➢   When I make a decision, do I use my conditioning or do I use current reality, as it is?
➢   Is it possible for me to do something entirely original?
➢   Is my identity defined independently of anything or anyone else?
➢   As a leader, should I seek to be different, or should I seek to find common ground?

An organisation that cannot detect change is unaware and unable to respond in a way that will keep it in harmony internally and externally. An organisation is a collection of people with contracts governed by law that tie them in to a collective effort, so it is with people that we must begin if we want to sustain the collective and the function/purpose of the organisation in a healthy way. Since you are a person, it must be your job to consider these questions before you expect answers from others.

Your identity is a matter of your relationship with external borders, boundaries and thresholds. That starts early in life with the emergent property of self, or 'I', and continues growing in detail and complexity throughout adult life. Layer upon layer of our self-descriptions, our rules, our guidelines, agreements, boundaries, systems of communication, ways of seeing, saying, and making, all these are forms of punctuation predicated on difference. People and societies maintain a delicate balance between what works and what needs to be renewed, re-evaluated, or rejected. This is not just in our day-to-day social conventions but, occasionally, in our whole worldview as well. Self-awareness is another manifestation of difference. Life is to be treasured and enjoyed in its finitude, imperfection, and impermanence just as much as it is to be valued in its creativity, abundance, and joy. The undifferentiated life, to twist Socrates a little, is not worth living. This is nicely summed up by one of my favourite quotes, from psychotherapist, spiritual teacher, and thorn in the side of anyone not wanting to enjoy life, Anthony de Mello, who said, "We see people and things not as they are, but as we are." I often share this with our Executive Master of Business Administration students on the very first day after we have run some exercises designed to get in the way of their flow of thoughts and certainties as managers.

Mastery of Difference

For the reasons put forward in these first three chapters, mastery in leadership is difficult to define. On the other hand, leadership is still something most of us know when we see it. People who are effective leaders roll with the ups and downs of the world, and they are usually able to do this because they can roll with the ups and downs of their own existence. As you read the remaining parts of the book, keep in mind the following:

1. The information you see, process, or create as a leader is the same thing as the continually changing relationships between elements in a system. We have evolved to attune to an analogue world, not a digital, binary one. Analogue means operating with variables that are gradients, or qualitative changes, as opposed to the quantitative on/off represented by the digital. In communication, the analogue (e.g. tone of voice, volume, or pitch) will carry more organising information to the listener than the digital of words.

2. Sense-making relies on complex and often taken-for-granted analogue patterns of information that loop back. The lens determines the pattern. Solutions contain the assumptions used to frame the problem. Transitions from one lens, viewpoint, mindset, or frame of reference to another can be disorienting but will result in new sense-making.

3. Learning follows a change in how we punctuate the world. This is a source of creativity in that the limits of our premises governing our choices are challenged. Of all the aspects of leadership, perhaps this is the most significant.

4. Tomorrow's leaders will probably be doing and thinking things about leadership that are a direct consequence of what today's leaders *think* leadership is. Unless we are self-aware, we are liable blindly to perpetuate the same thinking that created the problems we think leadership is the answer to.

The Integrated Leader must see through this. What Part 1 has attempted to demonstrate is that no matter our differences, we can always find common ground.[17] The starting point for personal development, and all learning and development, is awareness of

---

[17] Even if there was an absolute difference in all respects, we would at least share having nothing in common. When two things are not identical, then some difference must exist between them (at least enough of a difference to make a

the punctuation of the flow of events into experience. This is universal. Personal change is informed by knowing what triggers responses that will lead to learning. This chapter has proposed that all triggers, stimuli and information are questions of difference, so personal development is heightened awareness — and search for ever-wider categories to include things in.

The Integrated Leader, understanding that background and foreground constitute each other, will take care not to elevate themselves to the foreground at the expense of everyone and everything else. The chief executive officer who assumes the credit for having achieved their annual target forgets and excludes all the others who made that possible, and this creates not only an imbalance within the organisation but a pathology for its culture. They become attached to the success of the project and purpose of the organisation as being the same thing as their validation of themselves. Such a person is getting in everyone's way, including their own.

---

comparison). The opposite extreme, of absolute similarity would negate identity. If two things are completely the same, then there would not be two, just one.

Reflecting on the Integrated Leader's Manifesto (Leading Self)

#3

'Keeping up-to-date in my knowledge and skills through inquiry and study is my obligation. It is not a choice, but a responsibility I have. I'm happy to revise my practice and assumptions every day. I'm happy to listen to others, and at the same time I'm grounded in my convictions and values.'

Productivity and competence go hand in hand at work, and every organisation is built only on what people know. It's no surprise that acquiring knowledge and skills and then keeping them up to date are important, but this is not just good advice; it is an imperative.

Expertise is not an end state. Experts are authorities because they have devoted time to combine their experience with developing a skill. When you look at how true experts behave and in what they believe, you notice how few of them stop learning or concede that there is less ahead to know than there is behind already known. People who have trained hard to do a job, studied for years to attain a profession, or practiced endlessly to master a skill often not only keep a hunger and enthusiasm for learning, they deepen it. It is reflection in experience that teaches us the value of keeping up with current thinking, even when we may believe that our knowledge is complete.

Why is it our duty to do so? There are two ways of looking at this; keeping up to date as an extrinsic duty, and as an intrinsic duty.

An extrinsic duty is a pressure on us from outside (by others) to show or prove what we know and demonstrate that we remain competent in their eyes. A person can develop a genuine appetite for learning this way, but the motivation is from a duty to others, and the appearance of authority. Sometimes, this is explicit and well-accepted, for example, the further training and development of professionals or skilled workers such as doctors, accountants, or airline pilots. The consequences of a failure to keep up with what is current can be disastrous in some jobs, or for some organisations. This kind of learning is often codified and mandatory.

Sometimes, however, the extrinsic can mask a weakness in the learner. If we are driven only by what we think others will think of us, then we are displaying new learning to fit in, and to find validation and respect. This is a restless and unthanking kind of urgency to learn because satisfaction is outside our control. When Shakespeare has King Henry IV say 'Uneasy lies the head that wears a crown,'[18] he feels what a burden it is to carry the expectations others have of us.

An intrinsic duty to learn and keep knowledge fresh considers others and their well-being, but starts from a more self-assured place. Learning, when it is intrinsically motivated, doesn't need external validation for it to matter, and even when there is feedback (communication about performance) from others that it is appreciated or effective, that is not its point. Intrinsic means the energy to find out, to keep informed, and to enquire just must come out. What is incumbent on the Integrated Leader is keeping mentally fit and healthy so that they can maintain their natural curiosity, and to be self-aware enough to notice when it fades or gets side-tracked to please others. The stance for intrinsic duty to learn is an acceptance that whatever level of knowledge you have now, it is still a place of ignorance compared with what there is still left to know. There are many types of knowledge and many paths to harvest it.

---

[18] Shakespeare, History of Henry IV, Part II, Act III, Scene 1.

Part 2

Getting Out of Your Own Way

*For fools laud and love all things
more which they can descry hidden beneath twisted
sayings, and they set up for true what can tickle the ear
with a pretty sound and is tricked out with a smart ring.*

Lucretius[1]

Part 1 invited you to get in your own way just enough to be in the stop and think zone. Once you accept current reality, you know where you are, where you start from. Movement in any direction is possible when you are honest with yourself about this. Part 2 is about removing restraints. Now it is time to get out of your own way.

Many of the obstacles to navigating life as an Integrated Leader begin with the limitations of language. The word 'leader' cannot lead, any more than the word 'lunch' can nourish you. Yet mistaking the menu for the food is exactly what many leaders do.[2] Similarly, the word 'leadership' is a category, a convenient placeholder for many ideas that we debate and shuffle around to fit our

---

[1] Lucretius, *On the Nature of Things*, Book 1, II, 631–661.

[2] In 2020 during the COVID crisis in the United States (US), the former US President, Donald J. Trump repeatedly mistook the number of tests for the virus with the number of cases of positive results. This was akin to believing that the number of tests causes the number of cases. A categorical error.

understanding and experience.[3] Handy as labels, 'leader' and 'leadership' are maps of a system and not the system itself. A map is useful when it systemically codifies the ground, but no map carries everything in the territory. It will inevitably contain deletions and distortions. How accurate are our maps? What do they simplify, leave out, or distort? The territory of leadership is dynamic, with flowing patterns of feelings, opinions, facts, relationships, and decisions made in response to an environment that is constantly changing. Maps gradually become obsolete as the territory (or map-making) changes. We may be led astray by out of date references.

The four topics we map in Part 2 are:

1. The defining of leadership
2. The nature of purpose
3. The narratives of image
4. The question of self

Organisations are complex adaptive systems (CAS), which are dynamic networks of relationships where agents can all adapt, and influence each other's adaptations. As partially open, they cannot only be explained cumulatively by their parts. In a CAS, precise predictions of what will happen in a future state are impossible to make. The art of leadership lies in being okay with this constant motion and finding ways to work. You are going to get it wrong if you think you know what will happen, and you are often wrong about what has happened. One part of leadership is being good with this fallibility.

We will get in our own way and trip ourselves up numerous times before we attain wisdom, and we need to. A leader who brags about their results has stopped being one; they have mistaken the label for what it signifies and have lost their own way.

---

[3] The word 'leadership' might be analogous to the word 'menu' here. For more on this, see Gregory Bateson's classic essay 'The logical categories of Learning and Communication' in Bateson, G. (1973). *Steps to An Ecology of Mind*, San Francisco, CA: Chandler Publishing Company (pp. 279–308).

Chapter 4

The Leader Complex

Good-morning, good-morning!' the General said
When we met him last week on our way to the line.
Now the soldiers he smiled at are most of 'em dead,
And we're cursing his staff for incompetent swine.
'He's a cheery old card,' grunted Harry to Jack
As they slogged up to Arras with rifle and pack.
But he did for them both by his plan of attack.

'The General', by Siegfried Sassoon[4]

Learning About Leadership

We love to study leadership. Our appetite for it in recent decades has become a voracious search for people who identify as leaders. In countless Master of Business Administration classrooms, leadership is contrasted to and compared with management and perhaps this is one way of seeking its boundaries. Management, almost by design, is a more measured and measurable concept. Compared to leadership, management is a younger and more prosaic concept, forged in the furnaces, factories, and mills of the Industrial Revolution in Europe around 200 years ago. Management is workaday and specific, while leadership is broad and imaginative. Romantic, even. Management wears a suit, leadership rocks up in jeans. Across the board, management is defined as responsibility

---

[4] Copyright Siegfried Sassoon by kind permission of the Estate of George Sassoon.

for the creation of measurable value through the efficient and effective use of resources, in line with the goals and restraints of the organisation. For leadership, a similar consensus has been absent and when it comes to pinning down what leadership is, certainties are few and a complete definition still eludes us.

There are three ways to learn about leadership, only one of which recognises the transformational potential of the self[5]:

➢ Vicariously: through someone else's experience

➢ Rationally: via theories, models, frameworks, and constructs

➢ Directly: by the application of skill, imagination, awareness, and intellectual curiosity to your own experience

Looking at each briefly in turn:

Vicariously, from a distance, means we are perceiving leadership via the actions of other people. This might be in first-hand accounts or second-hand narratives, and sometimes as parables.[6] From the story we infer what leadership is (which suggests that part of our conception of leadership is concocted). Does this explain why so often we identify leadership as the person of the leader? A narrative is supposed to be a simple retelling of an order of events, but a major downside is that no matter how detailed the story, it can never cover everything, or be free from bias in the telling. There may be hidden or unspoken filters, biases, agendas, and assumptions on the part of the storyteller (or hidden biases in the leadership story itself), and there will be the same shortcomings possible on the part of the recipient (the listener or the reader).

---

[5] By the way, transformation here just means change, and there is no inherent judgement about whether a transformation is good or bad, intended or not, right or wrong, successful or a failure. Transformation is a neutral description of a natural process of being in one state at one time, and then being in a noticeably different state at another.

[6] A short, didactic story designed to teach something instructive. They are best seen as illustrations to run alongside another narrative to reveal a deeper meaning.

A narrative is at least one remove from the story it recounts and is never received unmediated or unfiltered, and exactly as it was for the author. In addition, we do not learn what leadership is from another person's experience, at best we learn what the experience of leadership was for them. These are not quite the same things. Vicarious leadership learning is fertile ground for punditry and training, but the best it can offer is imitation, not originality.

Rationally, through reasoned explanation, theories, and models, is what academia strives for. Theory should be arrived at with rigour. Management theory also needs relevance. Leadership is meticulously constructed and examined in a measurable (falsifiable, perhaps) pattern of working hypotheses. Most of the major concepts of leadership derive from this intellectual tradition (and sometimes, but less so, from the field and in practice). Having a comprehensive set of principles for leadership is not a bad thing to aim for. Leadership is after all an idea. But most leadership theory is stubbornly descriptive and very little is prescriptive.[7] We have many theories but have found almost no underlying, axiomatic truths of leadership. In fact, it has become very difficult to say anything original about it to advance the field because every new argument contains the structure of the old one it is a reaction to. When we appreciate our current situation with all its economic, social, political, and environmental issues, we can ill afford to study leadership in the same backward-looking and self-referential fashion as now. The study of leadership has not been transformational for the study of leadership, and although theorising about leadership is not a bad idea, it may not be enough. Because our instincts are biased and our knowledge fallible, we must develop the theoretical alongside the etiquette of practice. Conscious instruction is therefore needed.

The third way is to learn *directly*, which is the application of imagination, awareness, and curiosity to experience. This does not

---

[7]Prescriptive means it would be enforceable as a rule or method. A description rarely works well as an instruction, for reasons outlined in the section on vicarious leadership.

negate either the anecdotal or theoretical, which have their place, but the application of self-awareness to practice is the only true way to be transformational because it is how you will discover what leadership means for *you*. The catch is that this must happen without the filters, prejudices, and myriad thinking biases that might otherwise distort experience. There can still be a role for the educational process in this. Higher education and the business school can provide the right space for reflection and deep learning about leadership. Learning does not start in ignorance of theory or ignorance of conventions, it starts in ignorance of how you think, see, and act. The antidote to ignorance is curiosity, that insatiable yet trainable sidekick to awareness. If leadership exists, and if it can be understood, and if it's not just another social convention and convenient buzzword such as 'boss', 'performance', or 'servant' (the list is long), in short, if it matters, then it must be something that each person discovers in their own way. Leadership is to be defined and lived by in a way coherent with your identity and without compromising your self-esteem. This self-confidence must, however, be bound up with endless wonder.

We must be open to exploring leadership from every angle, with no preconceptions. When leadership comes from a rational understanding of how the world works, perhaps a scientific one of how the social world works (though this has so far still largely eluded us), then it may be said to emerge from education. When leadership comes from a place of self-awareness, and emerges genuinely, unmediated, and without labels, then it may be said to emerge from our nature. The art is perhaps to see that being genuine can be a route to becoming educated and that being educated can be a route to becoming genuine. The purpose of a leader is to make their organisation better by keeping it well. Defining 'better' in terms of 'well' leads to many possibilities and many choices of paths.

It's a crude research tool and pretty meaningless, but if you search the word leadership on Google, you can safely guess what will happen. In spring 2021, in less than a second, the search engine returned just over three billion results. The phenomenon of the age. Where did this interest come from, and what is feeding it?

The Leadership Industry

The United Nations Educational, Scientific and Cultural Organization (UNESCO) data suggest that more than 2.2 million book titles are published worldwide each year, of which roughly one quarter are produced in the United States and United Kingdom. If just 1% of those are about leadership, that is more than 5,500 titles per year (or 15 new books a day). We are hungry to be fed answers. On the academic side, this appetite is reflected in the growing number of peer-reviewed academic journals that publish research on leadership. Are there so many books and journals on leadership each year because we know what it is, or because we do not?

Leadership is an idea, and it is surely important to subject all ideas to genuine and critical scrutiny. All too often, though, leadership as it is taught in an academic environment feels more like a guided tour through a museum. We start with the early works and origins and walk through a series of rooms stuffed full of a progression of different schools and epochs, ending up in the contemporary (or abstract) section, just before the gift shop. For the tutor and the student, there are some advantages to this chronological approach. Students assume that the teacher knows something they do not, and teachers assume that students need to appreciate who said what in order to answer the questions in the examinations.[8] Professors, authors, and some practitioners are trained in this way, even while they know (or at least strongly suspect) that no real-world business or management situation ever entirely conforms to a single theory. I am exaggerating, a little. Models and theories of leadership certainly do give people a common vocabulary, which helps with sense-making, and they do reduce the risk of having to take complete responsibility for your own conduct when justifying leadership decisions. Leadership is a business. The popularity of leadership as it is taught in the business schools and training rooms of the world is fuelled by two things:

1. Growing demand from corporations for practitioners with the badge

---

[8] This is valid to the extent that the teacher sets the questions.

2. Increasing supply from academia of such badges in terms of management theory and degrees, as well as in-company training and development courses

In the early days of modern management in the 1920s and 1930s, companies made profits, but business practices were often idiosyncratic and chaotic, and productivity remained low. Higher standards and better methods to achieve efficiency were needed, and specialist functions for controlling work and implementing plans started to appear. This was the first period of scientific management, where managers were trained not just for current job functions but also for more practical and efficient methods of future production. This era set up many organisational principles, norms, and standards that are still in use today. The Second World War further shifted interest to the science of management from its craft, and after the war the extra productivity available fed a more sophisticated market. This demanded a more sophisticated manager, and with the social realisation that people were a vital element in delivering profits and value, this in turn led to the codifying of psychological principles as they related to work.

What is Leadership For?

You could be having a successful career and never have given this question a second thought. Possible, but unlikely. People are naturally curious and ambitious to know more, and when you have mastered your craft and learnt its principles, the only restraints left are your assumptions. This is not a new question or a fully answered one. There are some conventions about which all agree, and therefore leadership is not entirely subjective, but academics have so many ways of framing responses that managers may justly ask how they are supposed to know which one to follow to become better leaders. One possible area of agreement is that leadership requires a meaningful, moral, and satisfying objective. Leadership, in that light, exists for that objective. Leadership is movement towards an objective of health and well-being. If it is not that, then it is not leadership. For the most part, however, the field of leadership is more one of difference than common ground between theories.

Let us approach it this way:

If leadership is the answer, what was the question?

I think I can see four[9]:

1. Who's in charge? (or, who *should* be in charge?)

This is about communicating stability in hierarchy, power, and control, and this question permits leadership to operate in a structured and organised way. "Who is in charge?" isolates gaps and priorities for actions and decisions, but also reduces confusion and anxiety in troubling times. Leadership here is a question of certainty *and* control, and the acceptance of the chain of command within the system. Such leadership activity invokes the requirement to create tasks, distribute work, distribute rewards, and impose sanctions. In this sense, leadership is the exercising of power, organisational influence, and decision-making control. The underlying moral question to be answered is then framed as 'what is the best way for those in charge to arrange things?' Leadership development and training spends much of its time in this sphere and on that question. Resources are invested in looking after talent identification and the leadership pipeline, and on performance management of those in leadership roles. This feels pragmatic and fits nicely with the idea that good leadership = a good leader, or the notion that if you get the 'who?' right, then the rest will follow. Yet that would be only one aspect of a complex question. An oversimplification of what leadership is focuses everything on the individual and how they fit in (or how the organisation fits in with the celebrity boss) and on how this maintains the status quo. 'Who's in charge?' rarely provides a complete enough answer to allow leadership to be disruptive and different. If leadership is more than a game of 'I'm the boss', there is another question we need to consider.

---

[9] There will be others, given the fluidity of the concept.

2.   What could be?

In most business contexts, 'what could be?' is a differentiator between management and leadership. When all other things are equal, leadership deals with what is currently in place versus what is not yet here and will never be here unless action is taken. This is the aspect of organisational existence where the novel is needed at one level to continue the status quo at another, existential one. If you are alive on a boat and the boat starts to fill up with water, getting off the boat (changing state in a changing context) will preserve your life (your status quo). Leadership is the answer either when there is a need to move to something new in response to real and urgent threats or opportunities in the external environment, or when there is a desire to move towards a new and compelling idea. In this aspect, because leadership is the articulation of what is required when simply carrying on with the current situation is not sustainable, it has become a question of innovation, growth, and change with a flavour not captured in the hierarchical response to 'who's in charge?' A vision can forge purpose, connectivity, togetherness, excitement, and action without a chain of command, at least at first. For a vision to thrive, a structure will be required, and Question 1 will emerge. Nevertheless, a question such as this can influence, inspire, and even move to action, through only the power of the idea and not necessarily through role or chain of command. The impetus generating 'what could be?' may be environmental (i.e. the question is figuratively — sometimes literally — in the air we breathe) and so leadership can be the answering of a call to action from context. For example, now that the global climate crisis has arrived as a present-tense issue, leadership could be defined as a paradigmatic change to the business model of the global economy. This is, perhaps, where the best of current leadership theory is now — at the cutting edge of what must be done.

A third interlinking element logically sets up a question that is rather obvious when you think about it.

3.   Whom shall we follow?

It takes two to tango, as the old saying goes. Leadership studied only with the leader in mind is like studying pollination by only looking at the flowers and not the pollinating insects. Leaders go with followers and followers go with leaders, or both are meaningless. To be a follower is an active position, and a connection to the human need to be part of something, or to have something to believe in. Followership is a deeply rooting element of identity and belonging, and when infused with enthusiasm and belief, it can be the catalyst for leadership even before there is a formal leader in place. The lead up to that moment when someone says, 'I'm in!' can belie a lot of mental processing.

The three questions so far are interdependent and interlinked, as in the following Figure 4.1.

Where elements overlap, different connections are made. An intersection of 'who's in charge?' and 'what could be?' would be where visionary ideas meet the authority to begin to respond to and act on goals that are not business-as-usual. If these two

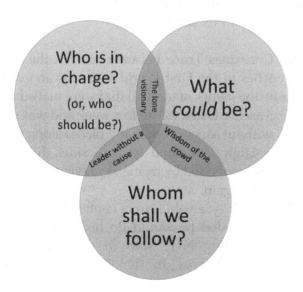

Figure 4.1.   Three questions to which leadership is the answer.

elements are the only ones present and there are no followers, then the result is 'the lone visionary'. In this case, leadership is latent potential. At the intersection of 'who's in charge?' and 'whom shall we follow?', on the other hand, there is realisable potential but nothing potent to be realised. This is leadership all dressed up but with no place to go, or a 'leader without a cause'. The third overlap covers 'whom shall we follow?' and 'what could be?' Here is a bottom-up need or call for change, and the result is 'the wisdom of the crowd'. The energy is there for movement, as is a general direction or conception of a goal, but either because it is early days in the process or because those currently in charge are suppressing or opposed to the idea of change, there is no hierarchical structure or secure access to resources to make things stick. Groundswell movements, where there is no obvious signal as to who is in charge, are more common in social situations away from the corporation (see Chapter 10 and Mintzberg's call for the plural sector) because organisations tend to be designed around a hierarchy. However, occasionally, lasting and fundamental change does not start with the boss, and in fact leadership emerges from the system rather is a snowball rolling down a hill.

Two examples of this last point:

(1) The 1914 Christmas Truce between men in the German and Allied trenches in the First World War was an event symbolised later by the games of football that were played in no-man's land. The ceasefire lasted for up to a week and was sporadically observed, without sanction, at many places along the line, over many days. High Command on both sides did not condone this, and they responded by trying to prevent anything like that from occurring again.[10]

(2) In April 2020, a 99-year-old former captain in the British Army, Tom Moore, decided he would do his bit to raise funds for charities supporting NHS staff in the national lockdown imposed as a response to the COVID-19 pandemic. He

---

[10] They never entirely succeeded, and small-scale truces or cessations of hostilities continued throughout the conflict.

committed to walk, slowly and with his frame, 100 lengths of his garden, and to complete this task before his 100th birthday. The family hoped to raise what they thought was the ambitious target of £1,000. Then his daily walk was reported locally, and within two weeks more than one and a half million people had contributed online to reach a staggering fundraising total of over £32,000,000. Beyond his immediate family, there had been no hierarchy or leader structure to plan or oversee this. The nation, it seemed, just needed something like this to rally around and follow. Captain Tom, who sadly died from Covid-19 in early 2021, became a national celebrity, but it was the context and not an organisation that denoted the leadership.

The intersection of all three questions, the still point of the turning world of leadership if you wish, is where capacity, outcome, and willingness combine. This can be an exhilarating and pleasurable experience (at least for a period) if all players and ideas are fully present and acknowledged, and everyone is on board and looking in the same direction. And where that direction is clear and sufficiently evidenced, most people would say this was leadership. The first three questions have all been widely responded to by management and leadership theory over the last 100 years. Leadership study has become more sophisticated over time, and has drawn from sociology, psychology, biology, engineering, economics, anthropology, systems thinking, as well as philosophy. An exhaustive review of all of this would (for academics) be a luxury (for academics) and (for most practitioners) unrealistic. For now, it may be said that:

➤ Leadership performs a useful social function and is a universal found everywhere.
➤ Leadership is concerned with utility. It is ultimately judged by how expediently the job was done.
➤ Only certain activities and contexts determine the field of leadership. Not everything is leadership. Not everyone *called* a leader is one; not everything a chief executive officer (CEO) does as a CEO counts as leadership. Not everything that could

be done should be done. Not everything a follower could follow is worth following.

Many models and frameworks of leadership track activity beyond the point of decision and preparation of goals to include implementation. There is a lot to be said for further training and development for both leaders and followers in the implementation of change. However, excitement and visibility in leadership tend to be front-loaded and interest will wane over time, even in successful projects.

Is knowing who is in charge, what could be, and whom to follow all that leadership is? Have we missed an aspect? I think so. In recent years, people have begun to extend the study of leadership towards the possibility that our actions in the present, which are our sole criterion for measuring what good leadership is, need to be evaluated through two more criteria:

(1) The system's capacity to retain its shape as it changes (resilience in duration)
(2) The legacy of unintended consequences on and outside the system of the organisation

The transforms of leadership and change reverberate inside and outside the organisation over time. Consequences may not emerge until after the original players have moved on or have been replaced. Leadership consequently is not a property of named people in the organisation, it is the context within which they and their successors work. This long-term aspect of leadership tends to be ignored or overlooked. Accordingly, I suggest a fourth question to which leadership is the answer:

4. What are the effects of what we do?

In times of change or renewal, everyone's energy goes towards achieving what can be measured and reacting to what can be controlled for. Whatever the context of leadership (and it is the approach here that vision, leader, and follower are all formed by

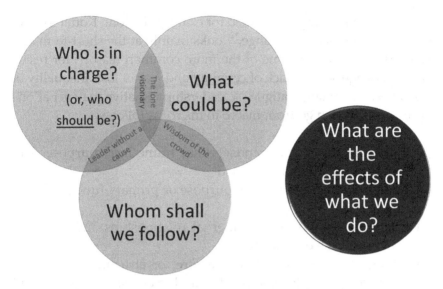

Figure 4.2. The fourth question to which leadership is the answer.

context), the story does not end even when the vision has been made a fact, the competent leader has played their role, or the followers have bought in and then settled into a new status quo.[11]

If there is one thing that is guaranteed to fuel the need for a new leadership direction or project, it is the consequence of an earlier one. One metaphor for this could be the pendulum; having gone one way and pursued one strategy, organisations will find they need to respond to changed market conditions (at least) and must pick this up from wherever their last venture, transformation, or CEO left them. They then swing (oscillate) back. Another metaphor could be the Russian doll, where every new initiative encases the old one in a new layer. If earlier iterations or previous generations have not thought through the consequences of their success, and if they have not looked at things holistically, it may be that change doesn't work because the system itself has lost its resilience and is unable to change — even if everyone is on board.

---

[11] And remember, most change projects are said to fail in their original goals, which will have rippling effects.

Leadership theory, as typified for example by John Kotter's eight-step implementation of change,[12] looks mainly at the short-term and its barriers, including some of the more common reasons for resistance to change such as lack of certainty and fear of loss, inequality of resources, and change fatigue. A leadership initiative may act at one of six levels, which go from macro to micro, as follows:

(1) Changing the global mindsets that frame *how* 'purpose' and 'primary function' are defined[13]
(2) Changing the definitions of purpose or primary function of the organisation[14]
(3) Changing the systems of internal relationships and interconnections in the organisation
(4) Changing the artefacts, architecture, or structures, including major processes, jobs, and roles, and even the people who fill them. The 'parts' of the organisation.
(5) Changing the processes and skills that guide or limit behaviours
(6) Changing events on the ground, getting different results

The list is hierarchical in that higher levels govern lower ones, and successful change at a higher level permits and supports genuine change at levels below. However, the effect does not work in reverse. For example, manipulating people's behaviours so that they do x instead of y might produce short-term results and tick a project outcome box but leaves intact any beliefs and belief systems that were there before the intervention, and which will probably resurface when the training is finished and consultants packed up. The likelihood of a holistic impact and sustainable change in that case is minimal.[15] Since each level is governed by what the levels

---

[12] Kotter International, The 8-step Process for Leading Change, www.kotterinternational.com/our-principles/changesteps/changesteps.
[13] Mindset will be a topic in Chapter 8.
[14] Purpose and primary function will be the topic in Chapter 5.
[15] Anyone who has been asked to do a best practice exercise as a strategic idea will understand the problem.

above are set up to do, the best way to bring about change beyond the superficial is to look at the purpose and primary function. Think back to your last experience of a major leadership event in your organisation and ask yourself, whether as leader, follower, or stakeholder, at which of the six levels was the change targeted beforehand. Then, consider at which level intervention *actually* happened. Most change projects have pressure on them to report on key performance indicators, even if the original issue was identified at a deeper and less measurable level. Interventions tend to happen at levels 4, 5, or 6, and no higher.

The crux of the matter for leadership is the following dilemma. An organisation should reduce or eliminate everything that does not directly contribute to the objective of its continued existence (survival). It should therefore not invest in anything that does not contribute to value creation. The logic of the short-term means that retaining anything which merely preserves a potential capacity for future flexibility should be stripped out because untapped potential is a waste. On the other hand, any organisation that eliminates its underlying ability to adapt will eventually face an ecological dead end.[16] When any unused ability of the system to respond has been given up, the organisation becomes more rigid. New contexts in the future will show up the deficit, making the achievement of short-term survival impossible.[17] Leadership does not happen in a vacuum, and the direction of travel has been a fashion for the lean and the short-term. Therefore the extra question matters — what are the effects of what we do? This brings us to feedback.

Feedback

Feedback is a process in all systems. What makes it special is that feedback is the effect of the information produced by the system at one time once reintroduced back into the same system at another.

---

[16] Ashby's Law of Requisite Variety.

[17] Anecdotally, the cutting out of mid-level administrative staff, often highly qualified and experience, in organisational change initiatives is a good example of this.

Feedback is a circuit, or loop, of news that comes back on itself and it tends either to heat things up (positive feedback) or cool things down (negative feedback).

When we apply this to organisations, feedback can be seen not merely as hindsight. That is, feedback appears not only as an explanation of how the past has caused the present but also as information about the present state of the system. We can think ahead to how our present actions will loop back later as either accelerators or dampeners in the system of balances and variations present in every system, whether organisation, market, economy, or ecology. We see this play out repeatedly in business. If a company is making a profit, it will in general seek to grow that ratio through investment or other measures but will find restraints on doing so beyond certain limits. Some of these are the relationships it has with sources of new resources, some with limits in the market for returns, including the effect of competition, and some with the limits of the whole economic system itself. The forces within the organisation propelling it towards growth will tend towards positive feedback loops (i.e. where a change in one factor in the system produces more of something else) until either it runs out of control and collapses, or it is acted upon by so-called negative feedback loops (i.e. where factors are imposed from outside the system) that constrain, diffuse, or remove the runaway conditions.[18]

Adjustments, which are part of the feedback process, are needed to remain in service of the purpose of the system, and this is where we find the link to leadership, and the leader. Feedback and adjustments in human life are another way of describing learning.[19] Learning how to be a leader uses the checks and balances of calibration to keep on course. If you have ever taken up a new role,

---

[18] Positive and negative feedback loops may be found in some instances of personal transformation, either through rapid or sudden trauma or where a person experiences relatively small inputs at very sensitive points of their experience, resulting in major and irreversible shifts of perspective. If you have experienced anxiety (panic) attacks, you will know this.

[19] This is not the meaning of feedback as in the first glossary definition, and how most people talk about it in the office. Here I am using a systemic definition.

moved to a new company, or been placed in (charge of) a new team, you will be familiar with the calibration feeling. Systemic feedback is more sophisticated than trial and error because as a leader you are surveying the context within which things work or do not work, and not just analysing the causes and effects. Learning is a non-linear process, meaning that the feedback (information) will not follow an exponential straight line of change forever.

As we have seen, information stays coded in the system and moves around in a circuit so that what occurs at one time is later re-incorporated to become new information, transformed in the time lag to become context. The function of feedback is to control flows of information to maintain a steady state. Going back to the six levels of leadership and change in the list in the previous section, and in terms of the organisation's integrity over time, the most noteworthy are those represented by the third level, 'changing the systems of internal relationships and interconnections in the organisation'. An Integrated Leader uses their influence to change directions of flow and availability of information to various parts of the system. A leader who intervenes at level three will be concerned with all levels below that, including the jobs and activities that people do to produce desired results. The difference is that those events are placed in the wider context and the bigger picture is available and communicated.

Navigating the Leadership Jungle

The Integrated Leader accepts the stewardship role in the system. They are stewards of the maintenance of a viable, ethical, and coherent enterprise in the present, and of the capacity of the organisation to access the resources it will need in the future. This is the bare minimum. At the point you first start to see yourself as a leader, you will work on three aspect of further development and practice in your capacity for leadership:

1. *Authority*: Your skills at being in charge and discharging the role and duties of a leader. Many people fail in the leader role,

and the majority of organisational change initiatives falter or never fully come to be. To an extent, this can be addressed through a deeper knowledge and understanding of the role, and of human interaction as they find their place in the system.

2. *Creativity*: Your vision and your talent for scanning the world and coming up with or identifying new thinking and ideas. It is the duty of the manager/leader to build and maintain in their organisation a readiness to spring into action whenever and wherever necessary, in accordance with the mission and purpose of the business (in line with founders, or shareholders, etc.), in response to context. The more you know about the total environment of business, the more you will know what to do. The more you care about the health and well-being of that environment, the more you will sustain it. The more you sustain it, the more it can sustain you.

   Senior management is about the creation of value, and value cannot be created in a vacuum. It requires a healthy environment. How do you proceed when these technical competences and expertise areas are achieved? Something else is needed.

3. *Wisdom*:   This third aspect of development is a critical look at awareness and understanding of who you are. The more you know and care about yourself, the more you can care for others. This includes being fair in your dealings with followers and being a wise follower yourself. Leadership success is no guarantee of wisdom.

To put all this another way, management and leadership are mastery of three things:

Practice: the things that you do and the things that happen in the world as a result.

Principles: the rules of the game, some of which are set beforehand and govern practice, others of which emerge to explain or explore practice as you go. Principles are captured in frameworks, models, and theories and tested in practice.

Stance: your character, attitude, personality, and moral outlook. It is the knowledge you have of who you are as a person and how you are present as a manager and leader.

These can become the point of entry for your personal and professional development. They permit you to seek guidance from mentors and information about the role of the leader. But the reasons leadership is complex is because no matter how much you have learnt the different names for leadership, how eloquently you've quoted all the models and theories, how effectively you've applied the models and frameworks, how sharply you've honed the behaviours, and how often you've been called a leader, you will still not know anything at all.

Reflecting on the Integrated Leader's Manifesto (Leading Self)

#4

'Becoming a transformative and integrated leader might be a slow process; I am willing to honour this rhythm.'

Some processes are difficult for us because they are complicated, some because they are not familiar, and some because the path offered goes nowhere. Most humans are impatient for transformation and in their rush for control, they have come to expect to be fed answers and fixes, not more questions and further puzzles.

Three assumptions about transformation are often required of you by authors and trainers in the self-help and personal growth industry. The first is 'if you wish it, it will be' and the efficacy of positive thoughts, the second 'it needn't take long if you know the short-cut' and existence of a path, and the third is 'you need a guide to get you there'. Are these so? Do they speed things up, or get in the way? Such authors may truly think that wishful thinking works, or they may merely believe that you believe wishful thinking works. Your guide may genuinely want to share their story with you in the belief that it will be a path you can walk without the time and effort it took them, but this is also an illusion.

Personal transformation or integration are not to be found in a model, framework, or theory. Nor do they reside in any method, practice, or 'way'. Our insatiable search for enlightenment in someone else's recipe and an appetite for rapidity of response are embedded in our culture. Anyone selling you this idea is selling you their own set of filters for observation and the only thing you're getting from it is their opinion of what your opinion should be. Searching for enlightenment this way is like looking for a lamp in the dark using the same lamp that you're looking for. This may result in the gross caricature of a leader to suit the views of others, rather than the complex picture of personal integration that brings the leader their authority. The problems start when your hunger for change and your expectation of speed of change bypass the necessity of you working yourself out entirely for yourself, independent of the opinion or example of others.

When you know that there is no other authority, that there is no secret that is known to someone else but not yourself, you can begin. Do so in tune with however long this needs to take, which may require travelling down dead-ends and making some detours.

What we have missed is that being a transformative and integrated leader is not an experience, it is a method of experiencing. It cannot really be prescribed, but it can be understood. Our starting place is our starting place and our finishing place is our finishing place and it will take forever to get there unless you realise that they are really the same place (that is, experiencing is always in the present) if you rely on other people's starting and finishing places. The reason transformation might be a slow process is not because it must be, but because we have first to understand our basic natures. People either move at their own pace or they are moved by the pace of others. The internal rhythm is the form in tune with the idea of integrated leadership.

Chapter 5

Today is Not a Stepping Stone to Tomorrow

Happy the man, and happy he alone,
He who can call today his own;
He who, secure within, can say,
Tomorrow, do thy worst, for I have lived today.

John Dryden, *Imitation of Horace (1685), 29th Ode, § 8.*

'What Business are You Really in?'

This chapter is on purpose. The question in the sub-heading was made famous by Harvard professor and marketer Theodore Levitt at the start of the 1960s in one of the most famous articles in *Harvard Business Review*,[1] and it remains one of the most powerful questions not just for those leading organisations but for everyone working in them. Then, as now, its strength and usefulness was as a wake-up call for any business with too-narrow a strategic focus in changing market conditions. The organisation that has not bound itself to the specifics of its current success will have retained the flexibility to meet future market needs while still retaining its identity. In his article (now over 60 years old), Levitt mentioned many businesses and industries that he saw as in trouble because of their narrow focus on product rather than the customer. Readers

---

[1] Levitt, T. (1960). Marketing myopia, *Harvard Business Review*, 38, 45–56.

were encouraged to analyse market size, industry growth, competition, and customers. This you can certainly do, but you may want to think about this question in a more philosophical way because the twin to focus is purpose. Focus is finite and exact, purpose is generative and broad.

Starting with your current product or service, ask yourself of what category is it a member? Of what is it an example? Then try to name the larger category to which that category belongs. Repeat, until you find yourself forced to be creative in identifying a larger pattern, something not necessarily obvious as to what its members have in common. As a critical thinking exercise, the chapters of Part 1 were preparing you for this.

By way of example, I prepare and fine-tune a subject module for an Executive Master of Business Administration (MBA). The module is a member of a category of taught modules owned by an academic department, and a member of a set of subject modules packaged as a single degree course. There are six departments in the faculty, which runs university-sanctioned degrees and courses in management, finance, economics, real estate and planning, etc. The business school is one of several faculties and every part of the university is focused on its own goals and outcomes, so operationally it does not appear to be confused. But is there a problem lurking? If I look at each nested category in turn, can I (a) answer the question 'what is .... for?,[2] and (b) are all answers aligned from top to bottom? What connects them all into one unit?

In other words, what business are we *really* in? Is the purpose of education the outcome, or the process? Does its essence lie in what is happening as it goes, or in getting to an ending? Is it about the future or the present? What should be the measure of education? I have my own answers to these questions,[3] as

---

[2] In my case, 'what is my module for?', 'what is my department for?', 'what is the MBA for?', 'what is the faculty for?', 'what is the university for?', 'what is higher education for?', 'what is education for?', and so on.

[3] My view: The purpose of education is for people to liberate themselves, and everything should align with that. The university should teach preparation skills, not planning or testing skills.

I am sure my students, colleagues, superiors, and various other stakeholders will all have theirs. That is not the point. The point is the asking, and in noting where hidden, false, or unhelpful assumptions are being made. Grades, diplomas, feedback sheets, rankings, research scores, are assumed to be the currency of education, but just as money is not wealth, education's statistics and targets are not freedom and a diploma is not well-being. If I were to venture to say what the interconnecting pattern is, I think that the purpose of university education is, and what business we really are in is:

1. *The art of the question*: The facilitation of learning how to think and not merely what to think, and the mindset of curiosity and learning.
2. *The principles of learning from practice*: A space to make mistakes and not be condemned for them, and a place to learn about work, productivity, and participation in society. Locating the right, sustainable resources for lifelong learning.
3. *The facilitation of self-awareness*: The discovery and development of personal, lifelong passions, and the promotion of wisdom, well-being, and mental good health. Stewardship for the future, and emancipation for the self.

Is there a category to which all three of these belong? What pattern do they share? This would have to be explored by as many people in the university (in this case) as possible, even though individuals can consider it. You may have noticed already that this topic generates questions. Here are some more:

Why do we do what we do?
Why one thing and not another?
What guides our decisions?
Is every decision and purpose conscious?
Is the track we lay as we go through life random in its direction and destination or are the tracks we lay according to a plan?
Is leadership purposive? Does it have a goal?

Defining Purpose

That last question above seems almost redundant, doesn't it? It is surely definitional that leadership is purposive, that it is there for something. After all, leadership is about intentionally developing ideas, adapting activities, and finding resources that are a resolution of a challenge or obstacle, or perhaps the realisation of an idea or dream. That is not possible without taking aim. On the other hand, there is a big difference between:

(i) *Purpose defining the system*: If leaders provide the purpose, then were it not for heroic and visionary people actively creating it, the organisation simply would not have direction. A danger of this interpretation could be that an organisation starts to wither away if it feels the wrong leader is at the helm to give it purpose. It gets stuck in endless rounds of corporate reinvention as each newly minted purpose introduced by those at the top demands a shake-up of existing operations and culture.

(ii) *The system defining the purpose*: This says that purpose is inherent in the fact of the organisation. Context inherently contains purpose, and this cannot be got rid of. Purpose can be lost or forgotten, and it can be discovered or rediscovered, but it cannot be changed or abandoned. The realisation is that evidence of purpose is synonymous with the organisation existing. If an organisation had no purpose, it would not need to exist. The danger here is that a great many organisations struggle to remember or rediscover what they are for and why they are there.

The topic of purpose is worthy of discussion not because we all understand it so well, but because our conceptions are not well enough developed for a deeper understanding of integration, leadership, and health and well-being in personal development. In general usage, purpose may be used to express either best explanation of direction (means) or best explanation of use (ends). It shares the same root as the words propose, apropos, and proposition, so we can see how purpose carries a hint of a suggestion or offer for the 'for what?' question. Small children[4] use 'why?' to discover and explore, and to learn general, social rules of life. Adults tend to think they already know those rules, and purpose becomes the intentions for what to do with those rules (for example, by setting up and running an organisation). At various times in leadership, looking for purpose both in the sense of childlike enquiry and in the sense of adultlike intention could be fitting.

Purpose is an abiding and interesting subject in both personal development and leadership, where it seems to have a bearing on existential happiness, and on well-being. It also relates to the justification of evaluating performance. The Integrated Leader merges these two, looking at how performance indicates the health of the system, where performance would be an indicator, not an end. Purpose suggests goals and reasons, and this brings in two aspects which may seem on first look contradictory:

(i) *Change and incompleteness*: Purpose is framed by absence, and therefore the role of the leader is as change agent. They are the stewards of flux.

(ii) *Duration and completeness*: Purpose is attained in the sustainable preservation of status quo. The role of the leader is to preserve something that already exists. They are the stewards of stability.

How are these to be reconciled? Only by the opposite poles being held simultaneously. Purpose is defined equally by changing while simultaneously not changing.

A Comparative Study of Purpose

A historical awareness of purpose may help to interpret the various ways people talk about purpose in everyday situations, and

---

[4] As many parents discover to their exasperation.

how it has become embedded in our culture. It may inform your thoughts about *your* purpose, as well because ultimately everyone must make peace with their purpose on their own terms. The four following approaches, Aristotle's final purpose, Stoicism, Taoism, and Totemism, have both ancient roots and contemporary relevance.

1. Aristotle's final purpose

For the Greek philosopher Aristotle, purpose is found in the final realisation of the function of an object, or of a person. The word for this is *telos*, which means 'end'.

Aristotle lived over 300 years BCE (Before Common Era) and led an interesting life. He was a star student of Plato at the Academy,[5] then a tutor to Alexander the Great. He founded his own school, known as the Lyceum. Aristotle was a polymath philosopher, mathematician, logistician, and biologist and like many such people was driven to consider the nature, organisation, and point of existence. An object's function, he said, is a virtue[6] it possesses, and this is a principle true for all living organisms. Its highest expression is found in humans and human endeavours, which uses a virtue unique to us — rational reasoning. Aristotle proposed that our central virtue is '*eudaimonia*', which translates to the chief aim or goal of living a good life; to flourish overall. This is the only purpose that does not lead to another purpose. Our path to this is by being a good example of whatever it is we have in mind we are, says Aristotle. This draws us back to our central question: what is leadership for? What is a leader for? What is a follower for? According to the Aristotelian view, the function (virtue, purpose) of a good leader is to embody those functions that represent what a good leader does. According to this, we must then evaluate good leadership by considering three aspects:

---

[5] An academy was an open-air gymnasium or sports area, while a lyceum was a garden with covered walks.
[6] Virtue means a property, not a moral aspect. For example, a virtue of a diamond is hardness, which makes it useful for what it is used for.

(1) *Character*: Excellence in those particular virtues that we associate with leadership, such as loyalty, communication, decisiveness, compassion, and so on. Linked to this would be enduring states of character that sustain excellence, and which can be cultivated. You might like to consider what *you* would list as such qualities of leadership.

(2) *Practical wisdom* (or *phronesis*): Getting closer to truth via the knowledge and judgement needed to do things. To reason, and act to attain goals.

(3) *Moral strength*: Overcoming blocks or barriers to action. Perseverance and resilience. Even if you had the character and the practical knowledge to be a leader, you still must set priorities and set off, overcoming adversity.

Don't forget that, for Aristotle, each category above is not an end but a means. To what end is leadership there for? Presumably, Aristotle would say that leadership, if it is for anything more than itself, is for *eudaimonia*; the fulfilled life. Yet that highest end, or final purpose, is still very difficult to define. What is a fulfilled life? What does it contain? Does attaining an Executive MBA degree represent fulfilment in life? This feels subjective because different people see this in different ways and behave in very different ways to get there. Aristotle rejected many possible candidates for ends, such as pleasure, honour, wealth, and excellence. None of these work because each can become the subject of a further round of questioning. The acid test is to find that thing, that final purpose, which is *not* done for the sake of anything else. Is this a good yardstick for leaders to evaluate themselves? Is it useful for evaluating what an organisation does? Once again, here is a chance to ask this question of yourself and of your organisation. Is the purpose of your company, and your role in it, a completely self-sufficient, final function?

We cannot say what Aristotle's response to our crowded, modern world would be, with its social and technological landscape so far from Hellenic culture and norms. Philosophically, there is a case to be made that in the 21st century purpose in leadership is still about the same three basic elements, and that good leadership accords with final purpose when you are the best possible exemplar of what a leader does. Despite its age, the descendants of Aristotle's version of purpose are relatively easy to spot today.

2. Stoicism

Stoicism is a simple yet durable set of philosophical principles that date back to the period immediately after Aristotle in Greece and then into the early parts of the peak of the Roman Empire, the political powerhouse that accounts for many core cultural assumptions in European thought today.

Stoic ideas are grounded in Hellenic philosophy, largely from the Greek philosopher Zeno of Citium,[7] a wealthy Phoenician merchant living in the third and second century BCE. Zeno is said to have survived a shipwreck on a trade voyage and, arriving in Athens, became enthralled with the multitude of philosophical schools there. He eventually set up his own under the colonnades (*stoa*) of the Athenian central marketplace. The main surviving tenet of the early Stoic approach to the question of purpose, and the one which took root in Rome, was the place of reason in both logic and in the means for living according to the virtues of nature. In other words, through reason you can discern purpose, and through rational behaviour you can be happy, and by being happy you can realise your true nature. This is a practical philosophy, well suited for those who have or will have positions of authority, power, or influence in a public sphere. These qualities made it ideal for expanding the influence of Rome in the first few hundred years of the Common Era. Among the most influential figures who wrote (or were written) about and who lived this perspective were a philosopher named Seneca, a former slave named Epictetus,[8] and the Roman Emperor Marcus Aurelius.

---

[7] Not the same Zeno of the famous paradoxes.
[8] We learn most about Epictetus from the notes left by one of his students, Arria. Epictetus, like Socrates, wrote nothing down.

The first principle of Stoicism is to live in harmony with the realities of nature and the vicissitudes of life, including pain, poverty, injury, defeat, and death. These are not in our control, so it is pointless to spend time and energy cultivating them, complaining about them, or trying to change them. What the Stoic can control and change is themselves and how they see and respond to the world. The wise person is the one who takes complete ownership of themselves and does not complain to others either about those things they cannot control or those things which only they can control. They are disinterested (but not uninterested) in anything outside their control. The world will take care of itself, but since you are part of that world, you must be involved and not shirk. This involvement is part of the same universal collective as everyone else.[9] The link to nature and natural processes is particularly clear here, and the result is that the Stoic finds no value in fearing what is inevitable, such as death, while at the same time they do not seek to hasten what is to come. A person's fulfilment, their purpose, therefore, comes from working on their own example, setting their own standards and principles, and being responsible for their own moral conduct in pursuit of the common good (a link to Aristotle there). And that is all.

In the case of the idea of the leader, they would place themself subservient to the greater good from this interior position of self-knowledge and authentic living. The only moral danger is in coming to rely on the outside world, the world which they have no control over, for validation. One's place in the world is to be found out, and lived, from the inside-out. Each is subject to, and accepts, the realities of the life they live. Epictetus was born a Roman slave but was allowed to study stoic ideals, which he spread in philosophical teaching when banished to Greece by Roman emperor Domitian. He lived much of his life with low social status and little authority or power as we would understand it. By contrast, Marcus Aurelius was the most powerful man in the most powerful region,

---

[9]Stoics are cosmopolitan in that they see their nature as shared elements of the cosmos, not as part of the *polis*, or city.

and who held almost unlimited and absolute imperial power for nearly two decades. What Stoics shared was mutual recognition of a common outlook on life and an appreciation of purpose, applicable by anyone at any time, and any level of status.

Stoicism contains few axioms. Its central ideas are highly generative and widely applicable by individuals in many situations, and simultaneously it does not get above itself. When combined with the Epicurean ideas[10] of the meaning of life in the face of our knowledge of its transitory nature, Marcus Aurelius was sanguine and humble in his admission in *Meditations*:

> 'Everything material soon disappears in the substance of the whole; and everything formal (causal) is very soon taken back into the universal reason; and the memory of everything is very soon overwhelmed in time.'[11]

Does that transience sound bleak to you? It should not. It is a call for rational self-examination of our mortality (more of this in Chapter 7), something that would be pointless not to acknowledge, and foolish to act in contradiction to. Purpose, say the Stoics, comes from how we act using reason and not through our passions.[12] We may experience ups and downs and have emotional reactions to these, but to base our actions on those feelings makes no difference to whatever caused them. Let that go. Further, say the Stoics, our emotions are not part of our highest nature, that of rational thought. Emotions are only opinions of things. We have no control over what happens or what other people do, only in how we choose to react. Focusing inward, the Stoic will exercise reason on themselves, and this then begins to look a little like our modern conception of mindfulness and of living in accordance with our nature,

---

[10] Chief among these was the aim to find meaning and purpose through cultivation of mental health and well-being in reasoning, identification of assumptions behind our choices and self-limiting beliefs.

[11] From Book VII 8, *Meditations*, translation by George Long.

[12] This word covers a lot, including suffering, intense emotional attachment, zeal, physical ailment, violent love, anger, etc.

which is part of nature. Elements of ancient stoicism have re-emerged to influence 20th century philosophy and culture, too. The existentialist movement of de Beauvoir, Sartre, and Camus in France (more in Chapter 7), the psychotherapy of Concentration Camp survivor Viktor Frankl, and even the closing sequence in the Monty Python film *Life of Brian*,[13] all explore the same territory of meaning, purpose, and attitude to life and society. Stoicism is at the heart of what many now think is our best definition of happiness.[14]

If so, then what might that mean for you as a leader in an organisation? For one thing, it suggests seeking:

Awareness of your emotions and choosing not to react to these in an irrational way.

Acceptance of the fragile, unpredictable nature of human life, and the inevitability of its finitude. Saying 'I don't mind' is not the same as 'I don't care'.

Being the best example and best version of what a leader should be in that role without attachment to external validation to judge that.

An appreciation of beauty in the natural unfolding of events, even when those events are negative or bad.

These European traditions from antiquity share some aspects and differ in others. Aristotle and the Stoics agree that humans use reason to evaluate and establish purpose, but where Aristotle emphasises purpose as externalised ends, the Stoics saw it as internalised means. The search for meaning and purpose has not been confined to Western thought. Equally complex ecologies of ideas

---

[13] Think of Eric Idle singing 'Always look on the bright side of life'.

[14] German philosopher Artur Schopenhauer had an interesting take on the concept of happiness. He saw the alternatives to a state of happiness, or joy, in life were pain or boredom. For the poor of the world, the movement away from pain and suffering was the same as a move towards happiness. But too far in the other direction, to excess of wealth, brings one away from happiness to boredom. When we need something, happiness is impossible. When we are too well off, we battle with having nothing to do, which denies us happiness.

are found across time and space and from among a range of intellectual outlooks that are stretched over ancient, pre-modern, modern, to post-modern eras, yet we have barely scratched the surface. How many unrecorded and unrelated human traditions around the world have either not survived to our times or remained too isolated or marginal to register in our cultural understanding? As far as we can see, and if we are looking carefully and compassionately, we always find the same basics being sought by humans, regardless of time or place. To compare is to find common ground with 'the other', and thereby understand ourselves more completely. While a complete map of human virtues is beyond the scope and purpose of this book,[15] clues can be found. Every society weaves into their present existence threads of thought and action from the past,[16] One of the most interesting examples of these is a cultural and philosophical tradition from China, Taoism,[17] which dates to around 400 years BCE, incorporating much older folk traditions.

3.   Taoism

Even acknowledging an increasing awareness and cross-over between East and West, direct (or exact) comparisons and translations from one system to another are rarely advisable because there is so much leeway in interpretation from one system to another (and from one language to another). With sensitivity and a little poetic understanding, however, we can access very valuable lessons about purpose. Few traditions or ways of seeing the world are

---

[15] I recommend *Sapiens* by Yurul Noah Harrari (Penguin).

[16] We are closer to the past than we think. If a generation is 25 years, then we are only about 16.5 generations from the first ever performance of Hamlet, in London in 1609. If you imagine someone in that audience aged 15, who at 100 years old then gave an eye-witness account of what they saw to a 15-year-old, and then this person lived to 100 and did the same, and this pattern is repeated, then there would be only 4 generations between you and direct experience of Shakespeare (the latest 15-year-old now being only in their 70s).

[17] Many of these intertwine their influences and their differences with others with surprising ease (compared to the West).

Figure 5.1. The component parts of the Chinese character for tao.

as simple and as wide open to interpretation as is Taoism.[18] *Tao* has been translated variously as 'way', 'discourse', 'path', 'route', 'principle', 'habit', 'conduct', 'text', or 'reality',[19] and each choice can make sense depending on how you interpret the original text, which is notoriously mischievous and playful.

One of two core Taoist texts[20] is a short work known as the *Tao Te Ching*,[21] which consists of 81 short chapters purportedly written by Lao Tzu (the name just means 'the old master', so it is probably a composite collection of older Taoist texts). The most famous chapter is the first, a carefully worded and playful warning that when it comes to understanding what the Tao is, those who know, don't say, and those who say, don't know.[22] The ineffable quality of the Tao has captured imaginations ever since. That said, Taoism is a realist philosophy. Taoist thinkers of this period saw life as a harmony of interactions and relationships with the way, or the course of the universe. They were concerned enough with how this

---

[18] Pronounced 'daoism', and 'dao'.

[19] It is characteristic of the Chinese process of language that concepts may take or give many meanings depending on what they are associated with.

[20] The other is by *Chunag-Tzu*, which is a very readable and often funny book.

[21] Which might be translated as 'The Book of the Internal Character of the Way'.

[22] There is an interesting parallel to what we are told about the Socratic method in Greece at roughly the same time.

might be conceptualised to write it down, perhaps to contrast with the elaborate social rituals and duties laid out in Confucianism.[23] Taoism pares down and strips out all but the essential to return to one's underlying nature. Humility is one of the strengths of the leader under the Tao, but while this comes from a person recognising their proper place as a participant in a vast range of events that they did not begin and will not finish, humility cannot be cultivated. This is beautifully captured in a lesson on leadership in Chapter 17:

> "The best leaders value their words and use them sparingly.
> When she has accomplished her task, the people say, 'Amazing:
> we did it, all by ourselves!'"[24]

Leadership from a Taoist perspective sees background and foreground as equal in importance. There is accordingly an interest in the power of empty spaces, and in the gaps between things where relationships flow. Seen this way, an organisation must move with and not against the grain. Here we find an echo of what we discussed in Chapters 2 and 3, and a nice resonance with stoic philosophy. This is ancient and entirely modern. Quite independently, Taoism criss-crosses many seminal ideas in Western philosophy being developed at that time. It complements very recent attempts to reconcile the problem of sustainability of business in a dynamic and delicately balanced world.

Leaders need not shy away from the fact that they are actors in the performance, but they should not make the mistake of identifying the role with external reality. The way we see the world tells us only about how we are oriented to it, not what it is. It is therefore a waste of time (purposeless?) to look for validation. Leaders may be necessary for the harmony of society, but do not confuse the word with what it names, say the Taoists. To interact with the

---

[23] A philosophical tradition from China contemporary with the blossoming of early Hellenic thought in Europe in the 6th and 7th centuries BCE.

[24] McDonald, J.H. (1996). *Tao Te Ching: An Insightful and Modern Translation*, Qigong Vacations, with permission.

world without a need to control or dominate makes this perhaps the philosophical tradition best attuned to the idea of getting out of your own way. In our society, we must ask whether we have become confined in a narrow view of health and well-being distorted from the actual source of happiness and contentment. The best way into leadership, from a Taoist perspective, is to:

Watch: Let things be. Lead by not inferring from your conditioning.
Listen: Hear without trying to focus on any one thing. Let the world around you tell its own story.
Touch: Remain in close contact with the world and guide events by holding our touch lightly.
Integrate: Find multiple perspectives and combine them by allowing the scattered parts to find their connection.

Taoism focuses on relationships, and in this way feels systemic and not hierarchical. But we must be a bit cautious. It offers no moral code and is not prescriptive, except in an artful and poetic series of instructions for rulers in later chapters, so it can be made to appear to speak to a great many audiences depending on how it is interpreted and presented. Purpose under Taoism is never dogma, it is fulfilled by being unobstructed. Do only what needs to be done. Its use for the Integrated Leader is as muse, or aid to thinking, rather than a tool for doing. An interesting contrast in view is found in a family of (unrelated) human kinship traditions from different parts of the world, Totemism.

4. Totemism

A totem is a symbol or an emblem that represents something. Totemism takes an understanding of nature and then applies aspects of that as metaphors to the social world, and to the people in it.[25] It takes an emblem, usually from the natural world, and

---

[25] The alternative, of attributing human characteristics to living organisms, natural processes, or inanimate objects in nature, is called animism.

looks within that for features that become a source of wisdom and learning (in this, it shares something with Taoism and Stoicism). Adoption of an emblem symbolises belonging and shared principles, and those metaphors may even represent principles on which to build society, and regulate how it is conducted. In popular culture and New Age mythology, Totemism is associated loosely with First Nations' peoples in Canada and Native American peoples in the United States, now ritualised and spiritualised as escapism from modern materialistic values and consumerism.[26] Totemism is a category of cultural ideas found among peoples spread across the globe. Emerging in the nascent subject of anthropology at the start of the 20th century, a debate has been in full flow as to whether Totemism is a universal or a cultural phenomenon unique in every case. You perhaps need to be aware of your conditioning before making a judgement. If you think Totemism is archaic and primitive, and that our modern life is not reliant on the symbolic and the representational, think again. We are just as reliant on symbols that help us express purpose and meaning as our ancestors, even if we are not looking to equate nature with our reality in the same way.

Famously tribal, the totemic possesses the uncanny ability to unite people around the quality it has been chosen to represent, even in an international and globalised world. We see this in our fondness for the logos and loyalties we associate with certain brands, and in how we gain from a great many group identities. The fragrance of animistic and emblematic roots still lingers in modern marketing. For example, the top five most common sports team names in the United States are, in reverse order, Wildcats, Panthers, Bulldogs, Tigers, and Eagles.[27] Many organisations that have reached a critical mass of employees or that need to maintain a central and unifying culture across geographic boundaries adhere to a form of totemic and ritualistic use of emblems. Jaguar

---

[26] There are aspects of a symbolic connection with the natural world that highlight the alienation that many in developed economies feel in the 21st century.

[27] Mascotdb, Most Popular Team Names (Active and Inactive), https://www. mascotdb.com/lists/100-most-frequently-used-team-names.

cars, Red Bull, the Peugeot lion, the Evernote elephant, and even the Playboy bunny all were chosen because they captured qualities the founders wanted their products to have. One could argue that leadership is a matter of symbolism. The position of the leader is representing and embodying something much greater than themself reflected not only in the holding of office but through objects that connote expressions of power.

Integrating Multiple Dimensions of Purpose

This chapter began with a question about purpose in your business. With no real stretch of the imagination, the same question can be adapted for you as a person. Here, 'business' means how you spend your life and/or to what end. What is your life for, and do your actions reflect that? What business are you really in? In the personal sphere, regardless of whether we say purpose is to do with being, or purpose is to do with doing, it is immature to rely on others to do our thinking and answer for us. Maturity in adult learning needs courage because you must act on your understanding without the need for comparison or validation. You must find your own way.

To this we may add three important aspects worth considering for the Integrated Leader. As with all good learning, these generate more questions than answers:

Locus of control: Does your purpose as a leader come from within or is it controlled from without?

> Where is the organisation's purpose? Where is your purpose? Is it in the future, and the work today is done only because it is a stepping stone towards purpose? Or is it here, now, in the present and synonymous with the work done today?

Roles and identity: Is leadership all etiquette? What are the rules, and where do they come from? If I am a leader and no-one is watching me, am I still a leader?

Is leadership about stability or is it about flexibility?
In leadership, is the person more important than the role, or the role more important than the person?

Effort: How hard must I try? Should leadership be hard work?

The Purpose of Life is Not its Ending

The four views introduced in this chapter are ways of answering these and other questions. You may find your own way. This is to be encouraged, and the only thing that matters is that you see the purpose of a leader is to serve the organisation, and this role is at once both external and internal to the person. It is also a role only for the duration it is needed. A persona is not a substitute for having freedom of your own, but while we are playing the part, we should play it fully, and well.

Purpose can be about:

Tomorrow, where it locks on to an absence, and qualities not yet present. This 'not yet here' version of purpose often fits well to the leadership question 'what could be?'. However, purpose in this case is not necessarily about completion and arrival at a future destination because an objective reached would be a purpose concluded. It might sound paradoxical, but almost every organisation has this designed into itself. Leadership with tomorrow's purpose in its sights is always and restlessly seeking its next purpose. The function of leadership is thus constant reinvention. Failure to search for the next horizon is failure of leadership. The nature of an organisation is that it is on a neverending path towards ongoing future desired states. The desired future state relegates the present to a waypoint.

Today, where it locks on to presence, what is here-and-now, and to qualities already existing. This 'already here' version of purpose can inspire 'what could be?' as the key question in leadership. The difference is that the leader is getting creative for the future using what they have in the present. Purpose is about knowing yourself well enough to see clearly why you are in business. The function of leadership is living in the best harmony with what is, and failure in leadership is failure to be present in the here-and-now, where all the answers are. The nature of an organisation is that it is on a neverending path from where it already is. Today is the vital organising principle, for which tomorrow or yesterday may be useful as ideas or waypoints.

Both views may be sustainable strategies in leadership if practice is aligned to theory, and theory is aligned to reality (social as well as natural). There is hard work to be done in any case. Businesses can become obsessed with the achievement of singular and fixed goals rather than valuing a whole range of possible outcomes.

Which one works for you? That will require further reflection, probably. Both call for hard work and dedication, but they promote very different styles of leadership. In personal development, the choice is open to you. This asks you to think very carefully about what having goals and purpose mean in your life. To be driven teleologically by the idea of an ultimate end, still out in the future, as yet unattained or unfulfilled is one thing. To be driven by being in touch intrinsically with what is complete in you now is quite another.

My view is that purpose is about the formation of a present-tense culture of being fully prepared for what might come next. Today is not a stepping stone, it is the embodiment of purpose being realised as unfolding. As the Spanish proverb says, we make the road by walking.

Reflecting on the Integrated Leader's Manifesto (Leading Self with Others)

#5

'Judging others will not help them and will interfere in my ability to manage and lead. As a leader I therefore seek awareness of my own emotions in every moment. This awareness puts the emphasis on my capacity to support others in transition. We all have fears, doubts, and weak areas. In our vulnerability lies our power for transformation.'

It is common sense to observe that people are not the same. We hold different opinions, have different tastes, and want or value different things. We all seek meaning, but at the local level my meaning will probably be different from yours even when we share all sorts of common ideas and beliefs in wider contexts of community and culture. What do we do when we meet someone who believes something in another form than us? How should we deal with this? Is how we should deal with it how we do deal with it? How much control do we have?

This Manifesto point says that judging others will not help them. This might sound a bit odd, especially if you have been brought up with the idea that leaders should be seen, and that leadership is about influencing, convincing, and persuading. Can a leader help another person if she has no judgement of them? Many people will reject the idea that they judge other people and will say that their leadership style means that they are open to that person, accepting them as they are. Some research suggests that for basics such as attractiveness and trustworthiness we have already made evaluative judgements in a fraction of a second[28] of meeting another person, and that additional time merely confirms this first impression, over which we can have little control.

Judging others is another way of placing ourselves above or below. The role of leader comes built in with the assumption of hierarchy, but this

---

[28] Willis, J. and Todorov, A. (2006). First Impressions: Making Up Your Mind After a 100-Ms Exposure to a Face, *Psychological Science, 17*(7), 592–598.

way of establishing it is hardly useful for building consensus or working collaboratively, and very few of the complex tasks of leadership can be solved by the leader role without all roles being equal in their self-worth. The judging referred to here is not so much about our unconscious biases, although in time an integrated leader will work on those as well. Rather, it is a question of self-awareness of what conscious judgements you are making. In the matter of self-awareness, we are all equal. When we turn the question on ourselves, what stops us from self-understanding, deeply? What kind of enquiry needs to happen?

Becoming aware of how you got to your conclusions, positions, or opinions means first asking yourself what is necessary for you to understand yourself. This is nothing to do with what is necessary for you to understand other people, the main topic leaders worry about. You will not be able to understand another person for them, on their behalf; you will only end up judging them as if they were you. Rather, the job for the leader is to look at all parts of their conditioning, their self-interest, and ambitions, as well as their life and its problems, and their emotions and fears.

To be serious as an Integrated Leader you must take possession of the enquiry into who you are. And you must be honest. Your vulnerability and fallibility are just as much part of you as your otherwise admirable traits and qualities – the type that management journals and books endlessly write about. Others you meet are mirrors to look at yourself with, at your doubts and uncertainties. Your ability to lead is not a function of how well you can judge others. You don't blame a mirror for how you look; you study the reflection and try to understand it.

Chapter 6

Outside-In and Inside-Out

And since you know you cannot see yourself
So well as by reflection, I, your glass,
Will modestly discover to yourself
That of yourself which you yet know not of.

William Shakespeare (Julius Caesar, Act 1, scene 2)

"What's Special About You?"

This sounds like a very annoying question to be asked. It needn't be. As ever, perspective is everything. It is a very annoying question to be asked by someone when you're expected to show how much you can impress, how much you can brag, or how you take the judgement of others. It puts us on the spot to validate ourselves to the satisfaction of those around us. Adults hate being asked this.

Very young children are not phased at all by this. A five or six-year-old will tell you exactly what they think is special about them, and it will be an answer full of authentic wonder, imagination, compassion, and creativity. Somewhere along the line, we lose the ability to be ok with ourselves on our own terms and start to require being ok with ourselves on someone else's. By the time we reach the end of our regular schooling and are approaching the world of paid work, many of us have learnt to be very cautious about what 'special' means. We know that our answer may be interpreted as a judgement on us. Such is the importance of this that we are trained in skills to answer it to the satisfaction of, say, an interviewer or a superior. It might not be phrased in these words, but promotions, bonuses, performance appraisals, and social status all require us to blow our own trumpet. What this amounts to is an outside-in way of answering, one of two orientations possible, as summarised in Figure 6.1. The counterbalancing perspective to this is inside-out.

Outside-in and inside-out are not mutually exclusive. They refer to a shared boundary, which is the interface of you with the world, and of the world with you. To be in balance, the relationships of influence between an individual and their context come from both perspectives. Outside-in is when the outer world is turned inward, and Inside-out is when our internal self is turned outward. We often, when it comes to notions of our worth, tend to lose that balance. An extreme imbalance has consequences for our health and well-being. To live entirely in the terms of outside-in would make you a shadow puppet for the intentions of others. To live entirely and only in terms of inside-out might place you in a desert, isolated from society and therefore far from community nourishment.

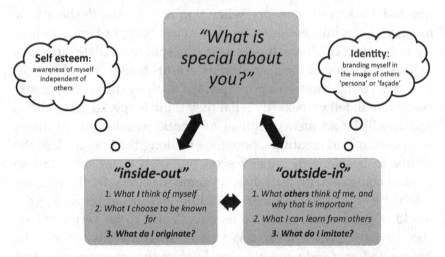

Figure 6.1.   Two perspectives on the question of what is special about you.

Outside-In

To know ourselves from the outside is to understand our façade as an outward projection. It is a version of ourselves that we inwardly think the world wants to see. A façade is our persona. A persona was the mask, a device to amplify the voice (in Latin, *per* = through, *sona* = sound), used in classical theatre by actors to identify which character they were playing. The point of a persona is to be clear to others who is talking, and in what role. We all use these to some extent in our networks, social groups, formalised roles, and in just about every basic interaction with other people. Many of us have well-formed and perhaps very precise personas in our jobs. At other times, our persona is our social status. Where 'leader' is a title in organisational structures, it is an assumed persona. We relate to significant others in our lives based on their personas, and when you think of someone you admire or look up to, are you looking up to (or down on) the person or the persona?

There are a great many outside-in skills that we learn, mainly from others, about roles and identities (professional, familial, interpersonal, cultural, etc.). Fitting in, doing well, and moving ahead provide the material necessities we need to live, and clarity of roles undeniably sets expectations for civil conduct and civic society that contribute to social and collective health and well-being. Few people live completely away from this for any great length of time. There are many examples of hierarchic belief systems that set expectations on the individual this way. Confucianism roots its appraisal of the ideal person in the strict cultivation of social rituals and ceremonies, for instance, as does Roman Catholicism. The practice of outward virtues, such as reverence for ancestors, (seen in the southern African social philosophy of ubuntu[1]), but more importantly of ethics, decorum, order, and governance sees everyone occupying their rightful place. The relational and hierarchical precepts of this heritage are still prevalent in many countries in Asia. Western thought has often been portrayed as more

---

[1] See Chapter 11.

individualistic in where it places the person in society, but if this is so, then it is relatively recent and perhaps not quite as unshackled as it sounds. The advantage of setting expectations for what counts as identity resulted in an overall stability that persisted for centuries, and this is hard to shake off. Most of us are quite content to operate with external labels. On the other hand, for all that is comforting and familiar, this is a world of meaning-making as measured entirely in the logic of the two questions in Chapter 3, 'compared to what?' and 'according to whom?' Free expression, investigation, and questioning of the order may not be tolerated if they threaten a fundamental premise.

Personas can be nuanced and sophisticated and may allow (if not encourage) variation in the rules and obligations for social conduct. Even where this is liberal, a restriction is that any evaluation of your talents can become limited to who you are in terms of what you imitate. If this is the only perspective or lens you use to evaluate yourself, then you will have hung your self-worth, and even your self-esteem, on the opinion of others. You will resemble a set of expectations of what you think you should or should not be, and very few of us are free of this self-definition in our work and career. Most of the systems and structures that are in place to evaluate, motivate, and reward you with praise, promotion, and performance targets operate 'outside-in', so to speak.

So we need a balance.

Inside-Out

The outside-in way is only half the story. 'What is special about you?' is a less confrontational (though still difficult) and more liberating question to ask of yourself from the inside-out, that is, without prior reference to anyone or anything external. Conceptually, inside and outside go inseparably with each other in the way described in Chapter 3. You cannot conceive of one without the other in your development. What usually happens is that because we rely so much on social ties to define ourselves, and because the apparent objectivity of an external measure feels more convincing, those who operate on their terms uncompromisingly from inside-out are rare.[2] Even in individualistic societies or in autonomous, creative industries, the idea of being true to yourself feels more like another way to fit norms than a simple statement of fact, independent of what anyone else thinks. The pressure to conform is enormous even when the subject matter is creativity.

Riding a wave of national fame following the success of their first album, on July 22, 1967, United States rock band The Doors made a television appearance on Dick Clark's show, American Bandstand. Between mimed performances, Clark breathlessly interviewed each band member, beginning with keyboardist Ray Manzerek. Their exchange went like this:

'Clark: How do you characterize your music? Does it have a name?
Manzerek: (after a pause) Well it's impossible, really, to put a label on it because of where we are in the music — being on the inside, you're only *of* the music, and all categories have to come from the outside. And so, someone else is going to have to say what our music is, rather than us, because we are our music...
Clark: (removing the mic) ...too much in it at the moment... now... (quickly moves on to Jim Morrison).'[3]

The contrast between the question and its response is worth remarking on. Dick Clark's frame of reference was that music comes in categories, and so a typology must be inherent in popular music. Once we can place it, then we know what it is. Outside-in. Manzerek's response does not reject the premise of the question, it accepts it as how many people make sense of their music and the music business, so this is not a simple contradiction (after all, rebelling against categories would simply be another label). Manzerek exhibits more awareness than a teen pop music show might have anticipated. Because they occupy their music, on the inside, the

---

[2] See Paul Newman's title character in the film *Cool Hand Like* (directed by Stuart Rosenberg in 1967) for a dramatic example of this point.
[3] See https://www.youtube.com/watch?v=dTkPOt2L7sI (3:22–3:48).

question of category does not arise. It is not essential for their identity and the music will speak for itself. How many of us can afford to identify ourselves at work, in our career, or in society this way? When founded on the opinions or expectations of others, leaders sometimes are identified (and may self-identify) as having qualities they do not possess.

The Inside-out way of answering the 'what is special?' question uses only the self as a reference point. Its meaning is emergent as a category therefore only when it meets the outside. This is where we get to understand the line:

'How can I know what I think till I see what I say?'[4]

We either shape ourselves to our environment, or we let our environment shape us. In either case, that image we carry of ourselves is liable to conditioning, so this is almost impossible to get right and balanced immediately. Introspection and reflection are required. The voice in your head that you think is you may have been leant by or learnt from others. If you have lived a large portion of your life influenced first and foremost by the opinions of others, through pleasing, fearing, or needing others, in co-dependency with others, in search of self through others, then those are the images that will form the foreground of what you believe is genuinely and authentically who you are. The shift is one of awareness, not of the reality of the social world.

Once found, inside-out should be an anchor for the locus of control when it comes to reputation, although for many people this is not the situation in their career. If reputation is what people say about you before you enter the room, then if they have not met you and if they think anything at all, their opinion cannot be you. If reputation is what people say about you after you have left the room, then the image they have can either be contrived by you (it's what you think other people should think of you) or contrived by them (not managed by you).

---

[4]See Chapter 4: Stages of Control in Wallas, G. (1926). *The Art of Thought*, San Diego, CA: Harcourt Brace and Co. (p. 106).

The outside-in says 'I am what I imitate'. The inside-out declares 'I am what I originate'. This ought to be a huge question for a person as they go through life, even if they do not have a ready answer. What do *you* originate? What starts with and only with you?[5] Or, put another way, is what you are known for dependent on others for its worth? In truth, we are all maintaining a balance between the inside and the outside. The Integrated Leader will operate along the continuum between the extremes of the poles. Their position may slide one way or the other (the moveable '?' in the following Figure 6.2) depending on whether the field of forces forming their identity predominates from others, or predominates from self.

Where a person's managerial identity is strongly influenced by what is coming from the outside, and where they are assessed and self-assessed on those terms, the slider will be firmly over to the left (Figure 6.3).

In middle management, most people find themselves pressed somewhere over to the left, where there is limited space for the individual to connect with their passion or with their inner world. By contrast, if a person is so dominated by their urge to pursue their own path, irrespective of the limitations and boundaries of their context, they will slide way over to the right (Figure 6.4), and risk having no following, and perhaps no social connection.

Figure 6.2. A person's position relative to inside-out and outside-in.

Figure 6.3. The position of identity formed from the outside-in.

---

[5] What starts with you may not finish with you, of course. That's kind of the whole point of being a leader.

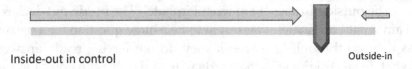

Inside-out in control   Outside-in

Figure 6.4. The position of a person's identity formed from the inside-out.

Too much force either way is unlikely to fulfil the role of the leader. For grounded, balanced health and well-being, that which is showing outward (your brand) should reflect the inward. In the right amount, the extension of your inward world into society can have incredible results. Due to our cultural addiction to approval and validation, this movement takes courage and self-awareness. The interplay of inner world and outer world plays out in a storied form, so one way of better self-understanding is the appreciation of what a narrative is.

Narrative Inquiry

A narrative is a collected series of statements that connect with a central theme or purpose. Conventions and style may differ among peoples but storytelling is a universal. And a fertile one. Stories hold groups together and transfer knowledge from one person to another and from one generation to another. The earliest narratives were oral and were legends, chronicles, clan histories, and creation myths. This has not completely died out. Your earliest memories are probably held, told, and retold as stories in family or community gatherings. This narrative thread stays with us as we grow up. Shared stories are a door to discovery, both outward for passing down wisdom and collective identity, and inward for the coherence of self-identity. Joseph Campbell's influential 1949 book *The Hero with A Thousand Faces*[6] was an exhaustive account of the stages of the hero's journey in mythology. Archetypal journeys of the ego (Campbell used Jungian

---

[6] Campbell, J. (1949). *The Hero with a Thousand Faces*, New York, NY: Pantheon.

interpretations for much of his work), such as separation from the world, a penetration to a source of power followed by a life-enhancing return, still form the staple of much of our sense of purpose today. Narratives combine familiar and shared patterns. We all expect that stories have beginnings, middles, and ends as well as open-ended possibilities for meaning. For this reason, they can be a great way in for personal development.

There are three useful frames to help you narrate your personal development: life stories, critical incidents, and discourses.

Life stories are themed biographies and autobiographies that stitch together fragments, artefacts, or memories to make a patch-work that eventually spreads to form a coherent whole. Life stories are blankets of lived experience embroidered in rich detail, and a good way to hold the pattern connecting separate elements. Passage from one stage or part of life to another, for example, often follows a recognisable script, so stories may have an important role in understanding things in changing contexts.

Critical incidents are selected episodes or turning points that stick in our minds or appear to us as significant in some way. These short scenes from life are markers, milestones, or waypoints. They are more akin to vivid short stories than whole novels. Critical incidents, unlike life histories, are compartmental and bounded. The study of a critical incident may be a systematic and forensic search for details that really matter. As such, they teach us something. Originally, critical incident was a research technique method-ically capturing and understanding the sequence and role of human behaviour in unwanted events, to investigate errors and improve process design.[7] The technique has since been used widely in health care, organisational efficiency studies, and market research. We now use the phrase more loosely, as a broad frame-work. A critical incident is a placeholder for an event sufficiently important to have explanatory inference for a wider system.

---

[7] The most famous proponent was Colonel John Flanagan in World War Two, who pioneered use of the principles and techniques of Critical Incidents in the United States Air Force to understand mission failure.

When you experience a critical incident, you know it. Your energy levels change, and probably your tone of voice. For some people, words may come tumbling out as they describe or put on paper what happened. You may struggle to pick the right word but there will be no mistaking the emotion. Critical incidents are not necessarily about life's hard knocks or lessons. They can be the uplifting ones, or the recall of moments where you were fully alert, and in touch with your passion. If you are a manager, you will know that this is true because (if you have been paying attention), you will have seen all these things from time to time in the people around you. You may be less aware of the same traits in yourself.

Discourse once referred to the thread of an argument and a line of reasoning as it moved forward, often in the flow of a conversation. Discourse still carries this sense of motion, or proper flow and sequence of events, but with the growth of formalised education and complexity of managing social interaction, it now denotes the ordered way that events are explained. Discourse is a description of the system and rules of how we are supposed to communicate with each other. More plainly, discourse is the unwritten set of rules of what gets included in a story and what gets left out, and (for example) what meets the criteria for a critical incident and what does not. It governs what is loud, clear, and pushed to the front versus what is kept silent or relegated to the background.

Discourse is how we learn to interpret meaning, and what we consider to be 'true'. If you have ever suspected or accused someone of having a hidden agenda, an ulterior motive, or a prejudice, then you have been inferring a discourse. Every story contains discursive assumptions. Conventional management wisdom is an example of a discourse because it helps direct leaders and followers through what would otherwise be extremely complex and risky contexts. Some discourse can therefore produce groupthink, which is a sort of herd mentality. Leaders who lead this way are choosing to act in line with convention because they are less likely to be blamed if things do not go well.

Narrative Identity

Narrative identity is the use of a story structure to define the self. It is usually thought of these days as working across three different aspects, with the function of maintaining flexibility for us to adjust to changing or challenging conditions without becoming so fragmented that we lose our cohesive sense of self. The person who first proposed this was Dan McAdams[8]:

> *Behavioural traits:* General dispositions and broad personality tendencies not specific to one individual that are independent of different situations. Very little of this can be relied on for a personal narrative
>
> *Characteristic adaptations:* Context-dependent, reflecting the goals, motivations, and desires of someone in certain roles. Experienced as personal and unique to that person
>
> *Integrative life narratives:* The task and product of adulthood and the life cycle or search for meaning, either as an individual or as a member of a collective

An integrative life story is a person-centred account of lived experience interpreted as a sequence of interconnected events which, as we have seen, emerges in patterns of relations with others. Our narratives serve a purpose. When healthy, they are a negotiation of who we are in respectful harmony with our environment. We can do this as private persons or in any of the roles or positions we occupy in the social web. In a healthy narrative, we can find our voice, but a narrative cannot explain the nature of the self. The deepest 'who I am' will probably remain out of reach in a narrative. Nevertheless, much of who we think we are is relational, and already embedded in the definition of self is the relationship with everything else. You experience yourself as a unique 'I', separate from the world around you, and at the same time this individual feeling only makes sense with reference to the rest of humanity.

---

[8] McAdams, D. P. (1995). What do we know when we know a person?, *Journal of Personality*, 63(3), 365–396.

There is no narrative, especially one defined by fixed dogma or shaped in the image of a self-help guru, that can get to the bottom of who you are behind your sense of 'I'. You cannot answer this except through yet another, implicit, 'I'…. and so it goes on *ad infinitum*.

When we shrug off the idea of using the self to see the self, we may be making a crucial step toward sustainable health and well-being. This is not the same thing as overcoming the ego, something many leaders are encouraged to do in contemporary leadership theory.[9] Such calls always fall short. This is not surprising; you cannot give up the ego *with* the ego. What is more, dropping the idea of the self would not release you from your reality. You would still need to pay the bills, cover the mortgage, send the children to school, and so on. And still, there you are with all the questions and uncertainty around how to live a fulfilling and meaningful existence. You can neither deny the sense of self, nor can you ditch it if you conclude that it is not real.

So if you are stuck with the illusion of being you, because the illusion also creates the sense of you creating it (it gets really circular), what remains the real question? Here is where reflection on inside and outside ideas of self is useful. The question is:

'What is happiness, and where can I find it?'

Many would argue that the answer has something to do with living authentically.

Authenticity

What would it be like to live completely authentically? It is an appealing thought, but it doesn't define whether authenticity is an

---

[9] *Harvard Business Review* has a fairly typical example of this in November 2018's article 'Ego is the Enemy of Good Leadership', in which the authors use ego as shorthand for hubristic self-importance, which works as a thematic device, but then the solution offered is to 'break free' from the inflated ego. And we're back to square one. See https://hbr.org/2018/11/ego-is-the-enemy-of-good-leadership.

end position or ongoing process. Is being authentic always a work-in-progress, or is it a threshold?

Something that is authentic may be trusted and believed to be what it says it is. In other words, it carries the authority of the real thing. When used in leadership theory, it usually refers to a person's intention to act with no hidden agendas. Closer to home, it signals that a person has a mindset of 'I am being true to myself'. Authenticity is the presentation of a person's self-awareness to the world. This sounds simple and straightforward... and isn't. The idea of complete, unfettered freedom of expression sounds attractive, but there are two versions of this, one of which is constructive and the other which is destructive. Here are three initial caveats and notes of caution:

1. A person can believe they are self-aware when in fact they are operating from a concealed wish to impress others. What they present to the world and claim as authenticity is a distortion of self-awareness. When any person starts to brag how authentic they are, it is probably the moment you know that they are not.
2. It is possible that authenticity is being used as a synonym for a kind of 'what you see is what you get' tactic of bloody-mindedness. When a person wishes to justify their stubbornness, an appeal to 'that's just me' might be a pre-emptive defence mechanism.
3. Tolerance of someone's authenticity is never entirely boundless and doing just exactly what you wish means either risking or choosing exclusion from society. Anyone who steps outside society's discourse unprepared soon discovers how immediate, volatile, and powerful this tension can be. The crossing of a threshold that is societal can mean not just loss of liberty but loss of in-group identity. Social forces exert many restraints on people, and there is no recipe for living genuinely as yourself. The constructive side of authenticity, however, is derived from the same confrontational source. Authentic living is a sort of exile, and this can — if approached with the right mental state — be an abundance of stability and joy for the person who goes out to meet themself without the requirement of

validation for self-worth and without the belief that the world must move aside for them.

Living authentically may not be a choice; we may be forced to discover and rely on ourselves in adverse circumstances and against our will. We can accept all of this and allow authenticity to be background rather than foreground.

All life is grounded in matter and all living things share the fundamental building blocks of chemistry, biology, and zoology. These are necessary but not sufficient for human life, which adds the defining, self-referential phenomenon of inside-out, subjective experience. The world as it is, reality independent of our perceptions, must include the potential from which such a capacity for perception of self can emerge. In other words, reality must be such that it has generated the capacity in me to see myself. I cannot experience directly how someone else experiences life, save vicariously through their reports. I cannot really know what the world looks like to you in the same way I experience my own existence, and you cannot really know how it is for me. Our epistemologies may be personal, but the capacity for epistemology is shared. We do not, however, have *direct* access to our biological nature; the lens of your eye cannot see itself. The closest the eye can get is its reflection in a mirror, and this may be the most useful metaphor for narratives of self. Knowledge is limited and fallible. Unmediated glimpses of another's life (let alone another's 'self') are rare and fleeting, so the best we can do is ask each other and compare notes. What is a healthy self? Narratives, stories, when constructed with awareness may have transformational benefits to the storyteller. An integrated narrative may end up being analogous to the underlying, generative structures of nature. Ideas can have their own narratives, too. A meta-narrative, or grand narrative, is a term that describes the narrative of using narrative in our lives. In education, for example, there is a grand narrative that separates the roles of teacher and student, often privileging the former over the latter. Throughout working life, management and leadership are woven into a grander story, which we label career.

Career Narratives

In management, narrative is a key aspect of establishing and sustaining a reputation, and it is how most people make sense of their careers. Career has been defined broadly as:

'the evolving sequence of a person's work experiences over time' (p. 8)[10]

This is short and sweet, and somewhat inadequate, like packing a big suitcase with only a couple of t-shirts. It suggests that the next step in a career should be more sophisticated than the previous one. That may be so, but that does not mean careers run in straight lines. Career development has been described as:

'a continuous lifelong process of developmental experiences that focuses on seeking, obtaining and processing information about self, occupational and educational alternatives, lifestyles and role options'[11]

This packs a bit more in. How leaders process personal goals in their jobs, how they see productivity and fulfilment, and what they perceive as barriers and obstacles to health and well-being are important in understanding and minimising stress and burnout. There is localised burnout (the kind of ratcheting up of pressure in a role or a period of time), and there is systemic burnout (the stress and strain of not being in harmony with the world). Traditional leadership has been concerned more with institutional structuring of work than fostering health and well-being through career success, except in some cases of providing relatively long-term and stable employment and a mutually beneficial and upward progression of skills and responsibility over time.

---

[10] Arthur, M. B., Hall, D. T., and Lawrence B. S. (Eds.) (1989). *Handbook of Career Theory*, Cambridge, UK: Cambridge University Press, with permission.

[11] Hansen, L. S. (1976). 'Career development education: Humanizing focus for educators', *Journal of Career Development*, 3(1), 42–48.

The career construct in the grand narrative of employment after the Second World War was to attract and keep talent to enhance the business and sustain value creation. The post-war version of career that emerged in Europe and North America over several decades of economic reconstruction in the 1940s, 1950s, and 1960s did so against a background of rapid scientific advancement, internationalisation, deregulation of commerce, and growth of trade across borders. In the 1960s, regional and global corporations began shaping our conceptions (and misconceptions) of career as something stable. It was increasingly non-vocational, too, in that people were no longer identified or confined to a trade, or repetition of what their parents had been.

During the 1980s and 1990s, some new models of career design with names such as protean, portfolio, or boundaryless assumed greater agency for the individual than the company. This led to a culture of leaders as mobile 'guns for hire' rather than integrated assets. Today, we work in a world that has become more interconnected *and* more fragmented than ever. The many cycles of turbulent economic recession, demographic and social shifts, corporate scandals, and macro changes in the spread and use of technology in business over the last twenty to thirty years mean we now need a more fluid understanding of the form and nature of career through the lifespan. Career today means being open to new ways of identifying such restraints and limitations to career success and fulfilment that might otherwise remain overlooked. This fluidity is nicely captured by Helen Tupper and Sarah Ellis in their book *The Squiggly Career.*[12] As Helen points out:

> 'creating an expectation of a 'good' career as one that gets progressively more senior and where everyone aims to reach the top, is not reflective of what people want from their work or what is available to them in the workplace. Instead, people are seeking

---

[12]Tupper, H. and Ellis, S. (2020). *The Squiggly Career: Ditch the Ladder, Discover Opportunity, Design Your Career*, New York, NY: Portfolio Penguin.

to develop far more individual and unique careers, where they explore multi-directional possibilities rather than follow rigidly defined plans.'[13]

Career success is supposed to come with quantifiable, measurable markers of advancement (salary, promotion, material reward, status, etc.). This may be true in its early phases, but a more circumspect view of job satisfaction and fulfilment will appear for many at some point. For an Integrated Leader, the traditional, transactional portrait of career success and its externally validated evaluation is not congruent with their lived experience. Their question is whether their work brings joy, meaning, and well-being to their lives and to the lives of others. A fresh perspective is required, though this will prove difficult to define. It has been proposed that when faced with a mystery, or with the unknown or the stubbornly uncertain, and direct routes have all been exhausted, there remain two ways of finding out what something is:

1. By stating and excluding what it is not. This resembles the Socratic method of a dialogue of discovery of presuppositions. By progressively finding out what something is not, our assumptions are tested and its true nature is revealed. The formula here is
   $x \neq y$ (the careful removal of anything that is not x)
2. By stating what it is like compared to other, known, things. This is the use of imagination and informed guesswork to find connecting patterns. An example of this method is metaphor. Metaphor is about getting at one thing through another and it is everywhere in human communication. The formula for metaphor is simple:
   $x = y$ (where the literal meaning of y reveals a poetic insight into the nature of x)

---

[13] Private correspondence, with permission.

Metaphor is a form of double description.[14] It reveals a truth (or something novel) by imposing a known pattern on an unknown one. Used imaginatively and sparingly, a metaphor can break a deadlock. Used unthinkingly and repetitively any metaphor can become a stereotype or cliché, but because it is such a creative device, it often appears in examples of great leadership, often in response to the leadership question 'what could be?' (Chapter 4).

Climb Every Mountain: Finding Metaphors for Career

Management writers are no strangers to metaphor in organisational or strategic theory, and this often extends into career and professional development. For example, Charles Handy coined the term portfolio career in 1978 as one of a whole bookcase of ideas to describe organisational life. Edgar Schein's career anchors were part of a wider project to map different types of organisational systems in the 1960s and 1970s. In fact, organisational metaphors often translate to career. The boundaryless career, for example, was borrowed from American multinational General Electric's corporate strategy in the 1980s. Classical myth and archetype is another rich source, as with the protean career[15] first applied by Douglas Hall in 1976. We should not forget that at its root the word career is also a metaphor. Journeys are often evoked to convey the passage of jobs over time. Visual metaphors tend to carry more information than the aggregated or generalised career metaphors mentioned above. If you have never done so, I would encourage you to get pen and paper and draw your career metaphor, something we do with our Executive MBA students. The images that emerge and the patterns they

---

[14] Double description (Bateson, 1989) is not just a question of making more than one comparison. It is how science moves forward in a combination of inductive, deductive, and abductive inferences.

[15] Portfolio, boundaryless, and protean careers each capture slightly differing aspects of the same thing: the person being in control of what they do and where they do it. The protean career adds the extra ingredient of being in service of the whole person and their purpose.

suggest provide many insights because they often contain indicators of the kinds of restraints or limits to sustainable health and well-being mentioned in the definition of personal development. We studied nearly 1,000 such images to find out what the main messages were, and noted they tend to fall into one of four categories:

1. Metaphors of positive growth
   Transformations, healthy growth, balance, and harmony (23% of the total). Images included butterflies, open doors, birds flying free, fields of flowers, forests, rivers, books, light bulbs, and rainbows.
2. Metaphors of turbulence, frustration, or restriction
   Obstacles, dilemmas, tricky choice, uncertainty, and stuckness (30% of total). Images included hamsters in wheels, volcanoes erupting (or about to), brewing storms, walls, ceilings, accidents/collisions, puzzles with pieces missing, crossroads or junctions, question marks (often on signposts), and a lot of mazes.
3. Metaphors of ends
   Rewards, goals achieved, journeys with endings in sight or in focus, races with finishing lines, competitions (14% of total). Images included ladders, climbing a hill or mountain, stairs, desert islands with treasure chests, and roads with a finishing line in sight.
4. Metaphors of means
   Ongoing journeys, travel, races, or travels with no end in sight, time and duration (26% of the total, only 6% did not adhere to these four categories). Images included many rocket ships, cars, and buses travelling from point A to point B, commuters, trains, sailing boats with the wind in their sails, rollercoasters, and running distance races (not sprints).

A career metaphor will work because it carries over a known frame of reference from one area and applies it somewhere new.[16]

---

[16] This effect can also be seen in a forced metaphor, whereby you select a random object (or someone selects for you, even better) and apply it as a career metaphor.

That can be a very useful thing to know when you are truly feeling uncertain or stuck about how to develop yourself as a leader.

The Perfectionist's Mirage?

A surprising number of otherwise well-balanced and well-qualified managers are stuck in their conviction that they must strive to be better because at present they are not quite good enough. Yet they never make any progress because they believe a change must be perfectly planned before it happens. The urge to perfectionism is a common malady.

A perfectionist is someone who demands the very highest standards in any given situation. It is someone who believes that being completely without fault or flaw is a theoretical possibility worthy of aim. There is more than one kind of perfectionist. The first says that imperfection results from an avoidable failure of effort. This person believes perfect is possible. The second says imperfection is our guide for choices and decisions on how to be better. This person believes perfect is just an ideal but a useful one. In both cases perfection is never a current state. To be a perfectionist is to be forever haunted by being imperfect.

If perfectionism is your outlook, then you probably find yourself applying one or other of these mindsets as your standard for yourself, as well as for other people, for your job, and for the organisation. These must generate at least some friction, tension, and conflict, since for the perfectionist their current state is not the desired state. The perfectionist is always chasing something and may see the pursuit of perfection as the only possible justification and the only worthwhile backdrop for measuring creativity, output, progress, and self-worth. Therefore, imperfection is the natural current state of the perfectionist. This may seem counter-intuitive, yet many managers and leaders behave in this manner and expect others to follow them in this thinking. Those who frame themselves as perfectionists use mainly their imperfectionism as their personal narrative.

Perfectionism can appear in a more benign form. Perhaps the best illustration of this is the tenets and principles of the Toyota Production System (TPS), first developed for use in the Japanese company's plants as a rigorous and meticulous means of continuous improvement in manufacturing. TPS works to eliminate waste, defined as any manufacturing activity not contributing to value. It looks at bottlenecks, defects, and work flows to optimise efficiency[17] along a production line assembled around the pull of resources through a system. Philosophically, TPS celebrates perfection as an ideal and acknowledges that complete perfection is an unobtainable goal, thereby saving it from becoming a dead-end of frustration from failure. The mindset of striving for perfection is the driver and this promotes immersion in what is happening in the present moment. TPS permits decisions to move to where the problem is. The individual is empowered to act where they spot an issue because they are part of a collective unified in the goal of seeking improvement. At the same time, it promotes decision-making made by teams, based on evidence that must be shared openly throughout the system. In this approach, there is a belief in the study and development of useful forms of resilience, creativity, and flexibility. In addition, and applied to specific and measurable outcomes, the team and social bonding fostered by a spirit of restless search for incremental improvement can carry benefits of health and well-being for the organisation.

Toyota knows that perfection is an impossibility. A lot of leaders do not. Perfectionism can become a compulsion and an unhealthy obsession, and in this form it is much less benign. This manifests as excessive expectation of flawless results from oneself and from others, and an overly, overtly critical evaluation when the inevitable happens and self and others fail to live up to those standards. Followers therefore get drawn in by the same impossible position as their leader.

The idea that performing better than in the past is a good thing is not controversial. Nearly all of us recognise this. Are we all therefore perfectionists? If perfectionism is more than this, then how does anyone know if they are a perfectionist? Researchers have posed the same question, with some consensus that perfectionism

---

[17] See the Japanese concept of *mottainai*, featured in the Glossary at the end of the book.

appears as a certain kind of persistent chatter, or self-talk, in a person's head, the origins of which may be a whole series of life events and narratives of expectations set when young. Typical drivers appear in mantras or mottos such as 'I need to prove myself', 'I must not make the same mistake twice', 'I have to compete and be the best', 'I have to work hard, all the time', 'how am I doing?', and even the 100 year-old mantra of 'every day in every way, I'm getting better and better'. The list is long. The trap for the perfectionist is that no matter what they do, it will never be enough, and it will never be here in the present moment. To be inefficient is a failure, but by definition a perfectionist is always inefficient. When this is a production puzzle, the stakes are seen in objective measures and are not too high. When this is a self-esteem question, the stakes are in terms of health and well-being, and very high.

A 2018 article in *Harvard Business Review* attempted to sum up the pros and cons of perfectionism from a meta-analysis of several decades of studies.[18] The authors found that although people who self-report on characteristics normally associated with perfectionism tend to be more engaged and work harder and longer than those who do not, there is no evidence to show they produce better results. They are significantly more prone to burnout and stress from an addiction to being at work, as well as poor mental health, anxiety, and depression. Is the answer that you should stop aiming for perfection and start settling for 'good enough'? That seems to keep the question tied to the way that the original problem was set. In other words, we return to the grand narrative. Arguably, because we now take it for granted, the grand narrative discourse of Western thought in the last thousand years has been that humans are inherently imperfect, and inherently incapable of perfection.

The counter presupposition is that the Integrated Leader has accessed a different personal epistemology. Their 'true north' is found within an Inside-out answer to the question of purpose. This is not a question only of mindset, but a more pervasive, holistic,

---

[18] Swider, B., Harari, D., Breidenthal, A. P., and Steed, L. B. (2018). The Pros and Cons of Perfectionism, According to Research, *Harvard Business Review* Digital Articles, 2–5).

multi-level, and relational way of being that transcends the dichotomy of perfection versus imperfection.

Perfection is in (Our) Nature

If there is such a thing as perfection, then it is most readily perceived in the aesthetic. The aesthetic is at its most obvious to us in the patterns and arrangements of nature. For example, a wave breaking along a seashore cannot do so in an unnatural or mistaken way, regardless of what shape it forms. Aesthetic refers to an experience accompanied by a feeling that something more is being perceived than appears on the surface of the senses. Life may be dotted with such moments of observation. For example, the light on a building at a certain time of day, a snatch of beautiful music being played by someone inside a building as you walk past, the bliss of the first cup of coffee late in the morning, the first steps your child takes, the top of the mountain above you lost in the mist, the discovery of a new skill at work, the first day of a three-year, part-time master's programme, etc. Any of these may be an aesthetic experience. With the right eyes, the moment to moment story of the organisation you are part of can reveal an aesthetic that goes beyond the bare facts. Whether that aesthetic gives you pleasure, provides you leisure, generates fear, or leaves you cold is in the relationship you have with the context.

Perfection should be our description of a natural alignment between what we do, how we think, and how the world is. This is found within the idea of integration. Not seeing this is a great source of anxiety and the trigger for an endless search for ourselves in the opinions and comparisons of others. The most difficult thing to discover is self-esteem without the need for comparison or validation.

Outside-in and Inside-out co-create each other. Leadership must reach out into the world, and leaders must have an inside to take out to be an influence and force for change. In this sense, being an Integrated Leader is already part of your nature. At the centre of this, as yet not fully examined, is the most elusive concept of all — the self. The next chapter will tackle the mysteries of the question 'who am I?'

Reflecting on the Integrated Leader's Manifesto (Leading Self with Others)

#6

'Each person takes 100% responsibility for their skilfulness, practice, and professional development. Equally, we share in a desire for learning, so we help those around us to find their own resources. Every team member has a right to freedom and decision-making in their evolution and practice, and I am happy to accept them just as they are.'

Earlier, we said that staying knowledgeable and following current thinking are duties and commitments that each manager must hold themselves to. We may recognise this duty and commitment in others, too, but we are not responsible for their levels of awareness nor how committed they are to lifelong learning and development. Each person must find their own way. This is difficult even for enlightened managers to take on board because, as leaders, they believe themselves trained to take responsibility for others.

What the Integrated Leader can do is recognise a fundamental truth; it is impossible to help another person stand on their own feet except through your conditioning. Even with the best will and intention, this perpetuates the idea of one person needing the validation of another to find out who they are.

If a team member, colleague, or boss is not there yet, then they are not there yet. They will have reasons for this and to intervene will be to invite resistance. Resistance on their part for having a desire to change and learn imposed from outside, and resistance within you because you are setting your conditioning up against theirs. If they are to find self-awareness, it can only come from them. If they see you, as an Integrated Leader, having discovered something about yourself that has changed your outlook and results, then resist the temptation to offer them a way or a technique to do the same. Their curiosity will be all they need to start, as was yours, but this cannot be imposed. It may be that they will get there, it may be that they will not, but in neither case will you make any real difference by intervening.

When you see someone who has truly taken responsibility for their development, quite independent of any instruction or coaching from you, support them. On the other hand, to travel alongside another in theirs and your learning is to create a companionship of equals who can use each other to help understand themselves. The Integrated Leader's approach in the learning of others is to take ownership only for their development, and not for those of others.

Instead, focus on your practice, your learning, and your wisdom. This will shine outward. Skilfulness is to bring together the thought and the action in one. You are not tied to how things have been done in the past. Any interval between past learning and present action is where your conditioning will re-enter. For the Integrated Leader, action and learning are one spontaneous movement.

Accepting others just as they are is practising non-judgement. Non-judgement is a core idea in mindfulness, which has now entered mainstream thinking in corporate and personal development. According to leading practitioner and Harvard doctor Jon Kabat-Zinn, mindfulness is 'the awareness that arises through paying attention, on purpose, in the present moment, non-judgementally'.[19]

---

[19] Kabat-Zin, J. (2017). Too Early to Tell: The Potential Impact and Challenges — Ethical and Otherwise — Inherent in the Mainstreaming of Dharma in an Increasingly Dystopian World, *Mindfulness, 8*(5), 1125–1135.

Chapter 7

The Familiar Self

My heart is heavy with the things I do not understand.

Mowgli, the Jungle Book[1]

Who Am I?

The microscopic, chemical complexities in water molecules mean that no two snowflakes are identical, yet every snowflake is the result of a simpler, underlying pattern in the atmosphere. If the conditions are present, the atmospheric system will always 'snowflake'. Is there an underlying pattern of culture in human civilisations also? This chapter is about three aspects of being an Integrated Leader — selfhood, lifespan, and change — that need thought before drawing conclusions about yourself. We begin with selfhood.

Most of us have a common-sense understanding of self as an 'I' that looks at a 'me'. If asked to define more exactly what that means, we may struggle to formulate a complete response as to who or what the 'I' is. The problem is not helped by the fact that we can neither avoid the question[2] nor answer it. In what sense does the self exist? Is the self the same as or separate from the physical body? During the European Enlightenment, during which

---

[1] Kipling, R. (1894). *The Jungle Book* (Chapter 6).
[2] Existentially, we exist. To deny this would presuppose someone who first has to exist in order then to do the denying.

French philosopher and polymath Rene Descartes famously deduced, 'I think, therefore I am', the self was understood as immaterial and pre-existing. This was in keeping with the accepted theological norm of the age. For many, the belief that the essence of who they are exists separate from their body is still a taken-for-granted. This is called dualism, which stands in contrast to monism, where mind and body do not just co-exist, they are co-dependent. In neither case are mind and brain synonymous. Cartesian dualism opened the door for the natural sciences to investigate the nature of the world without having to subject the self to the same search for natural explanation. As science progressed, and religion retreated as the sole provider of an answer to the question of the nature of the self, theories of the self began to emerge with increasing frequency and confidence toward the end of the 19th century. With almost exponential growth — if not with any real progress — this continued into the 20th century. Today, the world seems rife with speculation on the self.

Psychologists study the link between continuity of the self-concept over time with the development of emotions, the inner private world, and imagination. We are not born with self-awareness, but we are all born with the capacity for it to develop given the right conditions. It can be studied as a unit of analysis as it manifests during life, both from observation (induction) and experiment (deduction). By adulthood, the self is usually considered fully formed, and evidenced in three things:

1. Complying with accepted norms and standards of what selfhood is
2. Conceptualising a self-image in line with this
3. Projecting that self-image

There are two problems with this. First, as we saw in the previous chapter, there is an internal/external tension that many of us have balanced the wrong way. How we are complying, conceptualising, and projecting ourselves may not be contributing to our health and well-being (see next chapter) and it takes courage and a safe space to really explore the truth of who we are in those terms. Second, even if we become aware of the imbalance between outside and inside, and we re-balance, we don't know how to answer the question of what our self-esteem is based on. I believe this is because we cannot; each person has to answer without relying on others. We don't lack the intelligence. There are billions of us on this planet, each a complex and unique combination of characteristics, which includes intelligence. We see, feel, and experience. We think. We learn. Maybe we are a social species because we are intelligent, or intelligent because we are a social species, but either way it is certain that if the conditions are present, humans will always learn. And at the same time each person's answer to the question of selfhood is bound to be unique.

Uniqueness emerging from complexity is one of two basic features of learning; the other is continuity of the capacity for learning through life. Lifelong learning is not a means to an end. Life does not have a destination outside itself, so perhaps it is possible to say that the ends and the means in lifelong learning are one and the same. We might choose to stop actively learning, but we never lose the capacity, and the wisdom gained from experience will compensate for loss of cognitive plasticity. In sum, defining the self is almost impossible and almost irresistible. So, let's give it a try!

The Self

As we have seen in Chapter 2, many of us first understand the self in psychological constructs, and then perhaps we connect these to society. This is a view of selfhood that is relatively new, first rooted in the Renaissance,[3] and carried into the modern era with the Enlightenment. For centuries, the accepted notion of self had been fixed and unquestioned. In mainstream Western thought until roughly the 15th century, the individual was defined within society very rigidly on a hierarchy known as the Great Chain of

---

[3] A period of great social change and dissemination of ideas and thought in the 15th and 16th centuries in Europe.

Being,[4] a theologically mapped series of unchanging levels. At the top, on a tell-tale throne, sits the deity. At the bottom is the basest of the base minerals. In between comes everything else, with humans about halfway. Among humans in the Great Chain, there are further stratifications that — not entirely surprisingly — established a hierarchy of social statuses from God-anointed King to lowly serf. Everyone had, and knew, their place and, usually, were born and died at that status. Personhood was subordinate to a greater organisation of life.

The abandonment in the 18th century of the Chain as ultimate authority for understanding your place brought new opportunities for scientific and philosophical enquiry and discovery. Scientific principles now dominated philosophical meditation on the nature of the world. Although the natural world became explainable, selfhood was (at first) off-limits to the same kind of scrutiny. This is because it would mean rejecting the divine in any hypothesis of the mind and the self. In its search for the fundamental, natural laws of the universe, science eventually bypassed the divine and established a new root metaphor of nature, the machine. By the time social science managed to push its way into the picture, in the 19th century, it inherited the dualist notion of mind and body as not the same thing. Researchers who wanted to understand the mind could not reduce it to the material, and researchers who wanted to understand the body could not find mind in the material. Until very recently, this split has remained paradigmatic, and unsolvable. In modern times, there have been three traditions of self. The first stresses the inner, individualised, and introspective nature of identity. The second is social and looks at how cultural meanings from social situations determine a person's inner idea of self. The third focuses more on group-level processes within a larger, societal context where there is no self except in the context of the group.

---

[4]Lovejoy, A. O. (1976). *The Great Chain of Being: A Study of the History of an Idea*, Cambridge, MA: Harvard University Press.

Me, Myself, and I

At the heart of the Western view of the nature of self and identity is the problem of an essential 'I', a self that feels somehow to occupy its own separate space, set apart from material reality, distinct from the context of interactions with the world ('me'). In the late 19th Century, American philosopher William James proposed the two fundamental aspects of the self, the knower ('I') and the known ('me'), a theory informed by what German psychologist Wilhelm Wundt had pioneered in his laboratory experiments. The capacity of the 'I' to reflect on the 'me' is what results in self or identity. American philosopher George Herbert Mead developed this idea further in rejecting the Cartesian notion of the self as pre-existing the individual. The self, he said, is formed and emerges through social experience because for an act to have meaning, it must be part of a social behaviour that produces a response from another that signals they have understood what was in the mind of the individual making that gesture. The individual can only accomplish this if they can take the attitude of the other.[5] The self does not exist until it can produce and recognise this effect in the other. We are bound together in the understanding of who we are through our complex relations with people around us, even though it does not quite feel that way to us. Since Mead's time (early 20th century), the war between the self-as-isolated (an 'I' popped into existence and dropped into a cruel and alien world) and self-as-emergent (an 'I' growing out from and made by society) has resembled one of attrition where neither side has gained an inch.

Is this whole conflict another duck-rabbit situation? Well, yes, and no.

If you already believe that social phenomena are best explained in terms of individual psychology, then individual experiments and observable behaviour under controlled conditions is what you will set up. You will lean toward understanding the leader as the source of answers, and of potential for change. It may follow that

---

[5] This is known as Theory of Mind.

you advocate leader training as the way forward because you will view the leader as a *tabula rasa*.[6] Strength or competency-based approaches to leadership owe much to this, as do the reams of psychometric tests and personality questionnaires that managers are asked to fill out. We still have an attachment to the idea that leaders somehow embody what leadership is. Trait psychologist Gordon Allport was interested in the interplay of a person's current context and a list of descriptors or expressions of personality traits observed in behaviours. Traits make actions predictable, and this was turned into a quantitative definition of a trait as an enduring characteristic governing motivation and behaviour, which gave us the Sixteen Personality Factor Questionnaire (16PF). The same wish is now seen in the considerable interest shown by leadership trainers in anything labelled as neuroscience. There have been some astounding scientific advances in the study of the brain and the central nervous system, but we are still far from explaining what selfhood is.

Alternatively, if you already believe that the individual is best explained through social phenomena, then you may lean toward a more holistic, systemic, or gestalt view not just of leadership but of the leader, too. This favours the idea that 'I' is made observable through the lens of the system. The leader is a web of interconnections and influences in a social flow, and that is what the self is.

Is it possible to understand the self as undivided and also separate? This is something to consider for, as American novelist and essayist F. Scott Fitzgerald once wrote,

The test of a first-rate intelligence is the ability to hold two opposed ideas in the mind at the same time, and still retain the ability to function.[7]

The way out of the impasse of 'self' in self-awareness may involve developing this knack.

---

[6] Literally, a blank slate. The theory says that we are born without built-in mental content, and knowledge comes only from experience or perception.
[7] Fitzgerald, F. S. (1945). *The Crack-up*, Cambridge, MA: New Direction Books.

The Unconscious Self

One major obstacle is the influence of the interest in the unconscious in the first half of the 20th century. Condensing Sigmund Freud, the self consists of three structures.[8] There is the id, which contains our uncontrolled and unmediated instincts and primal urges, and which is submerged (or repressed) completely in the unconscious. Then there is the ego, which develops as children grow and which mediates between the instinctual id and the reality of the demands of the outside world. Finally, the superego, which is the inflexible, internalised parental authority of the self, telling itself what it should and should not do. If this feels like the ingredients of a feisty drama, many psychologists would agree.

With these as assumptions and starting points, a thick jungle of psychological theories has grown up around personal and human development. So much so that our default, taken-for-granted understanding of the self is now described as ego. This one word has now more or less taken the place of the Great Chain of Being as the seminal explanation of what a person is. Others have diverged from this in some very interesting ways. In seeing the self in spiritual terms and as regulated by myth, symbols, and archetypes, Carl Jung's analytical psychology introduced the collective unconscious, which are universal patterns. Jung's work, informed by visions he experienced during an intense period of psychosis as a young man, concluded that people have innate predispositions to one side or the other of three opposing attitudes of perception:

(i) Whether a person gains gratification and energy in life primarily from internal, subjective content (introversion) or gratification and energy primarily from content outside themself (extroversion)

---

[8] It is unfortunate perhaps that Freud's translator to English, James Strachey, used grand-sounding Latin derived terms (*ego, id, super-ego*) instead of a more prosaic translation of *das ich* = the I, *das Es* = the it, and *das Über-Ich* = the Beyond-I, which might have deflated much of the pomposity found in psychology today.

(ii) Whether a person is affected by and takes in information about the world primarily relying on the senses (sensing) or primarily relying on hunches or channels unconscious to them (intuition)

(iii) Whether a person is disposed to decisions and decision-making primarily through intellectual concepts (thinking) or primarily on subjective criteria of their construction (feeling)

According to Jung, individuals unconsciously use these classifications to adapt to the lived world and the development of the self is via a lifelong process of individuation, a search for wholeness, which is the assimilation of the symbolism of the collective unconscious into the personality of the individual. American mother-daughter partners Katharine Briggs and Isabel Briggs Myers were inspired by (but did not win the approval of) Jung to quantify the personality in an expanded version of this typology[9] that is now something of a hygiene factor in the delivery of leadership training.

The Interpretive Self

Cognitive learning theory looks at the way people process information. This view, in its purest sense, holds that human behaviour is influenced by external sensory stimuli, but is defined by the processes of the mind such as thought, emotion, and experience as reconstructed from memory. Learning happens when information is converted into valuable and organised knowledge. This information remains available to the individual through self-scripts, memories, and socially mediated rules of behaviour. Abraham Maslow's work (Chapter 8) explored concepts such as internal motivation and self-actualisation to explain human behaviour. He said that learning is the result of drives to fulfil needs which are formed in a conceptual hierarchy of basic needs and meta-needs. Maslow's

---

[9] This is MBTI, which you may have been asked to repeat many times in management or leadership training. I feel for you.

hierarchy is both durable and easy to take shots at. There is, it must be said, little hard evidence to support many of his assumptions, and in his hierarchy the external context of the individual is not considered. However, it feels like common sense that we perceive ourselves at different levels of what we are going to be concerned with if we can. Cognitive approaches to learning in management education stress the importance of self-awareness and personal goal setting, as well as the structuring of learning processes according to the needs of the learner as they are in their stage of cognitive maturation. This places you (the self) at the centre of the learning process. On the other hand, is there a great deal of relevance in self-esteem if your stomach is empty? Don't worry if you can't get a handle on what comes before or after what in this self reflection. The point is to enquire. What is your view (now) of the self? Does it exist? And if so, how? Does the 'you' change from moment to moment and situation to situation? Does it change during life?

Birth and death are objective and definitional markers of what a life *is*. Practitioners and philosophers alike have long agreed, however, that it is what happens in between that is a measure of what life *means*.

Lifespan Development

Conventional wisdom says an individual will change and develop over time, and no doubt this is your own experience, too. A lifetime is the sensation (usually after the fact) of passing through chronological stages of development. The biological stages are the most natural and inevitable, but there are cognitive stages in which the mind as well as the body goes from one state to another. In cultures accustomed to the idea of life as a progression, perhaps this is also going from one level of status to another. There is an accumulation of experience and memory triggered by the social demands of the life stage or by the impact of collisions of events in life, some of which will be random. These general sensations of learning and change are synonymous with personal development over the lifespan.

The Danish-American psychologist Erik Erikson, in long-term collaboration with his wife Joan, developed a psychosocial view of ego development across the lifecycle in eight stages, each marked by an inherent and necessary crisis for the person (ego) to face and understand, each leading to a value that helps development and maintains healthy relationships with the world. Each crisis is triggered by an appropriate dilemma generated by a combination of physiology, social environment, and personal view. Erikson studied adulthood, which presents its own challenges. The years roughly from a person's 40s to their late 60s signal mature adulthood, where a person's attention is gradually drawn more to the question of how they can contribute to the world. This is the crisis between 'generativity', or the ego's concern for what will outlast it or what, if anything, will be its contribution to the next generation, and 'stagnation', which is the ego's inward-facing concern for legacy. Many societies have developed local norms to deal with lifespan development, but the underlying sequence is held to be universal and its challenges experienced by every individual. In Erikson's understanding of learning, the mature adulthood stage would correspond in a manager's career with the period when they are at their most productive and influential. Erikson's model punctuates life in a definite sequence of thresholds or transitions from birth, through childhood to puberty and on into adulthood, with a goal of reconciliation of the self with the larger order of the cosmos. Moving from one recognisable role or state in society to another prompts questioning and introspection and gives stability and longevity to a much more important aspect of the self, in this stage it is that of belonging. As part of an evolving adult consciousness, we look for emotional awareness and acceptance of ourselves as creators of our own destiny as we confront the myths and assumptions of our childhood or adolescence.

Where Joan and Erik Erikson emphasise the social context, another conception of lifespan learning is seen in the work of German psychologist Paul Baltes, who looked at the development of the individual from before birth to death.[10] Baltes agreed that it

---

[10] This is called ontogenesis.

happens throughout life but said that development is not a directional process toward completion of the self. Instead, it is our biological and psychological capacity to act in response to events and influences in life that give it its shape. Baltes is less concerned with the 'what' of development than he is with the 'how'. How we act can lead in many different directions (lifespan development is not linear), and we may see setbacks and periods of irresponsible actions as well as advancement and growing wisdom. Wisdom may be represented by both gain and loss, as the individual adjusts themself to the world around them, and the world within. The multidirectional nature of development in this approach means that lifespan and lifelong learning may be much more flexible and complex than traditional views have tolerated. Our biology makes us a lot more adept and adaptable than we may think, and our surroundings can and sometimes do play an important part in our learning through life — perhaps more so than our age, Baltes suggests. With the right environment, we all may blossom at any age, even later in life.

Overall, the case for a process of learning happening over the course of a person's whole life is compelling. Two patterns common to the various narratives of lifespan development are that:

(i) A person becomes a person in relationship with other people, and

(ii) They do so in the context of the finality of life.

A Matter of Life and Death: From Not Being to Being... and Back Again

There are many occasions in a leader's development where they should focus on appreciating life. The corollary of life is death, which is rarely talked about in leadership studies.[11] Life flows, but

---

[11] Except poetically as analogy or metaphor for the passing of ideas and concepts. We talk of the death of projects, companies, perhaps industries, but we almost never stop to consider our own mortality.

a life is finite, and death is what allows life to have meaning. Death is something that we all share, yet the discussion of its inevitability is off the agenda when we come to the most persistent theme of leadership study, purpose. Privately, for example, when we are dealing with the loss of someone close to us, we may have close and personal experience of death and therefore of reflection on life. Professionally, we often feel it unhealthy, unacceptable, or fruitless to have a discussion. We may shy from it because it would seem gloomy and defeatist in a society built around longevity and the individual. But we are missing something.

Death has a place in a book about leadership and personal growth. As mentioned, it defines life. A life that goes on forever, open-ended, and unfinishing, would eventually become a real problem. Immortality would be unbearable. We are not evolved to outlive our lifespan, and not only because eventually our biology degrades in its ability to sustain and regenerate. Even if we were to maintain health and vitality, we would still need a psychological narrative with a structure of beginning, middle, and end. Our beginnings and endings are hard bargains with reality, but they are what make the middles worth it. Survival cannot equal never dying, but it can come to mean always living fully.

When we think about the finitude of life, we should not be morbid. For the novice, this is difficult. In Hamlet's famous To be, or not to be soliloquy, Shakespeare inserts many reflections on the constricting power that fear of death has over our actions:

> 'But that the dread of something after death,
> The undiscovered country from whose bourn
> No traveler returns, puzzles the will
> And makes us rather bear those ills we have
> Than fly to others that we know not of?
> Thus conscience does make cowards of us all'[12]

Does fear of the unknown properly explain how we tolerate unpleasant realities and resist letting go of limits and restraints to

---

[12] William Shakespeare, *Hamlet*, Act 3, Scene 1.

our potential? Dealing (if only momentarily) with our emotions and the fact of our mortality is important for our mental health and well-being, and that is intrinsic to personal development. In a sense, death is as much behind us as it is ahead. The years we have lived in the past are dead in every way except in memory, and that too will fade. Being and non-being, permanence and imperma- nence, meaning and meaningless are philosophical poles, and lead- ers who shy away from these will not fully understand one or two fundamental truths of organisational life.

As we saw in Chapter 3, existence implies non-existence and if you want to test this perspective, try this simple thought experi- ment. Imagine yourself dead. Gone. No more. If you can picture this, what is that? Do you imagine a version of you in a vast, empty, dark void?[13] Whatever vision you concoct cannot be a true representation of death because death is unimaginable. Or, to put it another way, if there is a way of conceiving 'dead', it is the same as the 'not alive' state lasting the age of the universe before you attained self-consciousness after you were born. Being dead and thinking about being dead are not the same thing. A thought is the result of physical phenomena, which are only possible when you are alive and, presumably, death is a state following the ending of our physical life. Think about this for long enough, and you will further realise this is an epistemological problem, not an ontologi- cal one. Upon death, you end. That thought is a contemplation many of us deeply dread and fear because of its implication for the ego. How do we cope with this? I think there have been broadly two speculations:

(i) We do not end at death. The extreme form of this argues that we cannot end at death

(ii) We do end at death (except, temporarily and vicariously, in the memories of others). The extreme form of this argues that we cannot survive death.

---

[13] Other post-mortem mindscapes are available, depending on your culture, beliefs, and conditioning.

Both forms may lead people to dwell on the meaning and purpose of life, and both have consequences for how we define what counts as a good life. As a reader, you will have to formulate your own response. For my part, the first is wishful thinking for immortality, the second is experience of life as dominated by an immense, bleak shadow cast by death's inevitability. Is there a third? A transient awareness of being in the present? In Japanese aesthetics, the expression *mono no aware*, which might be translated as 'wistfulness toward things' captures well a certain feeling in the face of the impermanence of objects and the ephemeral nature of life. You may want to keep in mind the first line of Samuel Beckett's play *Waiting for Godot*, where the tramp Estragon, unable to remove his boot, says 'Nothing to be done'.

In acceptance is the freedom to do everything. The French philosopher and writer Albert Camus was part of a new wave of enquiry into the nature of the meaning of human consciousness. Writing against a background of global conflict and social change in the middle of the 20th century, he proposed that human beings always search for meaning in life, but they are doing so in a meaningless universe. If life has no inherent meaning, asks Camus, then what is the point of existing? Whatever humans settle on as meaning has as its source consciousness, and nothing more. 'Meaning' is meaningless to a cosmos that does not have a plan. The absurdity of a meaningless existence, Camus concludes, is exactly what we must embrace to live freely. The key to a good life, and the only choice we can make in between being and not-being, is to take life for what it is, and as it comes, and embrace it completely.

Others, during the same period of a world at war, were becoming interested in those experiences and how we make sense of them. A contemporary of Camus, Jean-Paul Sartre, attempted to answer what might be a follow-on question; how should we live? This is a direct connection with the theme of purpose that we have met several times concerning leadership. The purpose of human artefacts, Sartre said, always precedes their existence. That is, first we have the idea, then we craft the world to realise this. In this way, the purpose of an organisation exists before it exists in reality.

Purpose dictates form, and leadership is the name of the role within the organisation to bring this about. There are limits, therefore, to what a leader can or should do to fulfil that purpose (leadership is not only given boundaries, it is also about setting them). That is the role, but the person is not the role, and Sartre was at pains to draw this distinction in philosophy and the conduct of civil life. We may have a purposeful self, but we are a part of nature, and nature does not begin from purpose. For humans, existence precedes purpose. It is entirely up to us to decide, create, or realise our purpose, a freedom that, said Sartre, we are condemned to. When we define our purpose, however, we are also responsible for the outcomes as they impact others, and as they impact the environment.

In keeping with this thread, and taking us into the current era, Norwegian philosopher and academic Arne Naess emphasised the connection and integration between a person's actions, their lifelong learning, and the natural environment. The phrase he used for this, first in 1973, was 'deep ecology', whereby you recognise the self as an interconnected part of everything in nature. How far has this pervaded the corporate world? It is difficult to say, but outwardly at least, there is hope that corporations are willing to do what politicians have so far abrogated and prepare for a future built on different assumptions of consumption. We are now at the point where even fossil-fuel businesses such as Shell are claiming they will achieve net-zero carbon emissions, and actively promote a change in consumer behaviour to match this along the way, something its chief executive officer admits will be an extremely tough process.[14]

Learning and Personal Change

Is this how most of us think or act in the roles we play at work? Does it make sense to put life off until after death, or to run from

---

[14]Public statement by Shell CEO Ben van Beurden, October 2020, https://www.shell.com/media/speeches-and-articles/articles-by-date/can-shell-transform-yes-and-we-will.html.

life because death feels so dreadful? Every manager's ambition is to contribute value through their actions while at the same time living a fulfilling and good life. But how? Another French philosopher, Maurice Merleau-Ponty, was interested in the nature of the mind as it is experienced in the everyday — as a phenomenon.[15] For Merleau-Ponty, mind and body are not separate, a position which is in alignment with much present-day scientific investigation and opinion, following advances in neuroscience and study of the brain. To understand ourselves more, we need to break with our inbuilt assumptions about our experience and see it in a new way.

We come again to the thorny topic of personal change and transformation, but this time in the form of three modes of learning, which may be described as incremental, transitional, and gestalt.

Incremental learning is better known as trial and error and it is what most of us have in mind when we think of learning as a process. It is what most models of learning assume, regardless of their philosophical antecedents. Change happens in incremental steps, built cumulatively from little bricks of knowing. We work on something fixing, improving, tweaking, or simply extracting more from it. The point of this type of learning is to reach an objective in the best way possible. Perhaps the best known and most ubiquitous form of incremental learning is David Kolb's experiential learning cycle, which, (albeit in a somewhat watered down and circular form[16]) has gained cult status among educators and trainers. The sensation that learning is a gradual and iterative accumulation has become common sense. Incremental learning happens 'bit by bit', either from the top down or the bottom up, and we are

---

[15] A phenomenon is something that appears and is observed, or any occurrence accessible to the senses as an object of perception.

[16] The learning cycle includes four elements (concrete experience, reflective observation, abstract conceptualisation, and active experimentation) mirroring the scientific method, but struggling to match the non-linear complexity of phenomenological learning.

nudged along slowly in tune with that, accruing our identity over time. Incremental learning has spawned several large categories of strategy and tactics for lifelong learning, such as learning through emulation. Emulation, apprenticeships, mentoring, role modelling, and a certain type of coaching all exemplify the idea of incremental learning. Certificates, degrees, and graduations, memberships of professional or trade organisations, endorsements, and up-dated resumes, are all outward signs of a set of incremental goals attained.

Transitional learning is focused on identifying and then bringing about the change from one (existing) set of goals or end states to an entirely new set. Learning is made explicit by the processes used to make that jump. Within organisations, this may manifest in the implementation of strategic change projects, planned as a series of interventions that move the whole from state A to state B. This is not just incremental learning, it is a radical interruption to business as usual. The purpose of leadership here is to make this shift as seamless and pain-free as possible, and transitional learning will generally begin with a grand vision. The bread and butter of many strategic plans, transitional learning can become quite mechanistic and unable to adapt quickly to unintended or unexpected consequences. For an individual, transitional learning depends on several ingredients: (1) a framework for mapping change, such as a lifespan framework, (2) a willingness to recognise the limiting aspects of past experience, and (3) a trigger strong enough to overcome inertia. For many, these have been built during the course of a life time. Transitional learning is about identifying the appropriate response to forthcoming change, but it does not question the basic premises of the framework. Doing that means working at a whole different order of learning.

Gestalt is a German word used in English for the perception of parts as an integrated whole. Social science, as well as a great many change management, leadership, and business courses have indirectly been influenced or resourced from contributions of gestalt thinkers. The social psychologist Kurt Lewin is perhaps the most noteworthy of these pioneers,[17] and his Force Field Analysis is a good example of how his ideas of the dynamic relationship between person, behaviour, and environment (as one) can be put to work. Gestalt learning happens with the recognition of an emergent quality from the oppositional interplay of otherwise separate elements in a new context. It may be marked by the experiencing of an accidental, sudden, and complete re-ordering of order. The 'ah-ha!' moment where everything falls apart/comes together. Then it is the chaos that results in a new order, with completely new information that is in a new pattern. Chaos, it should be mentioned, in human affairs is subjective. One person's messy desk is another person's tidy filing system. The feature of gestalt learning that matters is that the re-settled situation is now just as coherent as the old, but in a different form. Learning that is a gestalt, holistic, or systemic type of learning is not the path to transformation (as in transitional learning), it is the transformation. The transforming is immanent in learning; they are the same thing. What 'was' can no longer be perceived as it was.

Learning and leadership intertwine. Incremental, transitional, and gestalt learning are therefore interconnected. However, there are two ways that this is so, and it is worth considering each for a moment for they each have something to add:

1. *Learning is water:* a single river in a continuous flow from source to sea.

    Different modes of learning are just descriptions of the same thing in different contexts. The flow of the river of learning passes in one unbroken line from its source to the sea, and as it moves, it seems to express itself in its changing environments in different forms. And as with water in a river, learning may be put to different uses on the route. Topology sees it gain more

---

[17] Not incidentally, the period post Second World War in the United States and Europe produced many advances in and advancers of systemic thinking. Urie Bronfenbrenner's ecological systems theory, Reg Revans' Action Learning, the multidisciplinary Macy conferences in the 1950s are all good examples.

volume and more (or less) energy while basically remaining the same substance. In this sense, the language of learning in leadership is about finding the right description for the context we are in. A different learning context would require a different term. Leaders need mainly to learn the right names for the right situation. This is the way that leadership is currently taught. Various theories jostle and compete to describe what this looks like. There may only be a vague requirement to check whether the description is what the river is actually doing. The disadvantage of this is that the map tends to become territory (rather than the other way round). When the framework no longer maps reality, the leader or the learner is forced to abandon the map and explore.

2. *Learning is a Russian doll:* an ecology of hierarchical relationships and levels of abstraction.

Learning is about change, and occasionally change is itself subject to change, so different modes of learning reveal an organisation of hierarchical levels of change. This is harder to conceptualise (and communicate) in day-to-day leadership but could be of critical importance because a leader is likely to want to see more than incremental, trial-and-error, change. The "what could be?" leadership question should be punching a hole in the boundaries everyone has been using in their thinking before now. Following the work of Gregory Bateson,[18] incremental learning would be one level (changes within boundaries), and transformational learning would be a higher level (changes of the boundaries). Gestalt learning might be described as changes in the changes in boundaries. You can see how this starts to get mind-boggling. The relationship *between* modes of learning reveals a classification of context.

These two ways of understanding learning are not mutually exclusive, and the same distinctions hold for all communicative

---

[18] The typology of learning first proposed by Gregory Bateson deals with specificity of response and preservation of a higher order of flexibility of a system.

processes that process information, such as lifelong learning, leadership, the experience of the self, and many other complex concepts. The leader who recognises the larger pattern is less likely to be sucked into the fray when there is resistance to change in their work and in their organisation.

This chapter has been about defining the self, and about what learning is. It is a quirk of nature that each needs the other. Finding out who I am requires learning, and learning requires a self for it to happen. Somewhere in all of this are hard questions to answer, and you may sometimes feel that it is too amorphous to process, or too peripheral to matter. Maybe so. On the other hand, the same existential questions are out there for us all to ask in life. They do not go away even if we ignore them. A journey of self-discovery can bring profound growth along with scary change. What we discover may be uncomfortable because it can mean leaving behind familiar identities, unearthing well-established habits, or releasing long-held beliefs.

Reflecting on the Integrated Leader's Manifesto (Leading Self with the Organisation)

#7

'Humility and tolerance are necessary for the health of my organisation. There is no human hierarchy — only different levels of experience and knowledge. An organisation is a creative space, not a space of followers. Each person has the intelligence and the capacity to take their own decisions, and at the same time remember that their behaviour affects the whole. Therefore, we act always with responsibility and integrity'.

We cannot help but influence our surroundings and other people as we move through life. It is impossible not to influence just as it is impossible not to communicate. You cannot anti-influence, as the attempt not to influence is also an influence.

No-one is without influence, and this creates followers.

In an organisation, there are several key ways that people legitimately influence or affect the decisions of others:

(i) *Through the power of position or organisational relationship. Influence equals responsibility and perhaps accountability for what happens. Power this way is based on the idea of leadership as a chain of command, which is effective in situations where decisive action is needed and where there is transparency;*

(ii) *Through the authority of what a person knows about a specialist or niche area.*

The influence carried by either the power of a positional role or the authority of specialist expertise should be separate from the person in the role or the person with the know-how. Frequently, however, it is not. We mix the person with the role they play. This is to make an error that eventually causes harm to the health and well-being of the system because a person who is their position or who is their knowledge will see the system as part of their ego, and not their ego as part of a system.

> *There is a third kind of influence, and this acknowledges the interconnectedness of the world.*

(iii) *Not tied to ego and not seeking validation or recognition, influence of the spontaneous interaction of all the differences that exist when two or more people get together. This is influence allowed from a creative space, and it needs to be allowed to flow through people selflessly.*

It is the potential of all available differences that matter here. Even the differences of knowledge and of authority can, when they are not identified with the person but with the organisation and its purpose, be resources and creative influences.

When the organisation is a space where difference is tolerated and in fact valued, and where the confusion between self-worth and role or expertise is resolved, then it will have rediscovered an older and better meaning of influence: to cause flow in, and to inspire.

Chapter 8

Universal Mental Health and Well-Being

The mind is its own place, and in itself
Can make a heav'n of hell, a hell of heav'n.

John Milton, *Paradise Lost (1667)*

Defining Mental Health

The World Health Organization (WHO) defines mental health as:

> 'a state of well-being in which every individual realizes his or her own potential, can cope with the normal stresses of life, can work productively and fruitfully, and is able to make a contribution to her or his community.'[1]

Every human being on the planet has the right to this; it is a universal. As with physical health, a lot of people naturally maintain reasonable levels of mental health and well-being as a matter of course over life, albeit with occasional setbacks and scares. Although some of those setbacks will resolve and heal themselves naturally, others will be more difficult to deal with. In recent years, attitudes towards discussing and acknowledging mental ill health

---

[1] https://www.who.int/mental_health/who_urges_investment/en/#:~:text=Mental%20health%20is%20defined%20as,to%20her%20or%20his%20community.

have changed and more and more people feel enabled to seek professional help when they recognise an issue. There is still much to do. Many who have a drop in mental good health may not recognise it. Many more know or feel something is not right but do not seek help as readily as with a physical ailment. Very often problems are ignored or covered over with coping strategies that can persist for years, and that starts to resemble the outside world's perfectly successful patterns of behaviour. Mental health and physical health are two sides of the same coin. Someone with a mental health issue is likely to have or to develop physical ailments, which in turn trigger symptoms that interrupt the ability of the mind to cope with stress.

Some tension is normal in life, necessary to be in tune, in fact, but there are thresholds which if crossed are harmful. Many adult mental disorders and conditions have their origins and roots in youth and adolescence, but modern working environments and practices are stressful and can lead to absenteeism, loss of productivity, and anxiety among people who are otherwise well-balanced. Some interventions offer valuable quick fixes and shortcuts in the short term, but for sustainable, healthy levels of well-being at work, what is needed is long-term and systemic solutions.

Mental ill health covers a wide range of identifiable and treatable conditions. The WHO estimates that one in four people in the world will be affected by mental or neurological disorders at some point in their lives, but evidence suggests that perhaps only 1 in 5 people who go off work for mental health reasons actually disclose mental ill health as the reason.[2] If so, this puts mental disorders close to the top of the list of reasons for ill health and disability globally, with subsequent loss of productivity for organisations. What is new in many parts of the world and in many organisations is better promotion of well-being and assistance for employees in their mental health. For this to work, however, a positive working culture is required. The Integrated Leader can play a pivotal role in the reduction of stigma and discrimination at work by starting in

---

[2] https://www.mind.org.uk/media-a/5823/managing_and_supporting_mh_at_work.pdf.

their own self-awareness of well-being. Otherwise it will be just another empty corporate policy with slogans paying lip-service to the times.

A more comprehensive definition could help. In 2015, a group of European psychiatrists published a more nuanced definition of mental health, which proposed that:

> 'Mental health is a dynamic state of internal equilibrium which enables individuals to use their abilities *in harmony with universal values of society.* Basic cognitive and social skills; ability to recognize, express and modulate one's own emotions, as well as empathize with others; flexibility and ability to cope with adverse life events and function in social roles; and harmonious relationship between body and mind represent important components of mental health which contribute, to varying degrees, to the state of internal equilibrium.'[3] (emphasis added)

There is a lot that a manager or leader might work with here. For a start, note the link in the first line to universal values, which we will examine later in this chapter. Actions are often said to reflect outlook or mindset, so we will begin with this, and then explore beliefs and principles, before joining up the universal of mental health and well-being with the universal fundamentals of human values.

Mindset in Stone?

'Mindset' is a straightforward compound word and a relatively recent addition to the English language. Typically, it is used freely to mean a person's general frame of mind as they interact with the world. In there lies a hint of a deeper durability, but we usually think of it as a person's general mood and frame of mind. For a more serious look at what mindset means, we must dig a bit.

---

[3] Galderisi, S., Heinz, A., Kastrup, M., Beezhold, J., and Sartorius, N. (2015). Toward a new definition of mental health. *World Psychiatry: Official Journal of the World Psychiatric Association (WPA)*, 14(2): 231–233. https://doi.org/10.1002/wps.20231 with permission.

Mindset is the window on a person's principles and beliefs, which are the rules and guidelines that set the limits on what they conceive as permissible and what they view as their general disposition over time. Why might two people approaching the same situation, where no one choice of action has objective merit over another, choose to act in different ways? Alternatively, why might two people with nothing in common quite independently choose to act in identical ways?

Travelling outside your home country affords the possibility to observe with a fresh eye how people go about their daily business. This is especially so if you are going alone to a completely different region of the world. A lot may strike you in broad terms at first, but with more time it is usually in how the small things are done that you begin to see, perhaps for the first time, how things are done where you come from and how, within that, you vary what you do. When away from home, you are left guessing as to the etiquette, the rules, and sometimes the purpose of life. Being a stranger is a gift for self-awareness. Any oddness is only odd in relation to your perspective. For the locals, this is ordinariness. What you are seeing (more exactly, what you are seeing through) is your mindset. Mindset describes your defaults for how to act, your safe assumptions, and consequently many of the background personal beliefs you rely on. Travel can either be a source of positive or negative stress for you, so the next time you have the chance to test this, notice the mood. Mindset has two notable aspects:

1. A prescription for an *individual* to experience their uniqueness
    The most common meaning of mindset is the unique set of attitudes, psychological traits, and beliefs that sum up who a person is and how they see the world. Mindset is a person's guide to judgements used in decision-making. This is a normative[4] view in that you should have a mindset, and it has become very

---

[4] A normative statement suggests something that ought to be the case. Normative carries a sense of value judgement in that it proposes something you *should* do. The alternative to normative is descriptive, which reports only how things are or how they look.

popular in recent years. We each have our own experience of our mindset, and it feels like something we own, perhaps something we created. Mindset is precise and specific. There is, moreover, hanging onto this the idea that a mindset can be worked on or improved to lead to promote desirable outcomes. Not all mindsets are equal. There is no shortage of people telling you what they think your personal mindset should be.

2. A description of how an individual conforms to a *collective* reality

Mindset could just as equally describe or predict how an individual will act or react in general and in given contexts. A person's experience is intimately bound up with those of other people, and so is their outlook. Thoughts exist in languages shared by others, in shared history, laws, education systems, organisational structures, economics, and so on. Collective mindsets are value-laden and based on principles that the individual never really needs to invent. Mindset is relational and is another term for the glue holding society together.

We need to look at each view in turn, because they have a bearing on what we mean by Integrated Leader.

Mindsets of Individual Uniqueness

In this perspective, mindset is a question of personal perception, interpretation, and intent. This self-invention echoes a remark attributed to Henry Ford in 1947,[5]

'Whether you think you can, or whether you think you can't... you're probably right.'

Belief in personal belief is one of the triggers for the popularity of the Positive Psychology movement, as well as being an element in Cognitive Behavioural Therapy (CBT). Because the field of

---

[5] Caveat: Henry Ford quotes are often things Henry Ford never actually said.

psychology is so open and the normative tendency of social scientists and management trainers is so strong, there is now a long menu of mindset recipes to try out. Perhaps the best-known example at present is Carol Dweck's *Mindset: The Psychology of Success*.[6] In summary, this says that if you knew you relied on your mindset to operate, would you really want to change it? And if you decided that you wanted to change, would you be able to? If you were able to, what elements would you change? Where would you begin? Dweck's observation and thesis are that humans are equipped to react to the world and its challenges along a continuum anchored at one end by the idea, more or less, that you are given a certain amount of talent and a certain outlook and that this can't change too much. Behaviours linked to this attitude include avoidance of challenges, lack of persistence after failure, and immunity to criticism or feedback. She calls this the *fixed mindset* and anyone rooted here will want to stick to what they're naturally good at. Success comes early, then plateaus, and is defended by a wall it builds around itself. The other end of the continuum is anchored in the idea that a person's attitude can and should be developed and improved, including their persistence, resilience, and disposition to failure. This is the *growth mindset*, and much of the book is about how this can be encouraged and what rewards it can bring.

There are at least two valid points made in this approach. The first is the observation that people exhibiting the definition of a fixed mindset are often found trying to resolve the issue of improvement in repeated attempts at validation, and manipulation of the context to produce results that could then be framed, comparatively, as a success. This is a form of denial and may be reinforced in corporate cultures where making errors or failing are not tolerated. The second useful insight is Dweck's conclusion that the flexible mindset is indicative of a willingness to embrace not knowing as a method of learning. Imperfection is not an error. An individual mindset is a description of how you meet the world, and

---

[6]Dweck, C. (2017). Mindset: The psychology of success, 6th edition, Ballantine Books.

you can choose to slice this in any way you please. Although they are grounded in psychology, even Dweck's fixed and growth mindsets are ultimately speculative and arbitrary in terms of their explanatory power. But is this individual perspective the end of the subject? Does getting only into detail of the gubbins in your mindset mean much beyond your context? Do you need to know about how any sort of individual mindset comes about in the first place?

Mindset of a Collective

You might say a 'collective mindset' is a misnomer. How can a crowd have an attitude? But remember, you are society. A collective mindset is another way of looking at the relationship between mindsets of individuals, and describes a category of overlap, similarity, and commonality among those individuals. This is a striking contrast — the variation between individuals is the main point in one view, but at the same time societies retain their identity through a certain uniformity among the group, which is the other view. This is another link back to how 'different' and 'same' are yoked together. An individual's mindset assumes a biology for there to be a mind to be set in the first place (this is a whole area being investigated by neuroscience) and on a shared system of meaning (punctuation) to express it meaningfully. Mindset unifies individual with society, and vice versa. The wrong mindset, however, will inevitably prove toxic. As Gregory Bateson said:

'The major problems in the world are the result of the difference between how nature works and the way people think.'[7]

Any mindset change must be a broader and more abstract awareness of mindset as a social phenomenon as well as a person's attitude. What might such an awareness be of? With awareness as

---

[7] Quoted in Nora Bateson's film, about her father, *An Ecology of Mind* (2011), with permission.

both of the individual and the social, as mentioned above, we might find the following useful:

(i) Self-observation and attention to your inner thoughts. Stepping into the world of your thoughts is one thing (we do this automatically just by thinking), standing back from and observing one's internal language from 'outside' is another;

(ii) Spontaneous action, by which is meant doing without deciding. This is not the same as acting thoughtlessly. Being thoughtless is rarely done without thought. Spontaneous action may require considerable time, practice, and skill to master. A metaphor sometimes used is the archer releasing the arrow without saying 'now' (in their thoughts). More prosaically, a car driver moving through a gear change without consciously deciding to do so. The spontaneous is where you did it without first thinking; it is both of your doing and of-itself-so.

The search to understand the nature of mindset is one of the functions, I believe, of personal development. The task of this chapter is to draw a line between a single person's actions as they align with health and well-being, and what would give those actions meaning. The idea is that actions are connected to values, but only as filtered through beliefs and principles.

What are Beliefs?

A belief is an acceptance that something in our awareness is what it appears. We accept much that we do not examine or re-examine too deeply. In other words, once we have reached a threshold of acceptance, we are uncritical and do not stop to question our beliefs until something happens to interrupt or derail us. To question a belief is to doubt, and we may change a belief through understanding our doubts. We may reinforce an existing belief by overcoming doubt. Doubt is therefore an important part of leadership because it makes you question certainty in your perception. You can only work with doubt by embracing it.

Our beliefs are not always reliable in their correspondence with reality. When we talk about a belief as a guide and rule for how we act, we do not usually mean a full belief.[8] Most of our beliefs are weaker versions where we are only reasonably confident that what we believe corresponds to reality. A typical belief is a mental representation that is close enough to do the job, and these may have varying degrees ranging from certainty, to speculation, to wishful thinking. The other side of this is that we may act in various ways depending on what we think other people's beliefs are. Many of our actions are the product of our weighing up the balance between what we think we should do and what we think other people are thinking they should do. Beliefs are often tactical and ad hoc.

If you believe it to be good manners to hold open a door for another person and the person you are holding it for is from a culture where no such belief exists, is your belief right or wrong? On balance, we are biased more toward trusting our beliefs as holding true than we are expressing doubts. This is sensible when not much is at stake, as in the example above, but potentially fatal when the stakes are higher. Even when we do deliberately test the grounds of a belief, we may be framing our doubt through the same conditioning that led to the belief. This is called *belief conservation*, a phenomenon like confirmation bias in that leaders often interpret new information in a way that remains consistent with their existing belief. This belief resilience makes shifting a belief even more of a tall order.

A self-limiting belief is an important sub-category of belief. The first criterion is that the belief is used and trusted by the person as an acceptable guide for their decisions and actions. Self-limiting beliefs appear as rational to people because they work when coping with the immediate situation. In the longer term, they limit personal development because they become self-fulfilling prophecies. Some, such as 'I am terrible at foreign languages', are fairly easy to spot. Others, such as 'I work best when under pressure' are not negative in their wording but are anchored in an underlying

---

[8] A full belief is when we are convinced that what we believe exactly equals the truth.

position that is fixed and potentially destructive of health and well-being. There are perhaps two reasons why our personal beliefs become so resistant to change:

1. We may apply them to reinforce our desires, and then imbue them with emotion to the point of creating a new desire. The liberating belief, for instance, of doing something as well as possible can morph into the imprisoning belief that not achieving perfection is failure. We become invested in our beliefs as part of our personality and character, and therefore as part of our identity.
2. We may be blind to other options or choices.

Individual beliefs have flexibility only within parameters of the principles we are using to define them. If you want to free yourself up for more useful beliefs, examine your principles.

What are Principles?

A principle is a norm that has been adopted and accepted by a collective or a group. Principles form systems of beliefs. Principles are systems for belief formation because they are generative and broad enough to create categories. Principles are a bit like the reference books in our moral and ethical library and they regulate what can and cannot become our beliefs. They are the basic rules that may have emerged from common practice over a long time, or from consent, declared and defined methodically. Principles represent a complete system of ideas that reflect a collective set of norms. Another way of saying this could be culture, although the definition of culture is enormously plastic. It is certainly true that cultural norms are very powerful, but they will vary from place to place and from generation to generation. An example of a prepared system of principles is the United Nations Universal Declaration of

Human Rights,[9] first published in 1948, which contains 30 articles and statements advocating an inherent human dignity. Where did such principles come from? How was it possible to draft them, and find common ground among so many of the members of the General Assembly with different cultures? This question moves us, finally, towards whatever it is that we all have in common as humans. Whatever that is, its nature must remain unchanging except over many generations. We are a social animal with the facility for both reason and emotion, but not an ability to pick and choose between the evolved fundamentals of our survival as a species. Whatever our different cultures and civilisations, whatever our heritage, background, and language, and whatever our interpretations of what is and is not desirable to guide our choices, there is a level of agreement and common ground. That level is where we may deduce universal values.

Universals

The American anthropologist Donald Brown defined human universals as:

'Those features of culture, society, language, behavior, and psyche *for which there are no known exception.*'[10] (emphasis added)

Brown put forward a long list of candidates running to hundreds of items, many of which have an evolutionary flavour to them.[11] The following are forty items, many adapted from that list. Some are worth highlighting for the Integrated Leader because they illuminate what we have been discussing so far (items marked

---

[9] For full information, visit https://www.un.org/en/universal-declaration-human-rights/.

[10] Brown, D. (1999). 'Human Universals', in *The MIT Encyclopedia of the Cognitive Sciences*, edited by Robert A. Wilson and Frank C. Keil, reprinted courtesy of The MIT Press (p. 382).

[11] A truncated and adapted version of this can be found in Appendix 1.

with * are referenced in other chapters in this book). As you look through, challenge in your mind whether or not each is a true universal. Remember, if there are exceptions, then it is not. On the other hand, bear in mind that it may be the capacity that is universal and not necessarily an example in you. Not every person is a leader, yet leadership appears without exception in every society.

abstraction in speech & thought, interpretation for meaning*

actions under self-control distinguished from those not under control*

attachment, desire

beliefs, false beliefs*

binary cognitive distinctions*

choice making (choosing alternatives)

classification*

collective identities

culture & cultural variability

Decision-making (including collective)

emotions

entification (treating patterns and relations as objective things)*

explanation*

future, attempts to predict

good and bad distinguished

in-group distinguished from out-group(s), in-group biases

intention*

leaders*

marking at phonemic, syntactic, and lexical levels

measuring

memory*

mental maps*

metaphor*

myths

narrative*

nouns

past/present/future*

person, concept of*

poetry/rhetoric

private inner life

rhythm

rites of passage, rituals

self, distinguished from other*

social structure

statuses and roles (ascribed and achieved)

succession

symbolism*

taxonomy*

time*

true & false distinguished

These universals are good examples of punctuation as

defined in Chapter 2, but what of values? Are they, too, universal?

Universal Values

When we reach the level of a value, we have encountered a different sort of 'why'. Here is where we must seek out the basic; that which is shared by all humans. That may not, of course, be easily expressed through language alone. Different languages lose a lot in translation because they are also cultural artefacts laden with meaning and conditioning. If they are universal, values are not a matter of choice, ambition, or priority. They are the ground and the soil from which different principles grow, and while we rely on such principles for identity, collective survival, and well-being, the fact that every society has a system for regulating politics, setting and enforcing laws, organising commerce, trade, and education makes an overwhelming case for something universal. Life may set up conflicts between one set of principles against another, but at the level of values there is no conflict, just interpretation, understanding, and awareness.

It may help to illustrate the relationship between action and values as a visual analogy, a volcano (Figure 8.1).[12]

Values transcend the individual, even though each of us ultimately draws from them our individuality. Beliefs are specific in actions and values are not. Principles are axiological, which is to say that they are about the process of choosing the right course of action and the ethical way to go. Universal Values are neither prescriptive nor moral, they just are. That they force the questions that result in ethics and morals, and in many other things, is intriguing but not surprising. Beliefs can change, principles may evolve, but

---

[12] At the mouth of a volcano are our actions, what we do. At the base, deep below, are vast, slow-moving, and powerful forces that are the heat that will eventually rise to the surface. Between that underground core and the open world, lava moves in relatively wide channels (principles) that eventually divide and branch into smaller pipes (beliefs) that vent into the air. Vents may change; conduits, less so. The core magma is moving but as one mass.

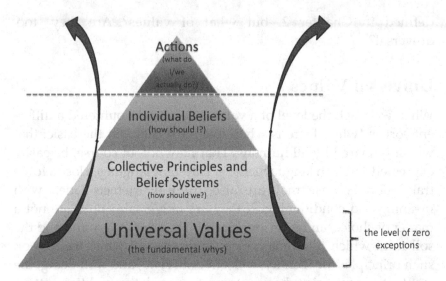

Figure 8.1.   The relationship between actions, beliefs, principles, and values.

universal values are not up for negotiation, and beneath values there is nothing divisible. They do not change because there would be nothing for them to change into without a serious redefinition of what the word human means. The most we can say is that we may not have yet reached the clarity in our language to express them in categories that cover all.

In contrast, most business, management, and leadership textbooks are happy to talk about values as a sort of pick 'n' mix exercise in selecting labels to wear as a suit of armour rather than as a device to establish common ground. My view is that asking what your values are is a redundant question, and we would be better asking ourselves what are our beliefs and principles. At any rate, what matters is the spirit and intent of the enquiry and whether the person is determined to follow it all the way to the limit of their self-awareness.

Frameworks of Values

Each of the three frameworks below takes a different approach to values and each attempts to get to the essence of a universality behind the question. Each uses 'why?' as a tool to dig.

Maslow's Hierarchy of Needs

Abraham Maslow's arrangement of different types of human needs in a hierarchical pyramid[13] is very well known and has been used many times in positive psychology. Values are the satisfying of different types of needs in our lives, says Maslow, and these run from the very basic and the bottom of the pyramid, physiological survival requirements such as food, drink, shelter, and warmth, through a sequence of levels (safety, belonging, and esteem) up to self-actualisation, or becoming a fully-formed individual in service of the needs of others. These are all proposed as universals. In Maslow's view, higher-level needs will generally not take centre-stage in our minds until those below have been met. According to this theory, people are only motivated by the bottom four elements when what those levels represent is absent or deficient in their lives. If you do not feel anything is missing, then you will not think about them until prompted. You will, however, be motivated upward to the 'growth' potential of whatever the next level is. The hierarchy hints at an end state, and the area above the pyramid represents a possibility, found in many philosophies and religions, of transcending the self, a subject Maslow explored later in his career. Critics have pointed out that a strict hierarchy is hypothetical and not easy to demonstrate or defend empirically. Even internally there is an admission that levels may overlap, and higher stages may be attained synchronously or even before lower ones. Maslow's categories may not stand up as hierarchical in theory or in practice, but they do provide a useful set of categories to start a conversation about health and well-being. This presents values as motivations or drivers. Contrast that now with values as desirable choices, as described in the very influential work of Shalom Schwartz.

Schwartz's Theory of Basic Human Values

If you are ever asked to take a values survey at work, the chances are it will be based on the work of Shalom Schwartz, a researcher who set out, iteratively, to map personal values as they are

---

[13] Maslow never presented them this way.

universal across cultures. He defined values as beliefs that connect with desirable goals, and as guidelines to select or evaluate actions in a way that made some more important than others. Originally, in search of trans-situational goals, he named 10 universal human values. These were later refined to make a set of 19 concepts arranged in a circular continuum of motivation grouped into four major types, as follows:

1. Openness to change
   Self-direction (with subdivisions of thought and action)
   Stimulation
   Hedonism (which crossed over into...)
2. Self-enhancement
   Achievement
   Power (subdivided into dominance and resources)
   Face (which crosses over into...)
3. Conservation
   Security (subdivided into societal and personal)
   Tradition
   Conformity
   Humility (which crosses into...)
4. Self-transcendence
   Benevolence (subdivisions: caring and dependability)
   Universalism (subdivisions: concern, nature, and tolerance)
   Underlying forces were arranged in two sets of poles, self-protection versus growth, and social focus versus personal focus. These poles are opposites and therefore conflictual (compare Chapter 3 and epistemology of tensions from difference).

This makes for an entertaining questionnaire, but the idea that what is held, constructed, and changeable at the individual level are values is a misconception. When you are presented with this as a menu, you will start selecting those that feel important to you. These were not your invention; they were conceived by another as having more, or less, 'value' (worth). If what we are trying to get at with the idea of values are really fundamentals, then they must all be universal, with no 'more or less', just differences in how and when. They should all matter equally and be beyond this kind of comparison.

Schwartz's model is a reasonable measure of an individual's opinion, but a questionnaire result already contains two sets of conditioning. One belongs to the person asking the question, the other to the person answering it. Schwartz's values are set up as localised phenomena, located in an individual's concept of selfhood. The implicit invitation in the survey is first to look for separate labels, but this separation then risks becoming internal oppositions. Although beliefs and principles can exclude each other, values, if they are universal, cannot. Further, the temptation will then be for people to identify themselves with a type, re-creating the duck–rabbit fallacies of 'more/less' and 'better/worse'. As soon as you have to rank a value, you have to resort to a set of principles to do so, and you have left the value level behind.

Schwartz does state that his values are grounded in universal requirements of human existence, and here we may be getting closer to the Integrated Leader. Schwartz names three such requirements; *individual biological needs* (think of Maslow's lowest segments), *needs for coordinated social interaction*, and *the welfare needs of groups*. A fourth, *spirituality*, he said he was unable to find sufficient data for in his research to include. I would agree that these deeper requirements are universals, and the level where I think we should appropriately be using the term value.[14]

(Dalton's) Values as Unspoken Universals

If basic, unifying aspects of human nature exist and these are not sets of individual goals, motivations, dispositions, or traits, then it follows that:

(i) Our biology has evolved to protect and preserve an innate flexibility to form social connections. We instinctively know what being in a group means.

---

[14] It may be that value is not the right word. Perhaps universals are just unnameable states.

(ii) Our biology has allowed us the cognitive capacity to express and recognise universal values in how we live. This flows through language, music, art, dance, poetry, humour, meditation, and so on.

(iii) Beyond our individual differences, we are all interconnected.

We must learn what the principles of our social group are, but we do not have to learn how to learn them. Every human can appreciate, deep down, that certain things matter, and every society sets itself up to raise their children accordingly. This capacity develops, matures, and grows through life. The working hypothesis of the Integrated Leader is that universal values are those essentials which hold, invisibly, every individual and every collective through life. If they are not visible, how can we detect them? Traditionally, there have been two ways:

(i) By a comparative study of the patterns in other cultures, and then looking for links at a meta-level (patterns of belief systems across peoples and cultures).

(ii) By observation or by interviewing people and identifying from their words or actions what matters to them. Then looking for patterns in that data, and either measuring against an existing theoretical framework or suggesting a new one from scratch.

Many serious thinkers, such as Maslow or Schwartz, first form an initial understanding of values in abstract terms or from a survey of sociological theory, and then move to investigate their hunches through data collected from observation and interview. The result is usually a diagram and a questionnaire. Others, such as Milton Rokeach, may begin with widespread interviews (based on current thinking in psychology), which in turn generates multiple themes and categories. The result is usually a diagram and a questionnaire.

This has led to three problems. There is a certain lack of clarity on definitions within the research literature and in corporate life.

Terms are often used interchangeably so that the difference between a value and belief is blurred. Additionally, the initial and very open search for the underlying pattern may be abandoned once the flag has been planted. Next, there is a tendency to present diagnostic tools and descriptive reports that obscure from the viewer some neotenous (juvenile and under-developed) assumptions. Finally, there is frequently a strong expectation that values are normative; that is, people should change their goal-directed behaviours according to what the instrument is telling them.

We can speculate and interpret universal values but not pick and choose between them. They all apply. Values must therefore be intrinsically linked to universal health and well-being, or they are not universal. When you think you have found a core value, you must still interrogate it with yet another 'why that?' If you can reply, then what you had was not the universal, basic value. Eventually, you will run out of language because of the limits of any language system to express universals. In expressing the richness of a universal concept, not everything that counts can be counted, and not everything that can be counted counts.[15] On the other hand, you can navigate from any surface aspect of the human context down to values.

Every society asks and tries to answer in its principles the basic questions of life to which universal values are the drivers. I believe I can see four such fundamental imperatives, which are aspects of one indivisible view of life, just seen from four different angles. I cannot claim these are definitive, nor that they are the only way to understand universal values. There will always be room for interpretation. For example, the Italian researchers who drafted the definition of mental health earlier in this chapter included the phrase 'universal values', which they say means:

---

[15] This phrase is attributed to American professor of Sociology William Bruce Cameron, in 1963. There is a lovely quote from *the Little Prince* by Antoine de Saint-Exupéry that sums this up, 'Here is my secret. It is very simple: It is only with the heart that one can see rightly; what is essential is invisible to the eye.'

'Respect and care for oneself and other living beings; recognition of connectedness between people; respect for the environment; respect of one's own and others' freedom.'[16] (p. 232)

While I like these very much as principles, the question is still there from where these emerge as categories. With that in mind, here are my four categories of universal values:

1. Being productive
   Am I competent? Am I contributing something?
   In different ways, all societies look to their members to find or develop their talent for being productive in terms of sustaining the health of the community and society.[17] The modern schools and universities we attend are designed around this central organising principle, preparation for work. Once in work, nearly everyone is formally evaluated in terms of whether their contribution is a net increase in value in the organisation. Some societies have developed sophisticated and organised processes for channelling ambition and the need to be doing something productive. Even without this social pressure, we would recognise what happens when we are idle for too long. If we're lucky, we will know the inward satisfaction and self-regard that comes from positive hard work. Finding joy in work is a manifestation of this universal value.

2. Being moral
   Am I doing the right thing? Am I good? Am I ethical and fair?
   Cohesion and co-operation in human communities require people to act in a way that preserves the delicate balance between giving and taking, and the fair and just resolution of any disputes and conflicts that may arise, whether on a large or

---

[16]Galderisi, S., Heinz, A., Kastrup, M., Beezhold, J., and Sartorius, N. (2015). Toward a new definition of mental health. *World Psychiatry: Official Journal of the World Psychiatric Association (WPA)*, 14(2): 231–233, with permission.

[17]What in fact needs to be sustainable is the *ecology* that supports the community and society. This ecology may be defined as the state in which all elements are able to propagate themselves.

small scale. No society is without a system for defining what is moral and ethical, and what is fair and just. Of course, it does not follow that all societies are fair and just all the time. The principles used in systems of justice change, but the question that generated them does not. Around the world, there are different sets of principles and even more examples of social norms for measuring morality. Numerous attempts to find common standards have been made as global contact and collaboration have spread in recent times. An individual may defer to the collective or develop a moral compass of their own.

3. Belonging
   Am I included? Am I worthy of love? What is my place?
   To belong is to be a participant in society, and to be part of an order. Finding your place in a system settles people. Generations represent the flow of lifespans from one to another, and this stream creates the context for identity. Family is the strongest and earliest such system of belonging, which reinforces the importance of this universal value in the maintenance of good mental health and well-being. Denial of membership, exclusion, exile, or forced removal are among the most psychologically damaging experiences an individual can face, so we will hold on to emotional ties as a core value. Many different systems of beliefs and principles have grown from this universal aspect, as many as there have been societies. These combine with social rules for obedience or dissent that are the two other aspects of being moral and being productive. All three universals listed so far are mutually intertwined and interdependent. Belonging is the only category we can experience as being a member of a set with no exclusions and no out-group (we are all human). This is our universal set.

4. Being Aware
   Who am I?
   The first three universal values are mirrors for the self-concept as far as it is socially constructed. One other universal needs to

be included, which is the inner desire to understand the conception of self. Not everything about the concept of the self is dependent on place, role, or position in the community, and in theory the introspective self can be looked for without comparison or validation. I can look for meaning in life with reference to nothing except the fact that I am asking the question. The question raised here is answerable only in self-awareness, not in other people's theories or experiences. It is the most important question you can ask because it is the basis of your health and well-being, and the basis from which you then answer all the other questions to do with productivity, morality, and belonging.

Humans are natural pattern seekers, and the pattern contained in the idea of core values is the same one we began this chapter

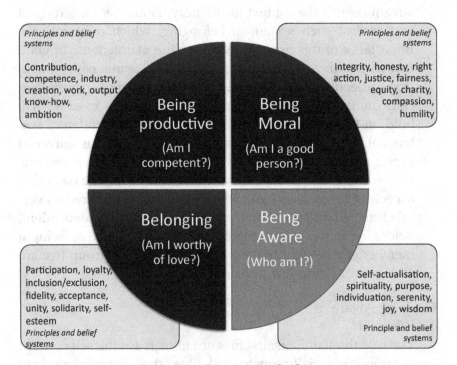

Figure 8.2.   Four universal values.

with, namely the search for universal mental health and well-being. The influence of universal values on actions is complex. They are evidenced in but not immediately evident from behaviour. Having passed from fundamental to principle to belief into action, there are many lenses of conditioning that may disguise why we behave the way we do or hide from us how we might change that. Each of us can, however, subject our beliefs and principles to deeper enquiry.

In closing, here are a couple of tasks that could help you tune into the themes of this chapter.

1. Pay attention over the coming days and weeks to whose voice you hear in your head before you come to decisions or take actions in various situations. At the same time, think whether you know anyone who might have your voice in their head before they act or decide in life.
2. Keep a diary of the following for a period of one or two weeks:
    i. How much sleep you are getting, and what quality sleep that is
    ii. How much you move, whether this is organised physical exercise/training, or a register of how often you get outside
    iii. How many times you are giving yourself 'me' time, and how clearly you mark boundaries for different things during the day
    iv. What sort of people you are spending time with and what energy those relationships have
    v. What you are eating
    vi. Whether you have access to people you can freely be yourself with

Reflecting on the Integrated Leader's Manifesto (Leading Self with the Organisation)

#8

'The organisation does not absorb individuals or own their personal paths and development — it supports people refining themselves through interaction with peers. An organisation is a community with its own culture. It represents that culture with its actions. What culture do we want to create?'

Employers ask too much of their staff if they demand that they put the company before themselves. Every organisation relies on the talent of those who work there, and in a healthy workplace this is supported without exploitation. Employees give too much of themselves if they base their happiness and self-esteem on the opinion the company has of them.

We have been following a train of thought in the manifesto concerning leading self with the organisation. The Integrated Leader finds health and well-being for themselves through awareness and humility. The Integrated Organisation must gain a self-awareness and humility of its own, analogous to that of the people who lead and work in it. The healthy organisation should not use people up and simply extract or exploit their people's energy with nothing in return. In contrast, the organisation should be a net generator of cohesion in life.

Is it possible to cultivate a culture? Many organisations believe that not only is it possible, it's desirable. But how does this work? Can an organisation control culture in that way? Because it is damaging when the culture of an organisation feels wrong, companies spend a lot of time and money studying and analysing theirs. Some conduct formal cultural audits, which usually involve looking at the behaviours, processes and systems, and resources, in the hope that enough information is forthcoming to suggest changes. The jump from an audit to the declaration of a new culture, however, is fraught with problems, and most attempts to repaint the culture run into serious problems quickly.

Trying to corral culture is like designing what a cloud should look like. The true culture of a group of people is discovered through careful, impartial observation, not through analysis. Analysis infects the observation with everyone's prior conditioning and punctuation. The true culture of your organisation is observable in the relations — the actual relationship — between its members, between it and its past, and between it and its competitors, customers, stakeholders, and so on.

Everybody who has a first day in an organisation will have a last. To be part of an organisation speaks to some deeply rooted beliefs, such as loyalty, conformity, and camaraderie, which the social side of the human experience needs to thrive. In between, may come involvement in the life, purpose, and direction of the organisational system as the dance of influence goes on, but no organisation has the right to require the individual to put the company before themselves. Toxic work cultures will see people jeopardise their health and well-being to live up to impossible expectations.

A different kind of culture would be one created from the spontaneous and the unfolding present, and not from artificial (literally, beguiling and imitative), prefabricated ideas. This sort of leap takes courage, but will always be of the moment, and ready to deal with the world as it is, not as it once was. In this way, we create a culture without contrivance; it is simply what we do.

Part 3

Don't Forget You're Change

The central task of education is to implant a will and facility for learning; it should produce not learned but learning people. The truly human society is a learning society, where grandparents, parents, and children are students together.

Eric Hoffer[1]

Without using the words leader or leadership, try and tell someone what makes your organisation move. Do this as if the idea of an organisation were completely fresh and new. Avoid formulas and jargon if you can. I hope just the idea of this as a task is enough to cause you to pause, think, and prepare (if only in your mind) how you might go about framing a response. How we communicate reveals how we see the world. If change is going to happen, then in some way it must be an embodiment of the people involved — starting with what you do, and how you go about deciding among the many possibilities for action which ones will make a difference.

This is encouragement to everyone to begin to communicate their essential thoughts and actions, with originality, and it is one of the outcomes of Integrated Leadership. In this part, we begin to reach the end of an arc in awareness described in Parts 1 and 2. The chapters in Part 3 integrate three normally independent ideas into

---

[1]Hoffer, E. (2006). *Reflections on the Human Condition*, Titusville, NJ: Hopewell Publications.

one central theme, the nature of health and well-being as it is lived and sustained by *you*. The three ideas are:

1. Time
2. Change
3. Uncertainty

These are aspects of you in the sense that your experience of them is what they are. The understanding that this is so may not arrive immediately, or even as the result of a process of logical reasoning, but that you are time, you are change, and that knowledge is limited, is not something you learn from following a method or walking in someone else's footsteps.

Chapter 9

Let's Meet at Infinity

Time is the thing I am made of. Time is a river that sweeps me along, but I am the river; it is a tiger that tears me apart, but I am the tiger; it is a fire that consumes me, but I am the fire. The world, unfortunately, is real; I, unfortunately, am Borges.

Jorge Luis Borges[2]

Who has Time?

This chapter looks at how ideas of time are relevant to the idea of Integrated Leadership. Time, like air, is one of life's great taken-for-granteds.[3] Moreover, time is one of life's great mysteries, even though every one of us routinely makes it central to our experience of life.

Ask a Master of Business Administration student what they struggle with most when trying to get to grips with their course in balance with the rest of their life and they will probably say time management. By this they mean they lack the effective management skills, the resilience, and the short-cuts to fit all their tasks into the day. So they search for received wisdom from others on how to become more efficient in their use of this valuable commodity. There must be a formula for this, they surmise, it is just that

---

[2]From Borges, J. L., translated by Simms, R. L. C. (1952).*Other Inquisitions: 1937–1952*. Translated by Ruth L. C. By permission of the University of Texas Press.

[3]That is, until we realise we do not have enough of it! In that sense, time is also like good health.

they do not know what the strategy should be. Perhaps. No doubt there are dozens of great ways to measure your performance using the metric of time, and this could cover the management part of clock time. Time is money. But that does not explain what time is; part of the equation remains hidden in the shadows. Many people set themselves up in opposition to time, imbuing it with an external reality quite separate and alien to them. Time is the enemy, time is against us, we often say. Time is running out. Time is wasted. It is a race against time. Perhaps these are all echoes in our consciousness that life is finite in its duration.

Look at the following list of statements. How many match or closely resemble your view?

- Time exists independently of me. It is universal, uniform, and absolute
- Time is outside my control. It passes and I have no power to stop it
- Time has a one-way direction from the past, through the present, and into the future
- Time is a measurable resource, a useful way to judge productivity or non-productivity
- The past determines the future; we are driven along by events in the past
- Time is not real. We make it real by choosing to count things in nature that occur and re-occur

As far as we know, ancient civilisations first conceived of and measured time as rhythms in nature, observed in the predictable and cyclical movements of transits of the planets, the revolution of the Earth through the year around the sun, and the experience of the diurnal–nocturnal clock from the rotation of the Earth. It looks true that life on Earth is in consequence of this light/dark rhythm because it turns out that the circadian rhythm is linked with many genetic patterns in humans[4] and our measuring of events by their

---

[4]Joseph Takahashi at the University of Texas Southwestern Medical Center in Dallas extended the work from fruit flies to mammals and showed that the system

repeatable duration is rooted in many of the signifiers in the basic levels of Maslow's hierarchy. Meanwhile, the moon is scarcely disguised in our calendar as months, although the origins of the word day are more camouflaged.[5] Marking time has a long history. Understanding time has long been a mystery. In his collected autobiography, *Confessions*, the theologian St Augustine of Hippo wrote around the year 400 CE:

> 'What then is time? If no one asks me, I know what it is. If I wish to explain it to him who asks, I do not know.'[6]

Fast forward 1,600 years and our appreciation of time as a concept in science has moved on considerably. However, many of us struggle with the same problem as Augustine, and the philosophical fascination with time remains unabated and unquenched.

We intuitively feel a circular form of time in the micro rhythms in our physiology, and we know that evolution needs inordinately long periods of cycles of genetic reproduction for macro rhythms to emerge as change. Time and change often seem so interlinked that they appear synonymous. In cosmic spacetime, Einstein's General Theory of Relativity shifted our view of time from a Newtonian definition. In Isaac Newton's work, time is an absolute, passing evenly, and independently of its measurement. Matter moves (or does not) relative to other matter, not in relation to absolute (mathematical) time. The physics of quantum theory showed

---

is remarkably conserved across species. Researchers have since tied the circadian clock to many aspects of mental and physical well-being. The links between the circadian clock and human health are so pervasive that medical schools should increase their focus on chronobiology, says Martha Merrow, chair of medical psychology at Ludwig Maximilian University of Munich in Germany.' Callway, E. and Ledford, H. (2017). Medicine Nobel awarded for work on circadian clocks, https://www.nature.com/news/medicine-nobel-awarded-for-work-on-circadian-clocks-1.22736.

[5]Perhaps 'day' began in a Sanskrit word which meant burn or glow, while the word night may share deep roots with another Sanskrit term meaning 'domain of the moon'.

[6]St. Augustine of Hippo, (c. 397) Confessions, Chapter XIV, 17.

that time and space are not separable. More about this shortly. In the smaller scale of a human life, though, time is still a linear and fixed concept, one that fosters a sensation that it must in some sense be real and outside us. Time is often seen as a line from past to future and as it passes, as it does, through now, it allows us to store information. That is why we use it as a tool for measuring the value of change, progress, and productivity. In business and management, time feels real enough when used as a marker to measure value. Not incidentally, this means time can be used as a rod for our own back. If time is money, then wasting it is a serious breach of a manager's fiduciary duty. In this way of thinking, every event happens in time, and occupies some of it, preferably with minimum waste. In business the clock is running, whether we like it or not, and we'd better make the most of it. It is only a small skip across a stream of meaning for us to believe that life's clock is running in the same way.

When we start to unpick this, we can see that we make a lot of assumptions about the nature of time and our experience of it in our lives. Here are three positions on time that have been influences on our perception and probably on our beliefs:

1. *The absolute view:* time as a fixed, lineal sequence.
   Time is quite independent of you and runs evenly throughout the universe. Depending on your view, it may have done so forever, or it may have had a starting point, but it is basically a real thing. 'Past' refers to events that have happened before the present and which still sit there as intact facts on a sort of conveyor belt going back. The future will be equally real, taking its place along the great line of time after the present. Events are happening in, but separate from, time.

   Is time absolute and independent? If your feeling is yes, it is, then your view corresponds to what Cambridge philosopher Jon McTaggart in 1908[7] described as 'A-series', where time is a fixed lineal sequence from past, to present, to future. The past has taken place, before the present, and the future occupies a

---

[7]McTaggart, J. E. (1908). The Unreality of Time, *Mind*, *17*(68), 457–474.

space taking place after the present. We move through time as a traveller along a road. In the A-series, as time passes an event's position will shift from future to present and then on into the past. McTaggart acknowledged the importance of this, but felt that time as objective and independently real from experience and events was an illusion.

He presented an additional way of conceptualising it, called 'B-series', in which a temporal sequence is set up between the 'earlier than' and the 'later than'. Before and after are summoned into being only with the event. Time is the localised phenomenon that results from this measurement of an event's position within our phenomenological experience of cause and effect.

2. *The narrative view:* duration of time and how experience is arranged.

This says that 'before' and 'after' cannot swap their positions, but both are intrinsic to the present and are relative to the event. Narrative time punctuates a sequence in this way to create a story where the viewpoint is always that events are either 'earlier than' or 'later than' something. Events are still fixed along the absolute timeline as well and will always remain so. World War II (WWII) happened in relation to World War I (WWI), and WWI might explain WWII, but WWI will always be in the past relative to WWII. This is historical time, which is the desire (in our society at least) for things to exist in time and be recalled in later time. Where we make these before and after incisions, however, is determined by nothing except convenience or convention. When WWI exactly began and when it truly ended depends on how we define our terms for (in this example) 'war', 'begin', and 'end'. Closer examination always reveals fuzzy boundaries.

A narrative view of time is very useful when we want to translate our ideas into action in a way or sequence that we know that everyone else will understand. When a set of experiences is arranged in time order, then any one particular experience will appear as if it were a component in the succession of a plot or story. Time is therefore another form of punctuation or marker of an order that creates the sensation of a narrative succession.[8] This applies as a dominant feature in a lot of people's personal development, which is firmly narrative, historical, and often teleological. Your resumé presents time as (i) your position concerning evidence of achievement in the past and (ii) concerning anticipation of achievement in the future. We are expected to make our mark in this way, and very little in our education system encourages deviation from this view. On the darker side, it is frequently a recipe for replication, not invention, and for analysis, not integration.

Narrative time measures duration in the same way that a centimetre measures distance, money measures profit, or high IQ measures intelligence. Time is symbolic in that it represents an idea but is a fiction — albeit a useful one.

3. *The emergent view:* how we make sense of our experience of time.

The emergent view of time says sense-making is a continuous activity, a present experience where we retain a just-pastness of one thing while simultaneously we anticipate the next. The present has wide horizons integrating both recollection and expectation. Time is experienced as emerging from events that are in some way organised, and the present is experienced as a whole, not as isolated parts. To put it another way, you bring into being your past and future alongside the present as you experience life. What you call the past flows away backward from the present.

This is not the same as the A-series view of time, which has the past occur before, not after, the emergent present. Nor is it the same as the B-series, which holds that the present is and always remains a before-then event regarding the future. Emergent time is phenomenological.

---

[8] Once the rules of how this is done are known, artists and writers can improvise or play with them, as we see in Joseph Heller's book *Catch-22*.

Time is Bound to Feel Like This

Time is experienced as emergent from events. We feel that we experience events because they have a duration. If there is a link between time, experience, and events, then how is time organised by the mind?

Music is a universal, but how are we able to perceive sounds as music? A piece of music is perceived as more than just a series of individual notes. This is not hard to grasp. However, is music a succession of experiences or an experience of succession? The experience of music is not the same as the experience of any of its components (notes, tones, harmonies, silences, and pauses). The same fundamental pattern must be at work whether we are following a conversation, reading a book, managing a career, leading an organisation — or just about any situation where we are sense-making or meaning-making.

So what is going on? The answer is complex and requires multiple levels of mental processing. In the first half of the 20th century, the Polish American academic Alfred Korzybski established a whole field of study[9] to investigate this. He concluded that humans have two remarkable and unique (as far as we can tell) capacities. The first is that biology and language combine to facilitate levels of abstraction in our consciousness. Not only are we aware that we are alive, we are aware of our awareness.[10]

The second notion is that we are the only animal that is time-binding.[11] This refers to our capacity to code and pass information

---

[9] General semantics.

[10] It follows that we are aware that being alive is a finite state.

[11] Part of Korzybski's operational classification of life, beginning with 'energy-binding', which is the ability to transform light into organic matter that can grow and reproduce, and make controlled choices but not move. 'Space-binding' is the power of controlled mobility toward specific goals such as food, or away from specific threats to survival. Space-binders can also transform energy to matter, but their existence is defined more by competition and interaction. 'Time-binding' emerges with self-awareness and is epitomised by the capture and use of information as knowledge.

and knowledge from one generation to the next. We can inherit wisdom, and cumulatively this perpetuates itself as more and more levels of abstraction. Accordingly, we know that 'music' refers to categories of sensations, experiences, and events that are related in a certain way. This is one way of understanding how the mind turns experiences of events into time. The discussion of time is also a discussion of history (that is, history as sense-making, not merely as a chronicle). Our modern view of history is strongly linear and teleological. Most people behave in accordance with the idea that, over time, the very practical business of management is part of a progress toward a desired goal or set of ideas. As we are seeing, this paradigm might need challenging given the global problems we face.

Next, how are we able to recognise sequences of notes as melodies? How do we construct our sense of duration? One answer came from the German philosopher Edmund Husserl, who saw that our sensation of time passing is a phenomenon[13] bounded by the data from our senses AND dependent on sets of abstracted mental processes embedded in our language, conditioning, and culture. Our lives are not segmented in separate chunks, independent from moment to moment. Somehow our consciousness in its present attention 'contains' what has just passed and what is expected to happen next. For Husserl, the three components of mental activity that compose our present tense are (1) primal impressions, (2) retentions, and (3) protentions. These are congruent but need a little explanation. Primal impressions are the immediate flows of stimuli registered in the senses in the present moment (here, think back to the fundamental notion of difference, or news of difference, as described in Chapter 3). This is the most vital and actual experience occupying

---

[12] Image from Wikipedia, https://commons.wikimedia.org/wiki/File:Fjordn_surface_wave_boat.jpg.

[13] To study a phenomenon as Husserl conceived, you must strip away all your assumptions and theories, which has echoes of the beginner's mind in Chapter 1.

the momentary now. However, this includes a 'just-pastness' which Husserl called retention. Retention is a natural and equally immediate facility, a sort of short-term memory which we can contrast with the long-term memory system of recollection (as described, for example, by Korzybski's time-binding) and which is a sort of recognition. This is not the same as a recollection or remembering, which is our consciousness of something that is no longer happening. Retention is linked to a living, present experience. In our present is also the anticipation of the future, or protention, and this is necessarily an integral part of our experience in the present. Perhaps retention and protention resemble peripheral vision around the focus of the eye when it takes in an object. Applied to how we experience an organisation or, for that matter, the way that leadership is experienced as a phenomenon by everyone in an organisation, Husserl's explanation goes some way to explaining how it endures without the need for constant restatement or reinvention.

The Physicist's View

The Italian theoretical physicist Carlo Rovelli[14] has written and spoken extensively about time. In a talk given at the Royal Institution in London in April 2018,[15] he gently dismantled several of our core conceptions of time. Here are a few of the ways:

> Time measures differently, relatively, in every place in the universe. On Earth, it demonstrably moves at a different pace between altitudes, for example.
>
> There is no universal 'now'. The distances we experience in the sliver of cosmic scale that is our environment are too small for us to perceive this, but the 'now' that we feel is the same now we all

---

[14] Rovelli, C. (2019). *The Order of Time*, New York, NY: Penguin.
[15] The Physics and Philosophy of Time with Carlo Rovelli, https://www.youtube.com/watch?v=-6rWqJhDv7M.

live in is only so if we ignore the distance between us. Rovelli says we carry a sort of bubble of now around with us, in which the present can have meaning, but there is no independent meaning of 'now' outside that. The meaning of ordering past, present, and future breaks down on a cosmological scale. Move into the almost unimaginable scales of distance in the cosmos, between solar systems and galaxies, etc. and the usefulness of a present time, universal now completely evaporates.

Time appears as ordered for us because of how we measure and narrate events. The concept of future feels inherently unpredictable, and the past inherently unchangeable because that is how we have defined the measurement of these as concepts. To an extent this is true; time could not run backward, says Covelli, from the end of an event to its beginning because of the second law of thermodynamics. The past is another way of describing the irreversible one-way friction imposed on anything with order. Our past consists of our present intent converted to activity, which is acted on the world around us, the ripples of which spread out and for a while can still be detected. In the United Kingdom, although weak, echoes of the Battle of Hastings in 1066 still form part of a national identity and sense of direction today, but none of that can influence the order in place in 1066 at the battle. Innumerable events appear to us in our present to be past causes for current effects. It is this perception that we use to distinguish past from future.

Covelli points out that the only difference between future and past is between order and disorder. The term used for this in thermodynamics is entropy, the dispersal of available energy (from heat to cold) in a system. Social systems are often described in terms of negative entropy, or their capacity to maintain order in their relationships over time. Rather than physical energy being the key, here it is budgets of information. The mental orderliness we see as homeostatic maintenance of the self, of the organisation, and society is how we conceptualise time. This could be another way of understanding what leadership is; the durability (i.e. negative entropy) of selected and socially useful structures or ideas.

The past looks ordered, but that is only from the perspective we choose for it. The past is another word for the identification of a relived pattern, which is certainly useful and may be necessary for maintaining a sense of self, but from which there is no reason to believe in the past as real in an objective, eternal sense. The past is therefore a form of inquiry or search about the organisation of human actions. The purpose of this as enquiry in personal development is to advance self-knowledge and understanding, though one person's ordered filing system of memories may to another person look like just a huge mess.

In physics, the properties of time as we commonly understand them become less and less distinct the more we zoom out, and the more we zoom in. The cutting edge of the theory of time these days is in joining relativity and cosmology to quantum mechanics. Somewhere between, in everyday human relations, time is a convenient way of sharing and counting events, and a question of perspective or framing. Nothing is happening in an absolute and independent time. What is happening in terms of your senses and your experience *is* time. There are serious implications in this for the very contemporary leadership mantra of seeking purpose.

Time as a Flow Through You

The chronological[16] sensation of passing that is created by our measurement of time can easily be dislodged. People who take long vacations (proper ones, genuinely spent away from the usual signals of marking time) soon find that they cannot quite recall what day of the week it is, how many days have gone, and how many remain. When our modern punctuation does not assert itself, biological rhythms of natural sleep and waking, and hunger and thirst reassert, as does the cosmological punctuation of the day/ night planetary clock. An hour does not exist independently of the idea of 60 minutes, although hours and minutes are very useful as

---

[16] Chronology derives from Greek words meaning discourse of time.

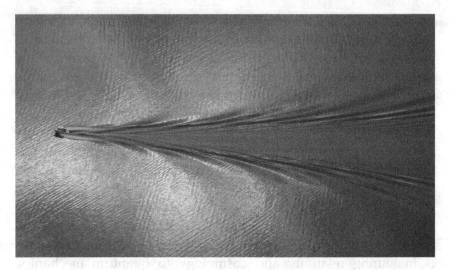

Figure 9.1.   The relationship between wake of the ship and time.[12]

agreed standards. Similarly, labelling events before our current experience 'the past', and events after our current experience 'the future' is useful punctuation to organise ourselves and each other, often in productive ways.

Now, however, let us encounter one of those moments which is often a course correction in perception, as illustrated in the metaphor of the boat on the ocean (Figure 9.1).

The boat in this picture is crossing the open sea. The first thing to note is that the boat is never anywhere else except where the boat is. It would be common for the people on the boat to have the feeling that they are travelling through time out of an endless past into an endless future. On the boat, it may seem that the present is a narrow, razor-thin moment of flow that comes and goes in an instant as the bow cuts the water. This is not the whole story. From the perspective of the boat, everything it sees or does (past and future) is all and only in the present.

As the boat travels across the surface of the ocean, it leaves a wake, evidence of where it has been. Close to the boat where the wake is recently formed, it is vivid and strong. From the boat, much about that recent past will be clear. As the boat moves further, in the wake perhaps other patterns, such as changes in direction, become possible to see, but the detail becomes less and less distinct. Eventually, the furthest part of the wake is not visible from the boat, and in fact, the ocean has returned to its undisturbed surface. For the people on the boat, the wake is valuable information about where it has been (that is, its past) but note that this information is only ever available to it in the present, where it is now. The past is a present tense phenomenon.

The area in front of the boat is completely clear. Regarding its future, the boat could now steer in any direction it chose. The area in front of the boat (that is, its future) and the direction it might move in are contingent upon what the boat is doing in the present, not what it might decide to do some time ahead of now. The future is also a present tense phenomenon. All the control is in the present, on the boat. This control can include selection of information from the past and about the future. However, this is not how most of us live our lives. For many, the wake of the boat is believed to have caused its current position, rather than the other way round. If you think the past has created the present, then you will feel restricted and controlled about where you go next, a problem made worse by the idea of a fixed outcome or destination. You have set an origin that is not in the present and an outcome that limits options. This view of the past is very prevalent in our society. We think a lot about our present position as if it were not our decision to get where we are. We will therefore feel that we have only a limited amount of choice, given the direction and momentum from the past, about what is possible in the future. As a result, when we look ahead we see only one direction in an open sea.

This should be your first wake-up call[17] about the nature of the present. The present contains the past and it contains the future. Your past is constructed in the present. You can select from the past anything you need to resource you in the present, including a sense of where your roots are. Equally, you do not have to hold on to anything from the past that does not resource you. The past does

---

[17] Pun intended.

not control your present, so it certainly does not define your future. If you want to see where you might go, look at where you are now, at the range of possibilities and opportunities around you, now. Your second wake-up call is awareness of the paradigm you are using to understand the fundamental nature of time.

For many, especially in the Anglo-Saxon business world that dominates the global network of organisations and careers, time is something we actively move through as if travelling along a line or a path. We make progress by consciously stepping forward into the future, as if it would not come into being if we did not. This is the basis of our core narrative — that life is a journey, and that the successful are those who boldly step into it with a plan. This is a universe where one thing follows logically from another in one orderly direction. This view encourages us to make plans, have goals, think of destinations, and even postpone the enjoyment of living until we get to the destination. What we do here is done to get there. This can lead to happiness postponed, our passions held on ice, and a present filled doing things we do not like, do not want, or do not agree with. This happens quite subtly and most of us remain quite unaware this is where we have ended up.

But what if you were to switch this around? What if, instead of you moving forward through time, time moves through you? You can only be where you are, in the present, and if you are aware of this then you will see that the future always comes to you and is passing through you. That is what time is, *the passing through you of events.*

This is a radically different perspective. You are not advancing into the future; time is the sensation you experience as the future moves through you. You can no more stop time moving than the early English King Canute on his apocryphal throne on an apocryphal beach could command the waves of an incoming tide to go out.[18] The only thing you can do is be as prepared as you can to experience it. In this paradigm, it makes no sense to plan. No plan

---

[18] Canute was a humble king wanting to dispel flattery among his followers who thought he had absolute power.

ever works out exactly as envisaged, and to focus only on a plan is missing out on life as it is happening, in the present. Planning is like wearing blinkers. Blinkers may keep the focus on a destination or attainment of a goal (usually someone else's goal), but the possibilities of the present stretch in all directions. You can still have goals, of course, but now every goal is connected to what is happening in the present. You begin to see that there is no way to a goal that does not start in your very next decision, thought, or action. Now you are open to greater possibilities and opportunities, and goals are redefined in the context of now. When you know how to stand confidently in the present, you can turn to face the past and take from it anything that resources you (leaving what needs to stay there to look after itself), and you can turn to face the future in any direction because it can come to you in all directions, not just one.

Time to Stop and Think

All organisations have a beginning, and every organisation will eventually have an end, despite the best efforts of whoever is in charge to elongate lifespan by various and creative means. The markers of birth and death in business are juristic. That is, birth and death are set out in law, where birth is a registration of a charter or articles of incorporation and death is recognised in liquidation or winding-up. Just as for humans, life is what happens between those two points and this is firmly where leadership sits, governing flows of stability and renewal. Legislation may define its existence, but time is the heartbeat of every organisation. As a human heart beats without a person needing to make it do so, the organisation endures in status even when those working for it have gone home to sleep. Leadership is the care of the health of that heartbeat. To carry out that task and to have agency,[19] a certain amount of theoretical knowledge of core principles is necessary for

---

[19]The ability or capacity to act or exert power and the intervention that follows from this.

both leaders and followers. From the past, they must accept what is. They should acknowledge what this history has given them, as well as what can be let go. They must continually and conscientiously find their place as the context and situation changes. Done incorrectly, there is a danger that leaders may be tangled in loyalties from the past beyond what might be rightfully theirs. This restricts and restrains their freedom to choose among all possible assessments of what course of action to take. How we understand the past, future, and present can make a difference to what we do. Time is found in the perspective we take, in the sum of the events and our conditioning. It is in the anticipation of our human wish of becoming, psychologically, something other than we are now.

Reflecting on the Integrated Leader's Manifesto (Leading Self with the Organisation)

#9

'Creating a new culture requires time, dedication, intention, and patience. New habits and behaviours are necessary for personal development to be born.'

'Let's create a new culture!' is the rallying call for many leaders of organisations. What do they mean? It may be meant in two ways, each a different path and different philosophy.

One sees a new culture as abrupt change, and a means to an end. The deliberate and forced change from how things worked before now, perhaps via the installation of a pre-determined and proscribed new way of working, does indeed take a lot of time and energy. Mergers and acquisitions often follow this pattern, and occasionally a single organisation can reinvent itself. Often, the organisation is seen as a machine with parts that can be re-tooled, but nothing will happen unless it is made to happen by the engineer.

The other sees the current culture as constantly changing and renewing itself. An abrupt or enforced cultural shift may go against the grain. The organisation is the river and change is the result of its resources and capacity to adapt while keeping its integrity.

Culture cannot be invented or decreed into existence.

In an organisation, 'culture' is the name for all the dynamic (and often hidden) relationships between people. Culture manifests in different ways. Edgar Schein[20] proposed it does so in three levels in an organisation, (a) visibly, in artefacts such as its branding, uniforms, structures, locations and so on, (b) publicly, in its espoused values evident via organised activities, documented rules, or written policies and procedures that explicitly explain 'why', and (c) powerfully, in its shared tacit assumptions, which are the unwritten and unspoken norms and rules and

---

[20]Schein, E. H. (1988). Organizational Culture. Retrieved from: https://dspace. mit.edu/bitstream/handle/1721.1/2224/SWP-2088-24854366.pdf?sequenc.

traditions that members actually observe (or risk expulsion by breaking). Culture, then, is the complex dance of assumptions, adaptations, and inherited norms of organisations as they visibly and invisibly try to maintain their integrity, purpose, and mission.

Cultures are identity and stability, and they are always in flux; they are never static. The Greek philosopher Heraclitus is often quoted on the subject of flux in the saying 'you can't step into the same river twice'. This is the modern version, but the original thought was more subtle. Heraclitus suggested the river is the same, but the water is not. A river is the moving, changing flow of water. A river maintains its integrity in the constant flow of new water through a relatively stable geography. At the same time, the action of the water also shifts the geography, and the river will change.[21]

So, the pattern 'you' remains even though your physical composition and mental state change, and even as the context moves. It is the same with culture. In organisations, larger, higher-order patterns are stable only in relation to the dynamic flow of relations between the various players involved as they define where the boundary of the system shall be. This is simultaneously and dynamically shaped by the larger systems outside. For example, the business school I joined in 2005 has existed as a system since 1945. No one working there now was working there when it began, and no one working there when it began still works there now, yet it retains the pattern and has a culture that we easily call, and others easily recognise, as 'the Henley experience'. Someone who studied there 30 years ago, arriving today would instantly understand where they are and what goes on there now, yet the culture is constantly new because the social world we live in is not at a standstill. Culture is a social object in the social world.

---

[21] Heraclitus. (2019). Retrieved from: https://plato.stanford.edu/entries/heraclitus/.

Chapter 10

Everything and Everyone Needs to Change[1]

One who brings
A mind not to be chang'd by Place or Time.
The mind is its own place, and in it self
Can make a Heav'n of Hell, a Hell of Heav'n

John Milton, *Paradise Lost*, Book 1

The Rise of Stewardship

A business cannot know its future. If it did, it would in effect have no future. You may need to pause for a moment on that one, especially if you work for or work in an organisation that seems to spend much of its (and your!) time convincing everyone that what it's doing is designed to beat the future by predicting it. If your organisation knew perfectly everything that was going to happen, there would be no such thing as decision-making, no such thing as choice, and no such thing as change. This is quite evidently not the case and nor would we want it to be. We do not know the future except as it arrives in the present, and we are superbly evolved to deal with uncertainty and change. We can make the case that it is when our not-knowing meets our innate capacity for finding out that we have the basic ingredients for progress, purpose, and

---

[1] Climate activist Greta Thunberg, speaking at the European Union, April 2019.

221

leadership. For tens of thousands of years in our history, our environment changed very little (beyond the effects of agriculture) and any change was relatively slow. Our knowledge processing requirements were maintained in balance. The story of the last 300 years, however, has been one of very rapid change. The environment is highly likely now to be in a rapid period of ecological change in response to the spread and influence of people, and the development of technology to exploit our cognitive capacity to adapt our environment to suit our needs.

It is said that the most important decision in business is the next one. This resonates with practising leaders and managers because it emphasises the unknown part of the present (which is what the future is) and it reflects one constant weighing on most manager's minds, 'how do I create value?' For many years, 'the next decision' in business could firmly and safely be anchored in the assumptions of the past. This is because the key to corporate value was incremental addition in whatever had been the status quo until then. This was the chief moral imperative for management. Such a closed-minded approach is no longer useful, even if it is still widely practised. The importance of the next business decision is shifting away from key performance indicators rooted in floating the corporate boat, towards those that do not degrade the environment the business relies on. The leading edge is now to consider business models that regenerate their environment. Integrated Leadership encompasses this wider concern and responsibility for sustaining the ability of the environment to remain a resource. If the next decision in business exploits a system's capacity for renewal so that the capacity is lost, then the organisation's health will suffer and even fail.

From now on, leadership must anticipate its own (unintended) consequences. This sense of care, duty, and subsequent long-term decision-making is the modern form of an old idea: stewardship. Typically, a steward supervises and supplies the resources that others need for survival, such as food, shelter, money, and so on, and stewardship carries a sense of doing something fundamental on behalf of others as a sort of service. The term is used in modern leadership theory (sometimes as an alternative to leadership), where what is usually emphasised is care for future generations.[2] Stewards think long-term when it comes to stability and order and this is an extension of the classical leadership roles of organising, planning, and rallying the troops to governance.

In 2015, all 193 United Nations (UN) member states adopted 17 Sustainable Development Goals, part of a concerted, diplomatic movement to address by 2030 many global challenges such as poverty, social justice, climate change, and ecological degradation. Each goal is ambitious[3] and the overall aim is about as radical as could be for so many nations to agree. Yet, because the scale of the task is almost too great to envisage, there is no guarantee that even if they continue agreeing on policy, and even if sporadic steps forwards by key and influential member states are made, we are very unlikely to reach the 2030 target. The 2020 interim report by the UN Secretary-General admitted progress as uneven,[4] and this was without factoring in the effects of the global COVID-19 pandemic that took hold in March 2020. Progress was reported in declining global poverty, falling rates of mortality among mothers and children, and international agreements on sustainable development. By contrast, action on climate change, prevention of famine and hunger, and increasing levels of social inequality and injustice were either reported as flatlining or in reverse. Public Health protection, ecosystem degradation, and economic recession look set to dominate the macro world of politics and economics for at least the

---

[2] A good example is Peter Block's *Stewardship: Choosing Service over Self-interest* (2013), published by Berrett-Koehler.

[3] No poverty; zero hunger; good health and well-being; quality education; gender equality; clean water and sanitation; affordable and clean energy; decent work and economic growth; industry, innovation, and infrastructure; reducing inequality; sustainable cities and communities; responsible consumption and production; climate action; life below water; life on land; peace, justice, and strong institutions; and partnerships for the goals. Retrieved from https://www.un.org/sustainabledevelopment/sustainable-development-goals/.

[4] Sustainable Development Goals Report 2020, retrieved from https://www.un.org/development/desa/publications/publication/sustainable-development-goals-report-2020.

next 2–5 years. That the UN is coalescing around these issues is perhaps neither new nor shocking. In recent years, several notable grassroots responses to social and ecological crises have sprung up that may be tapping into a feeling akin to the crossover point between the two questions relating to leadership as the answer mentioned in Chapter 4, 'what could be?' and 'whom should we follow?'. Examples include the #*MeToo* movement, Black Lives Matter, and Extinction Rebellion. These have manifested as mass, decentralised movements protesting, respectively, sexual harassment and abuse, systemic racism, and threats to the global environment in the climate crisis. As such, they are the latest links in long historical chains of locally organised, social actions for change.[5]

But What of Business?

The World Economic Forum (WEF, or The Forum) is an influential non-governmental organisation (NGO), founded in 1971 as the European Management Forum by Professor Klaus Schwab. At the inauguration, its avowed mission was that

> 'Business should serve all stakeholders — customers, employees, communities, as well as shareholders.'[6]

This was elaborated on in 1973 in the Davos Manifesto to mean long-term viability being dependent on economic profitability. Widening the mandate from just shareholders to cover many stakeholders would have been new but not controversial at the time. If there has been one single, key theme in Western business thought in the last 100 years, then it is that more is better. With that as a backdrop, the public image of annual Davos meetings in the Swiss Alps was of elites networking, power-broking (Davos has

---

[5] E.g. the United States Civil Rights Movement, anti-apartheid, universal sufferance, Jarrow crusades, gay rights movement.
[6] World Economic Forum Annual Meeting, retrieved from https://www.weforum. org/events/world-economic-forum-annual-meeting-2020/about.

become the photo-op for many world leaders), and panel sessions presenting the latest thinking in globalisation, new technology, and investment. These remain, of course, but in recent years the discourse has seen a crescendo of interest and speakers from sustainable development and the environment, social justice and equality, diversity and inclusion, the future of the world of work, and new models of economic development such as the circular economy. It is too early to say whether these are now mainstream for the Forum and its Davos visitors, but there may be a consensus reaching a critical mass that the tired theme of continuous growth must change. The Forum refers to the Fourth Industrial Revolution as a concept in its development and, from 2021, prompted by the public health crisis in response to the global COVID-19 pandemic, it intends to launch what it calls The Great Reset, a series of summits with

> 'a commitment to jointly and urgently build the foundations of our economic and social system for a more fair, sustainable and resilient future.'[7]

Is this radical and new change, or old wine in new bottles? Predictions of rapidly worsening ecological, environmental, and climate change are now turning into reports of it happening, with evidence. Should we look to something like WEF to lead the way on this? Its statements pack a punch, but can the Forum be the change they want to see? Does collective change happen (paradoxically) only at the level of change in the individual firm?

Every organisation changes. This feels obvious to say, but what does that mean? What sort of a thing is change? Are you measuring the properties, dimensions, and measurable facts of the organisation, or is change the relationship between you and what you perceive? If a company profitably makes rubber tyres at one time and

---

[7]The Great Reset: A Unique Twin Summit to Begin 2021 (2020). Retrieved from https://www.weforum.org/press/2020/06/the-great-reset-a-unique-twin-summit-to-begin-2021/.

profitably makes mobile phones at another, then other than in the name of the product, has it changed? Is change objective or subjective? Objective, quantitative change is what occupies us when we try to relate to change, but this makes very little sense. A practical issue for leaders and managers is the nature of change in terms of chains of past cause and effect, but if the organisation is in good health, this can be left to the realm of management. More liberating would be to delve into how we understand and act on change as emergent and contingent, which means looking at it qualitatively and subjectively.

Two Views of Change

There are two modes of thinking about the nature of change in leadership and management.

(i) *Change starts with an idea, and then the idea results in action.* First the interpretation of meaning, then a move to make it real. The way to change something is to get on top of it. In this mode, ideas are the engine for sustaining a business, because business is an idea. Someone, usually an individual and usually a male (which makes this narrative of change a good fit with our current picture of leadership and leaders), comes up with an idea. Then they turn this into a goal that can be achieved by getting people to act on it in a coordinated way. The idea contains the goal. It follows that the coordination of efforts by those who have understood the idea is what produces a result. Any other result, consequence, or side-effect of this planned set of actions is not considered part of the idea and therefore assumed not to be the responsibility of the leader.

(ii) *Change emerges from action, only later coalescing into an idea.* First the right ingredients, then the interpretation of meaning. The way to change is by getting underneath it. In this mode, the leader waits to see what the idea is, knowing that they only need to know the best way to work with what is already clear must be done.

How change is framed will determine how leaders interact with followers. There are many possible ways of looking at this, but two may be more relevant for the Integrated Leader.

Dialectic Change (Thesis — Antithesis — Synthesis)

In a dialectic, any idea that exists, or any idea proposed, necessarily sets up its opposite, or its negation.[8] We therefore may understand an idea by what it is not. When someone proposes a change in an organisation, they use the present situation to do so. This might explain why there are relatively few genuinely original ideas in business in comparison to the volume of ideas being proposed overall. The current state must in some way stand in contradiction to the proposed change, and very often we see that leaders try to use the current state as a force for change. In this way, the planned change will try deliberately to be very different from the current state, but the change will always be coded with the present situation. If planned changes do not work out, then its alternative is brought into play using the same dialectic process. This to-and-fro is familiar in many organisations that zig-zag from one change initiative to the next. It is exhausting for employees, stakeholders, and often for customers, too.

In the dialectic, however, the forces of opposing ideas are eventually resolved in a sort of progression of ideas or synthesis. A synthesis is supposed to be a new and more advanced idea that has transcended the first two by resolving their differences. In plain English, things sort themselves out and settle into a new steady state in theory. This is said to be how progress is achieved, and it has been a very influential concept in economics, politics, and social justice since it was elaborated in European philosophy, most notably by Georg Hegel in the 1820s as an idealistic process to get to truth.

---

[8] Another way of saying this is that any idea is already proposed by its opposite.

Crudely put, this describes one way of justifying the whole concept of leadership as the process of facing, managing, and resolving possibilities to design and then realise 'better', or 'more', or whatever we have chosen to define as the desirable future state and goal. In this view, ideas are information and have a causal power. They are the mechanism for organisational becoming. This is popular and powerful in modern strategic management and, if you think this way, it will follow that you look for and champion people who sound like they have strong ideas that stand in (positive) opposition to the current situation. When you combine this with the conventional wisdom that the purpose of business is the efficient and effective exploitation of the environment to achieve the organisation's mission, you have a recipe for a non-stop and neverending search for perfection and size. This is part of our culture now. Change leadership when based on ideas before action sees ideas as principles that matter not because they are in tune with how things are, but because they can be applied for competitive advantage.

The principal objection to change as a dialectic processing of ideas is that it does not seem to work very well in open systems. As stated earlier, most change initiatives do not resolve the contradictions that people face as staff running an organisation one way while simultaneously being implored to run it another way. Further, planned change often produces a whole host of unintended consequences that no one saw coming because everyone had their eyes on the tensions between past and future.

Holistic, or Systemic Change

The second approach says that change is what we call our perspective, later, after it is clearer what has emerged. Change is therefore a by-product of the act of sustaining a business, something we make as we go and discover when we look back (as the wake of the ship). This means that our actions do not necessarily rise from a thought-through progression towards an end goal or state. There need not be a 'why' to explain change, nor leadership of change, except in hindsight. Systemic change is never wishful thinking, nor is it unfulfilled. It is real.

With this circumspect view of change, the organisation never remains static, and its story is shaped and formed by constant adjustments to context, which is a complex description of relationships. One presupposition is that what the organisation does impacts the environment and what is going on in the environment impacts what the company does. A consequence is that the boundary conditions between organisation and environment are those where all the shots are called. The leader's skill is in reading and understanding those, much as a sailing ship's captain might understand not just the resources and skills of the mariners on the ship, but also the total conditions of sea and wind to navigate. The organisation maintains a certain amount of autonomy and cohesion from within but is not a closed system. This is an important point because how the organisation relates to and treats its environment is the same as how it relates to and treats itself. Damage one and you destroy the other. This organic and systemic view of an organisation (and perhaps of a society) would define what a leader is very differently from the dialectic, as was discussed in Chapter 4 with the overview of theory in leadership studies. Change is the default state of nature, a flow, and the ground-state of how we sense the world (back to the importance of difference in our epistemology in Chapter 3).

The dialectic view of change and the systemic view would both be consistent with the approach that, for example, diversity and inclusion (D & I) matter. In the dialectic, D & I would matter mainly as a contrast to the current (non-diverse and exclusive) situation. Action, leadership, taken by the organisation would be understood as an objective sign of progress. Furthermore, the individuals in the organisation would see themselves as being agents in the outcome. In all systemic or holistic views of change, D & I matter because we should always be able to find within us a recognition of their relevance, and not just because they might be currently absent. That awareness is the recognition that D & I principles do not need to be imposed, they are already there in a healthy, balanced system. If they are absent in the system, then there is a systemic issue, and just focusing on the introduction of policies to fill the gap will not work. The individual does not define the problem at the level of individuals because that would be to carry the pattern of the original problem into the solution.

The assessment of the result may be the same, outwardly, in both cases, but inwardly these are two very different interpretations of the health and well-being of the organisation.

Business stability is the fiction that the organisation exists in a steady-state, perhaps as a sequence of fixed states that are occasionally interrupted only by managed processes of reinvention, initiated and led by those at the top of the organisation's hierarchy. Alternatively, sustainability in business is the realisation that the organisation exists in a flow state of co-evolution with its environment. However, no organisation will be able to sustain itself, coordinate its resources, and remain a viable and going concern (in tune with the flow) unless it maintains a sufficiently stable self-image. There is still much work to be done, even when we see through the illusion of control and we allow everything to take its course. This is the art of Integrated Leadership.

Now reflect on your own experience. Think about how change is seen by your organisation. Which version do you see talked about? Which model do you see in reality? Is what you or your company says the same or different to what it does? And which view of its nature is closer to your personal and current conception of leadership?

Integrated Leaders move iteratively between a world of concrete, fixed states, and another of fluid relationships and patterns. The leader role, with one eye on being effective in the present and the other on being prepared for the future, fills the space created by the question:

"What is changing, and what needs to change?"

Perspective is everything because an organisation's alienation from its environment, usually to focus on satisfying the short-term demands of an internal set of stakeholders, can be its downfall. In the narrative of 'business as stability and continuity', time, events, and change are irreversible and linear. In the narrative of 'business as relation and emergence', time, events, and change are cyclical and oscillating. These are not easy courses to steer as a leader, not least because there are few cases where change, holistic or not, does not meet resistance.

Resistance to Change

Change is not an easy sell for individuals or organisations. There will be resistance and many change initiatives fail.[9] You have probably heard this last sentence before. A great many textbooks and nearly every academic paper on change and leadership include this as a caveat. What does this mean? Is it true, and if it is, why?

Explaining the whole (the complex) using the parts (the simple) sounds like it should work. But the simple (or the non-complex) is simple precisely because it is not what the complex is, and the complex is complex because it is not the simple. Reducing the complex to the simple often fails to deliver answers. To understand the complex we have to communicate another way, such as with metaphor, which is where one complex pattern has a useful resemblance to another complex pattern. The problem with metaphor in the leadership of change is that sooner or later the analogy will break down. It is impossible to 'do' change with metaphor if you see change as a linear process. Asking people to 'bite the bullet', 'embrace uncertainty', 'navigate', or 'get on board' when it comes to change are all signs that those in charge have missed the point. The environment is always more complex than the management and leadership tools we use to work in it. Kotter's eight-stage change model (Chapter 4) is an example of a good-looking recipe. The instructions for the cook are laid out clearly, but the ingredients are unpredictable. Not only might they not match the recipe, but you may find that they have minds of their own. Can this be a clue as to why so many change initiatives fail? Are they too crude?

---

[9] Usually the estimate given is that three-quarters of change initiatives fail.

Conventional wisdom in change management says that change initiatives run into trouble because people resist them. The reason they do not succeed is that people do not understand the need for change, or they feel the need to protect the status quo more. Sometimes it is proposed that trust is the issue, which is a devious idea that may be based on confirmation bias. The classic response to this is to hit employees and staff even harder with re-education and training, while also stepping up the charm offensive. If that stalls, then coercion may be the way to do it. People's actions tend to be a symptom, not a cause, so it is incredibly unfair — and inaccurate — to blame a change failure on them. If there is resistance, then the resistance is a good indicator that the thinking behind the change the leadership is proposing is forced. If a change project is there to allow the executives to justify their salary, differentiate themselves from their predecessors, or copy what everyone seems to be doing, then resistance may be a sign of a healthy organisational system.

This does not mean that the organisation will abandon the idea of adjusting or reinventing what it does. Nor does it mean that people will not change. When a change is organic, people get it. They may not have seen the need to change ahead of time, so the function of leadership as a call to action is still valid, but they will have a strong sense of whether what is being proposed as change is real or fake.

Wicked Problems

'Wicked' is a great word to describe a special class of problem or issue that is broad and involves many stakeholders and interests, and that does not lend itself to generalisation, simple analysis, or quick fix. It was originally proposed for use in social science in 1973 by Horst Rittel and Melvin Webber.[10] Rittel defined wicked problems as

---

[10] Rittel, H. W. J. and Webber, M. M. (1973). Dilemmas in a general theory of planning. *Policy Sciences*, 4(2), 155–169.

'A class of social problems which are ill-formulated, where the information is confusing, where there are many clients and decision makers with conflicting values, and where the ramifications in the whole system are thoroughly confusing.'[11]

The systemic nature of a wicked problem, whether large or small, evokes the fourth leadership question from Chapter 4, 'what are the effects of what we do?'. Only when we stop the game of 'where did it begin?' and 'who is to blame?' will it be possible to treat wicked problems in a way that starts to untangle their inherent insolubility.

The World Health Organization (WHO) declared the novel coronavirus outbreak a public health emergency of international concern on January 30, 2020. It is fair to say that the events around the globe in the remainder of 2020 and into 2021 were unprecedented in living memory, with many elements that were unclear, confusing, complex, wide-ranging, long-running, multiple, inconclusive, and inter-connected. This describes a textbook wicked problem because every part of society is affected, and no part of society has all the answers.[12] What is more, no single part of society can definitively state what the problem is... and this is rather the point. So how your organisation dealt with COVID-19 and the economic side of the pandemic will have been a very valuable learning laboratory for you as a leader. Now more than ever, it is necessary to think critically about change and leadership. We will be dealing with the political, economic, and social consequences of the COVID-19 outbreak for some time. What should the Integrated Leader's response be, in the presence of such doubt, volatility, and uncertainty in the economy? This is where we can usefully use the interruption to survey innovative and developing alternative business models. Here are two, by way of example.

---

[11] As cited in Buchanan, R. (1992). Wicked Problems in Design Thinking, *Design Issues*, 8(2), 5–21.

[12] Brexit, the climate crisis, obesity trends, population growth, and waste management are all contemporary examples of wicked problems. But organisations face their own issues that have the same sorts of insoluble characteristics.

1. The Plural Economy

In recent years, veteran strategy professor Henry Mintzberg has called for a rebalancing of three key sectors in society: the public, the private, and what he terms the plural (or civil) society. The plural sector is sometimes called the third sector, and it stands on its own, but any one of the three dominates, he says, the outlook is always unstable and unhealthy. The chief characteristic of the plural sector is that organisations within it are owned (or run) by those in them. A great many of society's functionalities rely on a healthy plural sector as it includes NGOs, support groups, community associations, lobbying groups, co-operatives, charities, foundations, and social movements. Mintzberg argues that in much of the developed world, the private sector has been so dominant that there has been a decline in (or ignorance of) the value of the plural sector. The private sector has incurred social and environmental impact which are unbalancing the overall system (except perhaps some of the financial institutions that measure and store wealth in money). We need a healthy private sector because most people work there, but they vote in the government-run public sector, and they live in the plural sector, Mintzberg says. The community, and sometimes the grassroots, needs to be encouraged to re-assert themselves in elements of civic society[13] and in social campaigns for change.

This may well be so, and there is often good evidence of stability in communities where all three elements are in a good dynamic balance, but this does not yet represent a blue-print for what companies should be doing or what the new business model should be if current business models are not appropriate.

2. The Circular Economy

Short-term planning goes with short-term thinking, but its consequences often tend to end up in landfills. Future generations, perhaps even beginning with the next one, will rightly wonder how on Earth anyone ever thought that the linear economic business

---

[13] There is a nod here to two of the leadership questions in Chapter 4 ('What could be?' and 'Who shall we follow?').

model, the 'take–make–waste' approach that grew in influence exponentially during the 1950s and 1960s, would ever be a sustainable idea. They might wonder why no one pointed this out earlier than the context forced them to. Perhaps it will be a case that we did not change our economic model because at the time we did not need to. Or perhaps because we could not convince ourselves that we needed to. Are we at an economic tipping point? Will forward-looking entrepreneurs, courageous policy-makers, and determined consumers force us to adapt to current realities? Has the circular economy's time come?[14]

A circular economy[15] has three distinctive features:

1. *Reduce:* Lowering and eliminating waste by designing it out. This is not just a move away from growth fuelled by the extraction from the environment of non-renewable resources, it is a move towards placing only sustainably renewable resources into the process, and of identifying how any waste product can be recycled or repurposed. This ethos runs through the supply chain vertically as well as horizontally. The idea is to do more with less.

This links to the value chain aspect of an organisation's business model. The next two points connect to the value proposition with customers and stakeholders.

---

[14] The phenomenon of multiple inputs is found in every complex living system. There are three prerequisites for sustainable living systems:

1. An ecology of sufficient robustness such that conditions may persist that sustain life. Destroy the environment and you end up destroying yourself.

2. A capacity and facility in living organisms to differentiate, process, and respond to the conditions of the environment while retaining the ability to remain adaptable. It's no use giving up your ability to change when adapting to a change.

3. A capacity for agreement on what conventions (punctuation) are useful, what hierarchy preserves those conventions, and how many there will be. If we don't come together in harmony and in tune with the environment, we are doomed.

[15] One of the best sources of information on this is the Ellen MacArthur Foundation, https://www.ellenmacarthurfoundation.org/explore/the-circular-economy-in-detail.

2. *Reuse:* Discourage the culture of single-use products (or services?). Prolong the life of every product and every resource used. Refurbish older products, designing them to be repaired rather than replaced, and repurposed rather than recycled (throwing away is not an option, ideally). Recognise that every waste by-product can be a new starting point for another circular process, as happens in nature. One industry's waste is another's raw material.

3. *Recycle:* Perhaps the most visible facet of a circular economy for consumers is the recycling of a product and the materials used to pack, ship, and contain it. Recycling schemes have been around for a very long time, picking up pace in response to very high levels of consumer use of materials. It has only recently become part of the design process back down through all elements of the supply chain, however, which could include sourcing raw materials that are made using recycled materials. Another way of phrasing the third feature is that we need economic systems that regenerate natural ecosystems.

These principles can be used to bespoke circular business models (CBMs) appropriate to large, medium, or small businesses, and different types of industries in developed and in emerging economies. Every case is unique, each economic circle a fit with a unique context. In the medium-term, CBMs may be measured by how restorative and regenerative they are. In the short-term, however, the task is for linear businesses to cross a threshold in their thinking that calls into question much of what they will have taken for granted. There is a lot of inertia to overcome, not least because theory around the circular economy has not emerged from mainstream management theory of the last 50 years. For example, the logic of 'reduce' goes against the grain of economic activity presupposed on 'more is more.' The circular economy is a coalition of ideas from many domains and it would be fair to say that it has yet to find its unifying exemplars. If it is not to become another variant of corporate social responsibility (CSR) and a footnote to the annual report, then the circular economy requires leadership equal to the task, and leaders who fit that space. Many current leaders do not have what it takes. Yet.

Liminal Spaces for Leaders

Resistance to change may be experienced within a system, but there is personal inertia to deal with as well. If the current paradigm is not sustainable, then change at the personal level will not be just to tweak the current identity; it potentially is a whole new identity. This means we can re-examine the personal development question. We do so in terms of sequences of thresholds to cross to get to strong self-awareness. The journey over a threshold often contains a point of no return, but the area on either side of that point also represents a shift or change in perspective where neither the past nor the future is concrete. This is the liminal space, that noticeable in-between feeling in life you get between one identity and another. There are three types of liminal change:

1. *Ritualised changes of identity (status)*
   Guided processes of change that usually happen in a community setting, that have a known outcome and a fixed duration.
   Liminality was first coined in *Rites of Passage* (1908) by anthropologist Arnold van Gennep[16] to describe how societies and groups transition members from one group membership identity to another. The process of crossing these thresholds has three steps: (i) a mental or spiritual separation from the old state, (ii) a temporary transition, and (iii) incorporation into the new. Many societies and religions exhibit planned movement from one life-stage or status to another, often in elaborate ceremonies. The result is generally seen as movement another rung up a ladder, and professions work with something like this as a presupposition. In truth, the same pattern is found

---

[16] Van Gennep, A. (2019). Rites of Passage, 2nd edition, Chicago, IL: Chicago University Press.

repeated at all levels of organised society. It seems we all tend to feel more relaxed when we can see where we belong vis-à-vis each other's statuses.

2. *Individual journeys of personal reinvention (deconstruction of identity)*
Change that feels revolutionary or chaotic, perhaps with an unsure outcome and timeframe. If guided, then only in a limited way, for example, by a mentor.

In the 1960s, a British anthropologist called Victor Turner revisited van Gennep's ideas of liminal states. In keeping with the times, Turner saw that betwixt and between in modern life was more like a bountiful confusion of possibilities under the control of the individual, rather than an organised transition within society's strata. A personal reinvention of identity is when we feel we are in limbo, lost in no-man's land, at sixes-and-sevens, or de-mob happy, in retreat, stuck in the wilderness, and so on. Here, personal identity is in flux and transition, but not in an orderly, structured way and perhaps not with elders to act as guides. Existing structures or certainties are being revolutionised. Not one thing or another, in this state, all is possible and everything up for grabs. Out of the chaos can emerge a new order of things.

Perhaps you can see how both version 1 and version 2 are present for individuals in the business world. Companies may replace the traditional community fabric, and have institutionalised rites of passage, such as promotion, where support, training, and mentoring are explicit in the process. These are recognisable narratives, with established plots, recurring characters, and roles that are repeated. When individuals experience passage from one identity to another internally, this sort of change is more haphazard and improvised, though just as profound. People go through personal moments of chaos that lead to personal change. In this space, you are writing your own script, even as you seek advice from experts or elders. Liminality usually defines itself between two stable states, but there is a third aspect.

3. *Being in a state of constant reinvention (rolling identity)*
Change feels like the norm and is guided by a flowing self fully in tune with context.

For some, there may be no pre-formed 'other side' to the threshold (or a need for one) and therefore no way to define the liminal state in terms of its before and after. What takes precedence in experience is the sensation of an unfolding quality of changing. 'From what?' and 'to what?' are left aside to be discovered later, and even abandoned. In business, any of the global and electronically connected worlds of commerce, such as fintech, could be studied as manifestations of open-ended liminality. In the personal sphere, if you learn to let go of the attachment for a coherent and explicable career script, with ordered, predictable, and objective steps, your world can become a rolling liminal space.

Transition can bring with it personal doubt, uncertainty, and confusion, and if you make doubt your foreground, then change events outside your control, such as being fired, or being hired, can leave you feeling marginalised and under-resourced. This brings us back to the whole subject of mindset for reflection, awareness, and the assumption of beginner's mind in Chapter 1, as well as mental health and well-being in Chapter 8. Are there any short-cuts to follow in this?

'Yes, and...'

We often think of transitions as treacherous and turbulent whirlpools. But equally, the frenetic energy in a whirlpool is also a pattern of stability in water. Liminal spaces can be hectic, and they can also afford time and space to craft more of your destiny, discover more creativity, see more opportunities, learn, work the world out, play, become more independent, and be divergent. The still point of the turning world, so to speak, is you, and around you there is a field in which life is continuously being created. The Integrated Leader's twin tasks are uplifting:

To care for the future and
To live fully while doing so

A good example of the second comes in the form of 'yes, and...' thinking. The idea is best known from the world of comedy improvisation (improv) and is a mindset that replaces a rebuttal with acceptance. If you audit yourself and those around you, especially at work, for how many times you hear 'Yes, but...' (or its equivalent[17]), you will begin to see why changing from *but* to *and* is such a powerful shift. 'Yes, but...' builds a wall of objection to block out a new idea, and 'Yes, and...' opens the gates to the new idea and welcomes it in as a chance to add. This process of accepting and not negating changes the frame. 'Yes, and...' not only disarms the external objector, but it also dissolves your internal negative voice. From here, it is almost impossible to be defensive. 'Yes, and...' is a creative step that raises everyone's spirits. This could be the single most influential and ridiculously simple perspective shift you can apply immediately.

Leadership is conventional in that it relies on agreement on what things are and what they mean. The agreement requires empathy and compassion. When we start a change, we select what we are conditioned to select. We react how we are conditioned to react. With awareness and with time, you can search beyond your constraints.

Tasks of Change

We have been discussing change, so here is a prompt for you. The following are four short experiments in how you act and react to change. If you decide to do these, then for each step note as you go

(1) How do you feel beforehand?
(2) How do you feel during the change experiment?

---

[17]Surrogates include 'on the other hand', 'however', 'still', or 'even so', as well as body language that deflects, defends, or deflates. Yes, and is not the same as being relentlessly positive or applying wishful thinking.

(3) How do others around you react?
(4) What is the learning, for you?

In ascending order of disruption:

Task 1: Eat a new food or drink a new drink. Choose something that you can safely consume but would never normally try.

Task 2: Make a noticeable and significant change in the layout in one of the spaces you use. For example, you could move furniture around at home, or in the office.

Task 3: Change something about your image or social identity. For example, wear something you would not normally wear, attend an event you would not normally go to, or switch a well-established work routine or habit.

Task 4: Confront something you have been avoiding, such as an unpleasant situation. This is context-dependent, of course, but could be anything from going out for an evening all by yourself, to speaking to a person you wouldn't normally go near, or to some-one you know you don't agree with.

Reflecting on the Integrated Leader's Manifesto (Leading Self with the Community)

#10

'Leaders have the power to transform and affect the world. I become a leader when I remind myself and others each day that the goal of collective transformation is a priority and more important than individual goals of personal success. True success is the success of the community.'

Does the individual form the group, or does the group form the individual? This may sound an odd question, but how you answer this has all sorts of implications for the role of leader.

It is impossible, of course, to apply a label such as 'leader' without implying the existence of an individual, a person who occupies it. But it is meaningless to call a person a leader in isolation. Leadership implies relationship, and relationship implies a 'between.' We usually think of this in terms of a relation between the person who is leader and the person or people who are followers.

Other relationships and contexts are just as important because the Integrated Leader must see and deal with them in terms of their ego. For example, there is the relationship a leader has with their predecessor(s), and with their assumed successor(s), which form the two ends of an individual's legacy with other individuals.

Another important connection is between the leader and the organisation as a whole, which is not quite the same thing as the relations with the people who work there. Understanding this is essential to see the point of interdependence in this manifesto item.

Integrated Leadership sees that the leader is in service of something beyond, more than, and independent of the leader. If the leader places themselves ahead of their organisation, their leadership role will have the opposite effect, that of disintegration.

The leader who places their reputation ahead of that of the organisation will spend their time and other people's energy proving they are in charge. This is stressful and will always take its toll both on the organisation and the leader. The leader who is centred in themselves, who sees their rightful place in the organisation, can occupy the role without ego and can preside over an organisation that can thrive. There is a compelling argument that the best and most effective transformational leaders are those that the organisation does not need to see all the time, who are rarely heard but are listened to when they speak, who force nothing, and who stop when the job is done. This doesn't mean they don't have their own ideas or their needs, but they first see the whole. Personal ambition can be shaped by that rather than the other way round. Equally, they view the parts of the organisation with empathy and compassion and can place others above their own without losing any of their authority.

The greatest influence comes when the leader trusts the organisation to know what is best, including the organisation's trust in that person as its leader. Health and well-being start from inside and move out. However, as a point of philosophical principle in leadership, you need to consider whether you should expect others to rise to your level of understanding and example, or you should lower yourself to theirs.

Chapter 11

The Principle Uncertainty

*The optimist proclaims that we live in the best of all possible worlds; and the
pessimist fears this is true.*

James Branch Cabell (1926)[1]

Because

We use 'because' in two ways. It can mean something coming to be
from antecedents or something that is going to be as a result. One
looks back to explain, the other looks forward to predict. These are
the two sides of why, cause becoming effect, and effect becoming a
new cause. For example, why this book? Well, this book because
there were hundreds of hours of workshops fuelled by an idea, and
then a publisher, and then hours of writing ('because' as cause).
And, because there is this book, its ideas can come into other people's view and then their thoughts, and perhaps into their experience ('because' as intent or future effect). 'Because' feels explanatory
and exploratory. It can also be circular.

What are the 'becauses' in your business? What comes to
mind? Presumably, your organisation exists because of its antecedents. But the fact of its existence serves many possible outcomes; it
can be the cause of things. Again we see how past and future are
just measures of the present. There is a rather lovely expression

---

[1] Cabell, J. B. (1926). *The Silver Stallion: A comedy of redemption*, Book four, Ch. XXVI,
London, United Kingdom: The Bodley Head.

from the Southern African cultural tradition and philosophy of *ubuntu* often expressed in English in the phrase 'I am because we are'. To fully appreciate its poetic importance, you must embrace both the why of prior reasons and the why of prospective impact and potential.[2]

I take as my challenge at the closure of the book to reflect on what I think are its 'becauses'. One 'because' has been to get closer to my definition of personal development.[3] My observation in that regard has been that in life the more you strip away, the more remains. That immediately feels problematic and inadequate, even if it does capture the process and intention of the writing. Perhaps I, along with everyone else, have been labouring under the illusion that there is something to fix, and that what needs fixing is inherent uncertainty about ourselves? We are in a world of much clutter. We horde intellectual objects every bit as much as we collect material ones. Our thoughts are sometimes piled so high, they block out the light and we trip over them in our darkness. And like many hoarders, we both admit the problem and find it almost impossible to part with any of it. Because you just never know when it might be useful. In many of our identities, most visibly when we are in leadership roles, the prevailing discourse encourages us when we communicate to be set permanently on 'transmit'.[4] Is this because in their search for what is wrong, others are encouraged to be set permanently on 'receive'? We are always looking up and outside for answers to questions from within. Anything we say and everything we hear is heavily filtered through multiple interpretations.

---

[2] Used on its own, 'because' can signify an end to debate, or a withholding of information. I celebrate and look for these sorts of subtleties and the uncertainties that carry the stream of meanings.

[3] 'Personal development is the identification and removal of those restraints that limit the likelihood of sustainable individual, organizational, social, and environmental health and well-being.'

[4] Don't be fooled by the inclusion of listening in leadership models. There's almost always an implicit 'in order to' hidden in there.

We see how it matches or adds to the piles of things we already have, but our minds are full.

Why? Because.

Giving Some Thought to Thought

You think. You have a mind. Thought is a neural activity, but not all neural activity is thought.

One of the because-prompts for me (I cannot put it more elegantly, I'm afraid) is that managers and leaders should learn how they think before they learn what to think. Mind is mental process. How we define mind ends up being how we define thought because thought is a mental process. The consensus view is that mind is an emergent property of brain activity and that thought is a special subset of that.[5] Mind makes thought possible, thought makes mind accessible. However, the definition of mind as neural brain activity falls short in some respects. If thought has a physical source, is thought reducible to matter and biochemistry? Thought is becoming mappable in brain activity, but if thought is brain activity, this becomes a tautology. What is more difficult is how the material functioning of the brain explains consciousness, and qualia[6] (subjective experience). How is meaning constructed, and how is it conveyed from person to person?

These are some of the most difficult questions to answer in philosophy. Some researchers believe that mental activity, (thought, feelings, self-concept, and so on) can only be material. We do not yet know what they are, but when we find the answer, they say, it

---

[5]This is a very tricky point, because we express thought in language, but we may not be sure whether there is such a thing as a thought that is non-linguistic. There must be, because there is mental activity to generate language, but it's the fridge light problem again.

[6]Qualia are properties or attributes, such as the sensation of 'greenness' of grass, the importance to one person of a particular friend, or any mental state that has no referent, physical quantity in the real world. Qualia convey what something feels like.

will be in material explanation. Others say we might well find out how the brain generates consciousness but that will still not tell us what consciousness is; we have not yet worked out how to ask the question. If subjectivity is not reducible to neurology, then what alternative explanations are there? How do brain, mind, and thought relate? One avenue has been to maintain, as dualists such as Rene Descartes and C. S. Lewis did, that mental states are not reducible to physical states because although they are real, they are non-material. Mind (the self? consciousness?) exists without the body. This argument begs the question in that it assumes what it is trying to find out (i.e. rather than asking whether there is a division, it assumes there is). I am not convinced.

Thinking is mental activity, and mental activity is systemic in the sense that it is inherent in, and characteristic of, a set of principles of organisation. Mental activity, cognition, is not the division of a whole into parts, but a description of the connections between parts. We cannot find consciousness in the brain, even though we cannot have consciousness without one.[7] Can we explain how we think by looking for similar patterns in other dynamic systems?

What would it mean to say an organisation thinks? Is there a way, if only figuratively, that an organisation has a mind? This is at once very easy and very difficult to answer. Easy, in the sense that organisations are social concepts, and it is people who constitute social concepts; in some way, an organisation is bound to resemble how we think. Difficult, however, in the sense that the culture of an organisation is complex and not purely the sum of the individuals within it. This is because the relationships between people are not properties of those people (as was pointed out in Chapters 2 and 3). A lot of the idea of leadership depends on bridging this gap. Formal similarities of patterns, metaphors, could reveal how an organisation maintains identity, holds a belief, adheres to a principle, or even exhibits an emotional state.

So, let us investigate. We start where everyone else does, in acknowledging that an organisation exists with something a little

---

[7] Although we can have a brain without consciousness.

more than a material basis. An organisation has artefacts and legal obligations, but these are insufficient to explain how an organisation is a system; bricks and windows do not have principles and mission statements. At the same time, an organisation's principles and mission statements are not identical to the beliefs and purposes of those who own it, those who work in it, or those who rely on it for their well-being. An additional idea is needed to explain how it is that a company generates a social field of its own. The (business) world is facing many wicked problems onto which our existing practical efforts, and our academic rigour, have failed to make much of an impact, so we must find this element by widening how we define mind. We should search for abstract, isomorphic patterns of relationships in common across different systems (that is a mouthful, I know). This may simply be a fancy way of describing what an Integrated Leader is doing. We need to challenge our thinking and stretch our minds (so to speak) a bit further.

Stop and Think: How do You Think?

People who speak more than one language fluently or to native speaker level can be thinking, dreaming, and conceptualising in different languages without translating. Are they having the same thought in each? Are they the same person in each? Holes between languages, the untranslatable, ineffable lexical gaps, are called *lacunae* and they tell us something very important about thinking because they suggest that language influences perception, which influences sense-making.[8] The literary critic George Steiner once said that every act of comprehension is an act of translation.[9] The fact that the famous Italian phrase *traduttore, traditore* crosses to English plainly enough as 'translator, traitor' while simultaneously failing to translate the pun of the original is a nice illustration of the

---

[8] This is sometimes known as the Sapir Whorf hypothesis.
[9] Steiner, F. (1998). *After Babel: Aspects of Language and Translation*, 3rd edition, Oxford, United Kingdom: Oxford University Press.

limitations of surfaced thought.[10] Anyone who creates, including a leader, is translating something into something else. Leaders represent a thought to achieve an outcome, and what gets to the surface is only a tiny fraction of what there is in the realm of thought. To have clarity of vision in creativity, the leader needs to know what is influencing their thinking.

Personal development is about health and well-being, so what are the possible biases you may have that might limit your sustainable equilibrium? There are three sources of influence on that kind of thought:

Social norms: The informal glue of the rules governing and constraining behaviour in society. Originally, the intellectual territory of the anthropologist, then the province of the sociologist, social norms are closely studied by economists, political scientists, marketers, salespeople, and philosophers (of course). Norms are usually said to be unplanned and emergent, although it is individuals that perpetuate them. Norms generally patrol the border between collective, social well-being, and self-interest.

Stereotypes: A stereotype is a single, reusable copy of something that would usually need repeated, re-assembly of several parts. The point of stereotypes is that they can be used regularly and quickly to save time. As shorthand, they can work well, but as they are fixed and unchanging, over time and with over-repetition they lose their accuracy, and eventually their relevance. Stereotypes will always set up preconceptions which become less and less accurate over time because contexts change (see what follows), and they carry less and less information until they are reified and become concrete, with the total loss of original reference.

Context: Context is scope. It has four aspects: the structure of a situation, the process of creation of a structure, the set of actions appropriate to a situation, and the frame for judgement of what

---

[10]Similar plays on words operate throughout the Tao Te Ching, a text mentioned more than once in this book, most notably in the first chapter.

does and what does not come within that scope. It is the ability to see the frame for what is going on, and most people are unaware of what their context is, or how to look for it. This is not a judgement, there are numerous unconscious biases that we all inherit. We do not know what we do not know, and we will not know until we are jogged with a little reality or discomfort.

If a leader acts in ignorance of these, the system will not tolerate that person for long. On the other hand, awareness of these does not amount to freedom from them, either. Norms, stereotypes, and contexts suck us in and pull us along, and for individuals as well as organisations, they create self-reinforcing patterns of beliefs and behaviours. If they are the only sources of identity and self-definition, they will cause us stress. Transformation is a buzzword in management and leadership. Yet, what organisation ever transforms its search for a new leader when the existing one fails? What new leader can ever practice leadership independent of the implicit expectation in the hiring process either (a) to do exactly the same as or (b) to do exactly the opposite of their predecessor? They are already drawn into the system even before they have started. The purpose of leadership often becomes stuck in whatever leadership pattern is already in the organisation.

Three Orders of Leadership

To summarise the point being made in this chapter, that of the difficulty of getting closer to integration, let us revisit a few of the aspects of leadership that have been covered earlier. In dealing with real-world problems, leadership manifests across three orders:

> The *first order* is the most common. Here, being a leader is a fairly mechanical component or a step/stage built into a model of management problem-solving. It is where leaders 'sort things out', 'get things done', or 'work out what we should do next.' It is a role we take on, and perhaps a persona we adopt, without necessarily seeing any deeper than the task at hand, or away from the

level of the organisation we are in. First order leadership seeks clarity and solutions, to calm things down, and to create or restore order and efficiency. Leaders use an internal definition of sustainability that equates mainly to keeping the organisation running well. Not restricted to senior, middle, or junior levels of responsibility, it can be found at all hierarchical niches and in any type of business. It seldom questions the context or general direction within which leadership is called for. Leadership of this order follows the rules with zero intention to rock the boat.

Second order leadership is forced upon the organisation when first order leadership fails. That failure may come from not reversing a general decline, not correcting for strategic drift, or not continuing an organisation's growth trajectory. Whatever the trigger, this is a demand for a change in the definition of what now counts as leadership. By this point, dwelling on the past story may be counter-productive and there may be a resigned feeling of 'we are where we are.' Second order leadership makes a new map of the known territory. It doesn't reinvent the territory, it reinvents the map. This requires sharp powers of observation and questioning of existing assumptions and context markers. If there is a systemic cause for business-as-usual failing, then this leadership may coincide with people being removed from the organisation. If done for the wrong reasons, the system will likely resurface the underlying issue by finding someone else's shoulders to put the problem onto, thereby creating a new cycle of first order leadership without addressing the underlying issue. Leadership of this order doesn't rock the boat, it builds a new one.

Third order leadership is a deeper challenge. It occurs when there is a need to question what sort of a thing leadership is in the first place. Whether it is up to the job, and whether there is any point to it at all. It asks, 'Is the problem that we face a leadership problem?' Third order leadership resembles an examination of 'the context *of* the context' within which problems are set. Third order leadership is revolutionary only because it wants to turn everything on its head. The usual leadership questions, models, frameworks, and theories have little relevance and are not good places to start. Third order leadership can generate reinvention, or deal with some very hard decisions, such as business closure. It can also be seen in cases where people leave one organisation to go and set up their own version somewhere else. We are squeamish about endings. Maybe the idea of an organisation having the same cycle of birth, life, and death that a person does is a little too close to the existential angst we feel about dying. Leadership of this sort queries why a boat in the first place.

The point is not the three descriptions but the link between them, which is an epistemological hierarchy. A taxonomy.

Transformation, integration, and peace of mind are very difficult to manufacture, even in a progressive and supportive educational setting. Most of us live a double life of contradictions and fragmentation. We maintain multiple selves and identities, we say one thing, do another, and believe a third. We do not live lives of deep integrity, complete and whole, untouched by a sense of alienation. Occasionally, we receive moments of insight, flashes of understanding, and some techniques may help practise the attention needed. Mindfulness, meditation, dialogue, and systemic learning can all do this, but because traditional management science presumes that problems are measurable and predictable, and that problem solving is an application of generalised principles, there has been only a limited version of integration on offer for most managers and leaders. Integration, wisdom, and health and well-being are often attained (when they are attained at all) despite and not because of the organisation and its culture. No one owes you any answers, no one is coming to rescue you from yourself. It is up to you, and it is down to you.

Untangling Integrated Leadership

The Integrated Leader is a human being. There is no doubt that being human is a prerequisite for being a leader, and little doubt a leader, in the end, only has what they and others know to bring the role to life. Human knowing is an emergent property of the rich and complex interplay of biology, sociology, and psychology. To integrate all that we know with all that needs to be done means working at a level where there is congruence between the organising principles we see in nature, those we see in organisations, and those we see in our minds. What drives everything going on in human systems is relational ('between'), not material properties. This is not difficult to understand if you agree that it's not the properties of a production department, human resource department, finance department, head office, salesforce, customer, supplier, inland revenue (and so on) that make a business, but the relationships between them.

As an educator, over the years I have developed my understanding of the process of personal development. I have come to question whether self-transcendence or self-actualization follow self-awareness, as is often suggested or implied in frameworks, models, and most self-help books. In part, the issue is certainly the difficulty in defining what awareness is, so I will start by speculating that the route to Integrated Leadership consists of three developmental descriptions of awareness, as in Figure 11.1.

1. *Entangled*

Being unaware or ignorant of something often makes absolutely no difference to quality of life, or appraisal of competence in a role. Much of the fabric of life can be safely assumed to be just that, a fabrication. We can live well oblivious to how much we are wrapped in this, up to a point. 'Entangled' means ignorance is

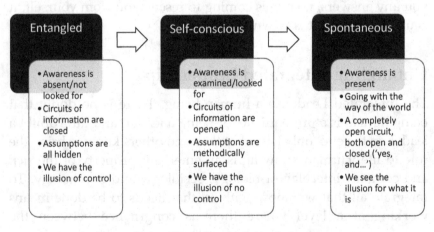

Figure 11.1.   Three descriptions of awareness.

becoming problematic because it is interfering with performance or with development. It is holding us back. An organisation led or managed by people who are in entangled states of unawareness may find itself lurching from one crisis to the next, with ever-more draconian change initiatives imposed by those who are trying to cure the symptoms and not the disease. As one process fails to achieve its goal, the next lurch — having started from the same prior assumptions — eventually proves ineffectual. And so on. Entanglement might not be seen, or seen only when the world around the leader or the organisation changes sufficiently to trigger one or more negative feedback loops on the system. The leader or their handlers may then notice and act to remedy the fundamental, erroneous assumptions. In either case, change starts when that threshold is crossed and not before.

2. *Self-conscious*
Understanding the pattern of your practice is key to personal development and bringing this to attention is a great step forward in self-awareness. Brought to awareness, you are asked to reserve your impulse to act, to solve, and close off the problem. But even then, you as a leader may be so entangled in your conditioning that you do not realise that any organisation-level reflection and rethink includes you. What is first needed is an environment for personal development where you replace or let go of your fix-it reflex. Conscious awareness begins in stepping back and examining one's inner life. In time, this critical thinking skill becomes a source of enlightenment in your management practice. The nature of conscious awareness is really what this book has been about. Multitasking is a myth. We can concentrate explicitly only on a very small number of things at once, perhaps only one. What makes it to our attention is very blinkered and narrow. You begin by focusing very intently on your practice and learn to question everything you once took for granted. This is the start, but self-consciousness can only take you so far.

Here is a leadership lesson, in the form of a poem that is over 2,000 years old. It has age, *and* it has relevance in today's corporate culture of performance management.

The need to win

When an archer is shooting for nothing
He has all his skill.
If he shoots for a brass buckle
He is already nervous.
If he shoots for a prize of gold
He goes blind
Or sees two targets —
He is out of his mind.

His skill has not changed, But the prize
Divides him. He cares,
He thinks more of winning
Than of shooting —
And the need to win
Drains him of power.

Chuang Tzu

Over-thinking the self leads to a new entanglement and can take you to the extreme of being unable to act because nothing can be taken quite as it appears to be. Becoming too self-conscious can make you lose the ability just to get back into the flow of the world that you were always a part of, even when you practised the art of being the conscious outsider, observing it all.[11] Self-conscious awareness can therefore end up as a stage of paralysis. If reflection replaces action entirely, a different kind of entanglement is experienced. The newly reflective leader is in danger of substituting unreflective action with reflective inaction.

3.   *Spontaneous*

Spontaneous action sounds as though it would be rather random, haphazard, and unprepared, but it is how you behave when you are completely in tune with the world around you. It is action without 'acting'. Actions arise naturally when we are in flow, and this is management practice where the leader follows the line of least

---

[11] Think of the tight-rope walker who effortlessly, thoughtlessly crosses the wire each night in their performance, until someone asks them how they do it. As soon as they think of it, they fall.

resistance. More accurately, they go with the grain. In spontaneous action, the leader fuses reflection and action as an improvisation between agent(s) and context. Improvisation does not contain the sub-category 'error'; everything is all right exactly as it is. Every action becomes a move in the right direction. This is a reminder of 'yes, and...' thinking and is a transcendent step for the Executive Master of Business Administration student (as it would be for a business school willing to reflect as deeply). It presents a paradigmatic challenge to "business as usual" without the need to set off a face-off on a battlefield. Leadership as a spontaneous state is unmediated, recursive, and immediate. Some of the themes within this, over time, become anchor points for a shifted worldview. Here are five possible such thinking points:

Mastery: Gradually becoming good at what you love doing (see the glossary: *kodawari*)

Alignment: Belonging. Fitting in. Finding your place

Legacy: The outcomes and achievements of your life, and the evidence you want to leave behind, or influence you want to have on others

Freedom: Choice in how you feel

Self-compassion: The most difficult skill of all.

The spontaneous is a return to the world as an intentional (business is purposeful), fully present, and active agent.

There is a seriousness in joking that the only way a person will ever know they did not need enlightenment is through becoming enlightened. That sounds flippant and is not. The same point is put rather more eloquently in the following quote, which comes from the golden period in the development of the Zen Buddhist tradition:

Before I had studied Zen for thirty years, I saw mountains as mountains, and waters as waters. When I arrived at a more intimate knowledge, I came to the point where I saw that mountains are not mountains,

and waters are not waters. But now that I have got its very substance
I am at rest. For it's just that I see mountains once again as mountains,
and waters once again as waters.

Ch'uan Teng Lu, 9th century[12]

This is one of my favourite quotations. Applied to leadership, it suggests that a leader who has a longing or wishful thinking that the situation should be any different than it is, realises that this is the way that sustainable change comes about. It can take a great deal of time for mountains and waters once again to be mountains and waters, and in career terms, that may only occur at or close to the peak.

The Furthest Reaches: Peace in Solitude

We have been given many freedoms in the 21st century, and fought for others. Most of us live without the worst of the outward deprivations of material poverty, lack of status, local and international conflict, and lack of treatments for disease and ill-health that previous generations were forced to endure. To have all this wealth and still squander the opportunity to live a full life inwardly is about as wasteful as it is possible to be. The question left when all other issues have been dealt with is 'am I free of myself?' This is the thinking of a quiet mind, one free of prejudice, bias, comparison, validation, and conditioning. This sort of thinking begins in itself when we have explored and exhausted all external routes of inquiry and found nothing there. It therefore will have no history. Solitude, which is the contentment of being alone with one's thoughts, even in a crowd, takes up no space and uses no energy because it sets up no resistance.

In the end, 'Who am I?' may turn out to be the ultimate rhetorical question. What are the characteristics of an Integrated Leader? I do not know for sure, but I start with:

---

[12] As quoted in Watts, A. (1962). *The Way of Zen*, New Orleans: LA: Pelican, p. 146; As quoted in Suzuki, D. T. (1961). *Essays in Zen Buddhism*, New York, NY: Grove Press.

> ➤ I do not see myself as separate and alien from the world. I no longer have the feeling that I am a stranger in a hostile world.
> ➤ I experience the world through its events. All my experience, even the conflictual and the painful, is framed by a wider pattern.
> ➤ I am true to my beliefs, and no belief I have is so fixed that it cannot change.
> ➤ I have peace with how things are. I start from there.

Keep the self-awareness question as open as possible. This is very difficult, as Jiddhu Krishnamurti pointed out:

'You are the trap. That means you have to break down your conditioning, yourself, the centre of the 'me' — which is the mainspring of the trap. It can be done without a single breath of effort. One who makes an effort to be free of the trap is further creating the trap. It breaks naturally without a single effort if you are aware of yourself as being the trap. Since you are the whole history of mankind, you are the embodiment of that trap. You cannot escape from yourself, you cannot run away; you have to see what you are. That is, you have to have self-knowledge, know about yourself — not about the higher self; there is no higher self — you have to know yourself, not through analysis but through watching, looking, observing.'[13]

Being this self-observant has enormous benefits. You reduce your stress levels, for one thing, and you tend to find that you are not as easily drawn into office politics or the minutiae of detail. It also leads to social development because systematically surfacing and questioning the basis of unspoken assumptions will, if taken to its conclusion, result in the broadening of scope beyond your interior world to your role and actions in society. A full definition of the Integrated Leader will not come simply from a naïve observing

---

[13] Jiddhu Krishnamurti, public talk 6 in Ojai, California, April 18, 1976, https://jkrishnamurti.org/content/you-are-trap-means-you-have-break-down-your-conditioning-yourse.

of leaders or followers, or from reading their accounts of their experiences. Or from this book. In truth, the enquirer must ask other questions and be prepared for an exploration into their own, innate uncertainty.

Personal development is about stepping out on your own to make your mark, in your own way. No-one can tell you definitively how to do this, or whether you will succeed. Are you living in your own way? For that, you must establish some principles without knowing for certain what they should be.

The principle uncertainty.

Reflecting on the Integrated Leader's Manifesto (Leading Self with the Community)

#11

'Willingness and attitude are the roots of our strength as a community. All members need time to reflect on the right balance of freedom and commitment. Spiritual maturity will give us the courage to move forward and grow. Every organisation works better in thought, word, and action when there is truthfulness.'

Between the extremes of having no thought or esteem for oneself and having no thought or esteem for others, there is a middle way. Needed for your well-being as part of an organisation, it provides a healthy flow of give and take in exchange and is the result of the type of awareness talked about throughout this Manifesto. It is epitomised in a spiritual maturity where there is an open and honest acknowledgement of four things to do with self-awareness, namely that:

(i) *Even if I notice my hidden assumptions, my conditioning will expect everyone and everything else to change, not me. I will not want to let go of my attachments to my beliefs and identity*

(ii) *There is no model, 'truth', or way for self-awareness, and no one is coming to the rescue. Understanding starts and ends with me*

(iii) *There is really nothing I can (or need to) do to change, except in how I react to the world*

(iv) *I admit I'm fallible*

People's needs and requirements are not static, or consistent. We all face challenges, downs, and moments of doubt or fear and vulnerability. Equally, we all have successes and know what it means to feel engaged, enthused, and creative. If everyone accepts this, and if the organisation embraces people as they are, and does not judge them or expect a pretence, then the willingness and the mindset for followership, even through difficult times, will be present. This includes recognising that things will go wrong, that people will come and go (and need to be acknowledged when they leave), and that eventually every business will end when its purpose is fully served.

For all that we try to explain things by breaking them into pieces, parts, and processes, an organisation is the best explanation of itself. To paraphrase the mathematician and cyberneticist Norbert Wiener, the best material model for a healthy organisation is another, or preferably the same, healthy organisation.

The Integrated Organisation is integrated when it is paying full and complete attention — to the inside as well as the outside — with no set point of view. It still makes mistakes, it still has successes, but is not concentrating on either in the same way that it used to. While experience before now is a resource, the Integrated Organisation safely dies to its past insofar as this is not the determinant of what it might do now, in the present. What the organisation chooses to do now in the present is what becomes its future.

For an organisation to reach its own sort of awakening, this truth must be lived by its leaders. This commitment to truthfulness, come what may and in the face of a lot of programming in corporate life that leads to hiding the truth, requires courage.

***

This was the last of the reflections on the Integrated Leader's Manifesto. Remember, the aim of each of the 11 items is for you to pay attention — over time — to anything that resonates with you or strikes you as important.

Then the question to ask yourself is:

If this is true, what changes do I need to make at work to live this?

Appendix 1

A List of Human Universals

Adapted from Donald Brown[1]

abstraction in speech & thought, interpretation for meaning

actions under self-control distinguished from those not

age statuses, age terms

anthropomorphisation

attachment, desire

beliefs (including false)

beliefs about fortune and misfortune

binary cognitive distinctions

childcare

childhood fear of loud noises

choice making (choosing alternatives)

classification

classification of kin

coalitions, co-operation

collective identities

conflict

conjectural reasoning

cooking

crying

culture & cultural variability

dance

death rituals

decision-making (including collective)

distinguishing right and wrong

diurnality

dominance/submission

dreams

emotions

empathy

---

[1] Brown, D. (1999). Human Universals, in *The MIT Encyclopedia of the Cognitive Sciences*, edited by Robert A. Wilson and Frank C. Keil, reprinted courtesy of The MIT Press.

entification (treating patterns and relations as objective things)

etiquette

explanation

facial communication (including masking/modifying of)

facial expression of anger, contempt, disgust, fear, happiness, and surprise

fairness (equity), concept of

family (or household)

fear of death

future, attempts to predict

gestures

good and bad distinguished

group living

habituation

hope

in-group distinguished from out-group(s), in-group biases

intention

jokes, humour, laughter

language

law (rights and obligations), law (rules of membership)

leaders

likes and dislikes

linguistic redundancy

making comparisons

marking at phonemic, syntactic, and lexical levels

measuring

memory

mental maps

metaphor

mourning

music

myths

narrative

nouns

numerals (counting)

onomatopoeia

pain

past/present/future

person, concept of

planning

play

poetry/rhetoric

private inner life

rhythm

rites of passage, rituals

sanctions

self, distinguished from other

sexual attraction

shelter

social structure

statuses and roles (ascribed and achieved)

succession

symbolism

taboos

taxonomy

time

tools and tool making

trade

true and false distinguished

turn-taking

worldview

Appendix 2

A Learning Journal Extract

This is an extract from the learning journal of an Executive Master of Business Administration (MBA) student at Henley (used with permission).

'A colleague of mine purposefully sought the help of a therapist during his MBA journey with Henley. This always seemed a bit excessive and indulgent. I've changed my mind about that, here's why:

The personal development that you go through in the first two years is substantial — at least, that was my experience. If it isn't, you weren't paying attention. Or perhaps I just reignited a natural curiosity that had become stifled by the demands of adult life! The downside of this accelerated personal growth is that you're alone in this — the change happens inside your mind, but the people around you aren't on the same journey. A personal challenge has been to not be overly critical of people who haven't gained the same level of insight into a situation as me because I had spent time studying different perspectives. At the same time, however, it is my strong conviction that you have an obligation to improve your understanding of any given issue by purposefully reading as widely as possible. It is absolutely necessary for anyone who wants to live an impactful life. Empathy is key to navigating this tension — with others as well as within yourself.

At the moment I'm reading Mastering Leadership by Adams and Anderson, where they discuss how leadership capability and adult development go together. It's fascinating reading, but I realize that like most people, I've gotten stuck at a level of development that enabled me to function effectively enough to maintain my life as it is, but is inadequate to do anything more, or to extract the full worth from life. It would have been impossible for me to even recognize this, let alone make a decision to purposefully pursue further personal development, had I not gone on this journey. I'd go as far as to say that I wouldn't have been able to grasp the full extent of the book's message, had I not already invested in personal development through this MBA programme. It is frustrating as much as it is gratifying!

I know without a doubt that this is only the beginning of pursuing further personal growth for me. I am optimistic about the future; at the same time, I'm not in a hurry. There is much still to learn, and a great deal to be gained.'

Glossary

Abstraction A type of thinking which uses a simplification to represent the complexity of the real world. Very often these simplifications appear as symbols. An abstraction is the deliberate and sometimes forced isolation of a concept away from the mundane (everyday) into thought (imagination).

The Anthropocene Applied from the science of dating rocks in geology, formally this term has been proposed as a new interval of geological time – a new epoch. This asserts that the impact of human activity on Earth is resulting in changes visible in the stratification of mineral sedimentary deposits (as distinct from ongoing changes in the chemical balances in living systems, atmosphere, hydrosphere, etc. perhaps attributable to human activity). Many now believe that the marker for measuring the onset of the Anthropocene is the middle of the 20th century, specifically the fallout globally of radioactive material from atomic weapons tests in the 1940s and 1950s.

Assertiveness To be assertive is to stand up for yourself and your rights without affecting the rights of or putting down anyone else. To assert something is to state a claim, usually in terms of a right or a belief, and then take action to protect or defend it.

Authority   In leadership, authority is the probability, overall, that a person (or a group of persons) will obey or comply willingly with a given instruction on the strength of a perceived superior position/relationship of the person (or group) giving the instruction.

Awareness   Awareness is awareness, and vice versa (OK, that is too little). Awareness should be direct and unmediated (which makes language a barrier). Awareness is an open and intelligent mind-set that looks without judgement at how meaning is inherent in our punctuation of events. Awareness is when the observed and the observer are perceived as the same thing. This may only be a glimpse at first.

Body of Knowledge   Each knowledge domain or accepted category of human understanding contains its own set of concepts and its own way of structuring and using them. This is the 'what you need to know' to undertake a task or perform in a profession (for example) and is often formalised in education or training. Because this changes and expands over time, staying up to date is a must.

Compassion   Starting in a shared human experience, broad in its content and deep in its roots, compassion is the state of mind whereby people feel an identification with the emotions of others who may be in distress. Compassion is action emerging from an appreciation for the whole and without attachment or expectation of anything in return.

Contingent   We normally think of this as 'depending on', but the better meaning is that things are contingent when they are touching each other. Contact of this sort creates many likelihoods and possibilities, and here the random may play a part. To say that something is contingent is to be open to the unexpected and the potential, not to the dependent.

Creativity   An innate human talent, and one that is difficult to define. To create is to give birth to an idea, and to bring something into being from nothing. This requires imagination and invention and is liable to need time and hard work just as much as it takes inspiration and playfulness. Creativity is a description of an ability and a process, not a judgement of the worth of its output.

Feedback (1) In management, and probably in leadership (if leadership is a thing), feedback is a technique used for telling someone what you think about them or about their performance, or asking someone to tell you what they think about you or your performance. Positive feedback equals giving them your positives, negative feedback equals you giving or receiving negatives. Very little of this is ever unmediated and straightforward.

Feedback (2) In living systems and social systems, feedback is the return of a signal in a circuit to its origin, but in a modified or adjusted form. Positive feedback will send a system into runaway until acted upon by negative feedback loops. These will tend to dampen or reduce an amplification in a system. Sub-systems are controlled by wider systems in this way. The Sub-prime mortgage crisis of 2008 demonstrated both at work. The climate crisis may be our biggest test of feedback loops.

Freedom There are three sorts of freedom. (1) Freedom *to* (permission), (2) freedom *from* (safety and liberty), and (3) freedom *in* (peace in solitude). The first two are about the dynamic agreement, disagreement, and negotiation of relationships between the individual and the collective. Of the three, freedom in is the most useful to the Integrated Leader.

(A) Fundamental Anything necessary for the construction of an explanation for everything else. For any discipline, area, or subject in — for example — management and leadership to be coherent, there must first be a discussion of what is necessary as a prerequisite for anything else to be understood. In the last two or three hundred years, social science and management education have struggled to produce worthwhile or valid fundamentals. In leadership, a fundamental would in effect define what can and cannot be said about it. It would be the language in which all leadership theories and ideas would be 'written'.

Hubris   When we think of hubris, it is usually looking at someone whose excessive pride has preceded their fall. Like many human faults, hubris often looks like a positive at the beginning, in this case, one of self-confidence. Ambition is a cultural trait we often encourage, perhaps over diligence, and in individualistic societies this is sometimes inculcated independently of its balancing twin, humility. As with so much, these must be understood together. To have hubris without humility is arrogance, and very dangerous. But equally so is having humility without hubris. You require just enough hubris to reign in your humility, and vice versa.

Imposter Syndrome   The feeling nearly everyone gets from time to time that they do not deserve to be where they are, have been elevated into a position without proper scrutiny, and worry that colleagues know more than they do. It is often accompanied by a fear that others can see this and will point it out, with ridicule and shame. Numerous remedies are offered, many involving the idea of re-scripting the narrative in your head. Few point out that it is a social construct, not a psychological reality. You didn't invent it, so you cannot uninvent it except through changing the context.

Integrity   Describes when nothing is missing, removed, or taken away, and there is a wholeness of entirety. In the world of physical objects, integrity means something has held on to whatever was its original state. In a world of thought, emotion, intention, and morals, integrity means there has been no corruption, compromise, or deviation of character, principle, or sincerity.

Mind-set   One way of describing your heuristic (rule-of-thumb) way of seeing the world. Your mind-set is a relatively stable short-cut that prevents you having to think each time before you act. It also is what stops you seeing other ways of acting.

Personal Development 'The identification and removal of those restraints that limit the likelihood of sustainable individual, organizational, social, and environmental health and well-being'.[1] This definition presupposes that the task of the individual is to contribute to the whole by being whole.

Power For all that we think of power as being a question of authority, strength, or influence from position, in leadership it is the probability, overall, that a person (or group) is in a position to take an action even in the face of any resistance to that action. Power is a prediction about a relationship. An abstract of an abstract.

Self-esteem Esteem is the judgement of the value of something or someone. Self-esteem is the level of opinion one has of oneself. We think of this in terms of high or low self-regard, confidence, worth, or abilities. Healthy self-esteem is important but, as ever, the question is complicated when 'high' and 'low' are defined by or in comparison to other people.

Sustainable In the 21st century, running a business should mean working to remain viable as an organisation meeting the needs of customers profitably, without degrading the ability of the system to do the same for generations in the future. This should now be the bare minimum for any business model. Principles defining sustainability could include: that renewable resources must not be used at rates that they cannot regenerate, that non-renewable resource should only be used until a renewable resource is developed to replace them, and that these principles must function at the social level in accordance with universal principles of equity and fairness.

Threshold concept Learning changes you. More precisely, learning is you changing. Some change is elastic, and you can reverse or

---

[1] Dalton, C. (2018). 'Reflection is embedded in my brain forever now!': Personal development as a core module on an Executive MBA. *Reflective Practice*, 19(3): 399–411.

slip back to where you were. Other sorts of change cannot be unlearned or undone and may be points of no return, either in your understanding or in your state of being.

Value   In business, value is the potential for future realisation of a promise made by an organisation, institution, or individual to a customer, and their willingness and ability to use and pay for a good or service. Because this is nearly always calculated in monetary terms (as a universally accepted store of value), a return on funds invested that is higher than alternative uses for that money is considered the primary measure of value. Valuation, what something is worth, is a key indicator of strategic decision-making, and a distorter of strategic vision.

The following is a brief selection of Japanese concepts I found compelling during my sabbatical year in Tokyo, where they could often be observed in action.

Ganbaru(頑張る)   Translates as 'do your best' and means persevering through troubling or hard times. Think of a stoical never-give-up attitude, a do or die mindset, or the spirit prized in narratives of the determined underdog. It may express the steadfastness of the sentinel or sentry, who will not budge from their duty. There is a kind of inward stubbornness in Japan's *ganbaru* that other island nations feel they recognise, and when combined with a passion or strong interest can result in overcoming the odds — or going quietly crazy obsessing over small details!

Kodawari(こだわり)   If you are tirelessly willing to put in the work, paying proper attention to detail, and if you lose yourself in this, and if you consciously and for no external reason just do your best in the endeavour, then you already have an idea of what kodawari is. Kodawari is not just doing a good job, it is about the inner pleasure of focusing on something for its own sake, with no cutting of corners, no looking for approval or validation. Doing something entirely and only for its own worth.

Ma (間)   The empty space between. Translating this as merely 'gap' would completely miss the point because in English a gap is an absence or lack. *Ma* is endlessly versatile and very fecund, and it can apply to all parts of life. In fact, without *ma* there would be no things, no noise, no reflection. Without this concept being a principle in modern Japanese life, there would be little chance to enjoy life. Japan is busy, modern, and restless, as the visitor witnesses upon arrival. However, what facilitates this is an appreciation for *ma*. *Ma* is far from empty.

Mottainai (もったいない)   An expression of regret when the full value of something is not being put to good use. In domestic life, it roughly equates to the English expression 'don't leave any waste', for example food on your plate. This does not do the idea justice, though, because *mottainai* fits beautifully into the emerging field of economics that deals with social enterprise, circular economics, and zero waste industries. The Nobel Peace Prize winner and Kenyan environmentalist Wangari Maathi brought the concept to the United Nations as a symbol for global environmental protection. It is telling that we do not have a word for this in English.

Index

absence, 25–27
aesthetic, 149
Aldwin, Carolyn, 48
anthropocene, 2, 267
Aristotle, 47, 115
    eudaimonia, 110, 111
authenticity, 138–140
authority, 99–100
awareness, 27, 29
axiology, 42–44, 46

Baltes, Paul, 162–163
Bateson, Gregory, 22, 171, 181
Beckett, Samuel, 166
beliefs and principles, 182–184
Brown, Donald, 185

Campbell, Joseph, 134
Camus, Albert, 166
career, 39
change, 40, 96
    status quo, 40, 90
Change, 109
Chuang Tzu, 256
Ch'uan Teng Lu, 258

circular economy, 234–237
    circular business models,
        236
Clark, Dick, 131
compassion, 268
complex adaptive systems (CAS),
    82
consciousness, 28, 49–51, 118, 129,
    209, 210, 247, 248
    unconscious, 50
consequences, unintended, 94
corporate social responsibility
    (CSR), 236
COVID-19, 223, 225, 233
creativity, 100
curiosity, 18, 28, 86

death, 163–166
de Mello, Anthony, 75
Descartes, Rene, 154, 248
dialectic, 227, 228
difference, 47, 61–65
discourse, 136
duck–rabbit, 67–69, 157, 191
Dweck, Carol, 180

Einstein, Albert, 205
entropy, 212
epistemology, 46–49, 140, 148
Erikson, Erik and Joan, 48, 162
existentialism, 115

feedback, 97–99
Feynman, Richard, 20
final purpose
    Aristotle's, 110
Fitzgerald, F Scott, 158
followership, 91
Ford, Henry, 179
Frankl, Viktor, 115
Freud, Sigmund, 159

gestalt learning, 169
Goffman, Erving, 34
Great Chain of Being, 155, 159

Hegel, Georg, 227
Heraclitus, 220
heuristic, 68, 74
Human Rights, United Nations
    Declaration of, 184, 185
Husserl, Edmund, 210

ignorance, 27, 28
imposter syndrome, 270
Incremental learning, 168
information, 46, 61, 63, 76, 98

James, William, 157
Jung, Carl, 159, 160

Kahneman, Daniel, 22
Korzybski, Alfred, 209
Kotter, John, 96
Krishnamurti, Jiddhu, 259

Lao Tzu, 117
leadership initiatives, 96
leadership narrative, 84
leadership, orders of, 251–253
leadership theory, 85, 87, 93
Lee, Bruce, 20, 21
Levitt, Theodore, 105
Lewin, Kurt, 169
lifespan development, 161, 162
liminality, 237–239

management, 3, 59, 71, 83, 88
    learning, 8
Manzerek, Ray, 131
Maslow, Abraham, 160, 189
Master of Business
    Administration, 12, 39, 83, 106,
    203, 257
McAdams, Dan, 137
McTaggart, Jon, 206
Mead, George Herbert, 157
meaning-making, 5, 34, 65, 66
Meister, Jeanne, 38
Merleau-Ponty, Maurice, 168
Metaphor, 143–145
mindset, 44
    collective, 179, 181, 182
    fixed and growth, 180
    individual, 178, 179
Mindset, 177–180
Mintzberg, Henry, 3
    Plural Economy, 234
Moore, Tom (Captain), 92

Naess, Arne, 167
Narrative, 134, 135
    career, 141–143
    identity, 137, 138
Naya, Diana, xi, 12

Newton, Isaac, 205
Noth, Paul, 68

ontology, 52–54

paradigm, 5
pattern, 107
perception, 59, 60
perfectionism, 56, 146–148
personal development (PD), xv,
    17, 18, 24, 54, 57, 246, 250, 260,
    271
perspective, 127, 130
presuppositions, 23
presuppositions, definition of, 22
psychometric, 44, 45, 158
punctuation, 35–37, 62
    naming, 33
purpose, 105–107, 167
    integrating, 121–122

reputation, 132
Rilke, Rainer, 52
Rittel, Horst, 232
Rokeach, Milton, 192
Rovelli, Carlo, 211

Sartre, Jean-Paul, 166
Schein, Edgar, 219
Schwartz, Shalom, 189
self-awareness, 25, 75, 85, 86, 107,
    138, 154, 181, 182, 196, 268
    persona, 129, 130
    self-esteem, 66, 132
sense-making, 5, 33, 34, 60
Shakespeare, William (Hamlet),
    164
Socrates, 29, 75

Squiggly Career, 142
St Augustine, 205
Steiner, George, 249
stewardship, 32, 221, 222
stoicism, 112–115
    Epictetus, 112, 113
    Marcus Aurelius, 112–114
    Seneca, 112, 113
sustainability, 73
Sustainable Development Goals
    (UN), 223
systemic change, 228–230

Taoism, 116
time
    absolute view, 206
    as flow, 213, 214, 217
    emergent view, 208
    narrative view, 207
tobacco industry, 69, 70
Totemism, 119
Toyota Production System (TPS),
    146
transformation, 102
Transitional learning, 169
Turner, Victor, 238

ubuntu, 129, 246
UNESCO, 87

values, universal, 187, 188, 193–197
van Gennep, Arnold, 237
vision, 90

Webber, Martin, 232
wicked problem, 232–233
Wiener, Norbert, 262
wisdom, 7, 48, 54, 100, 111, 203

Wittgenstein, Ludwig, 67
World Economic Forum, The, 224
    Davos, 224, 225
    Great Reset, the, 225
World Health Organization
    (WHO), 175, 233

Yes, and..., 239–240

Zen, 19, 257
Zeno of Citium, 112